This book is brought to you by:
hackneyandjones.com

Writers and Publishers of
fiction and non-fiction.

Scan QR Code

Copyright © 2024 by Hackney and Jones. All rights reserved.
No part of this book may be reproduced in any form or by any electronic or mechanical means, including information storage and retrieval systems, without written permission from the authors, except for the use of brief quotations in a book review.

CONTENTS

INTRODUCTION: EMBARK ON YOUR ADVENTURE!	1
MYTH BUSTING: BLAST THROUGH WRITING MYTHS AND UNLOCK YOUR TRUE POTENTIAL	8
GENERATING IDEAS: WHERE IT ALL BEGINS...!	12
GENRE: FIND YOUR PLAYGROUND	18
SETTINGS: PAINTING WORLDS WITH WORDS: THE ART OF CAPTIVATING SETTINGS	29
CHARACTERS: LET THEM LEAP OFF THE PAGE!	36
VILLAINS: EMBRACE YOUR DARK SIDE AND CRAFT COMPELLING ANTAGONISTS	43
ALLY: "YOU'VE GOT A FRIEND IN ME..."	49
GOALS: BUILD THEIR BOLD AMBITIONS	54
OBSTACLES: HELP YOUR CHARACTERS NAVIGATE THEIR JOURNEY	60
THEMES: DISCOVERING THE HEART OF YOUR STORY	68

CONTENTS

TITLES: PIQUE YOUR READER'S CURIOSITY...!   75

LOGLINES: HOOK, LINE AND SINKER: CAPTIVATING READERS WITH LOGLINES   79

CREATING YOUR LOGLINE: HERE WE GO! LET'S GET CATCHY!   85

CHARACTER ARCS: CREATING MEMORABLE CHARACTER JOURNEYS   92

CHARACTER DESCRIPTIONS

POSITIVE CHARACTER TRAITS	98
NEGATIVE CHARACTER TRAITS	101
BACKGROUND IDEAS	104
INTERNAL STRUGGLES/CONFLICTS	106
EXTERNAL STRUGGLES/CONFLICTS	109
MOTIVATIONS AND GOALS	112
OCCUPATIONS	115

CHARACTER PROFILES: CREATING UNFORGETTABLE CHARACTERS

MAIN CHARACTER (PROTAGONIST)	120
THE VILLAIN	131
THE ALLY	142

CONTENTS

PLOT TWISTS AND ENDINGS: KEEPING READERS ON THEIR TOES AND CRAFTING UNFORGETTABLE ENDINGS	153
ACTS 1, 2, AND 3: YOUR STORY'S LIVING, BREATHING SOUL	164
SHOW NOT TELL AND DIALOGUE: MAKING YOUR CHARACTERS SPEAK AND UNLEASH THEIR POWER!	166
YOUR OPENING LINE: START OFF WITH A BANG!	174
OUTLINES: PLOTTING YOUR COURSE TO SUCCESS!	178
WRITING YOUR OUTLINE: TIME TO GET CREATIVE!	183
LET'S PUT YOUR STORY IN ORDER	198
YOUR SHORT STORY CHECKLIST: HAVE YOU INCLUDED EVERYTHING?	211
SETTING TARGETS: OUT OF YOUR HEAD AND ONTO THE PAGE!	214
EDITING YOUR SHORT STORY: SCRAP THE CHAFF, KEEP THE WHEAT!	217

CONTENTS

GENRE TOOLKITS	FANTASY	228
	SCIENCE FICTION	254
	ROMANCE	278
	CRIME	309
	PSYCHOLOGICAL	341
	HORROR	369
	HISTORICAL FICTION	395
	YOUNG ADULT	417
	CONTEMPORARY/WOMEN'S/DOMESTIC	440
	PARANORMAL	467
GLOSSARY OF KEY TERMS: AN A–Z OF SHORT STORY WRITING		495

INTRODUCTION

EMBARK ON YOUR ADVENTURE!

INTRODUCTION

WHY ARE YOU HERE?

We are assuming you are here because you want to write epic short stories, right?
Maybe you have tried lots of things before or maybe this is your introduction to short story writing.

Either way, welcome!

THE AIM OF THIS WORKBOOK?

This workbook aims to take you from a blank page to a fully written story, step by step, and to enjoy it along the way.

It is a streamlined roadmap to creating an awesome short story from scratch – with never seen before techniques. We know this because we invented them!

Sound good?

THIS WORKBOOK IS MADE UP OF THREE PARTS

1- The theory – so you know what you're doing and why.

2- The picking – pick the best bits for your story.

3- The resources – we have created a HUGE genre-specific set of resources for you so your story will delight your readers!

INTRODUCTION

WHY WE ARE DIFFERENT

We have read books about creative writing, taken courses etc. but found them far too 'fluffy'.

We wanted actionable steps. Can you relate?

So this course GIVES YOU the actual content and ideas so that you have inspiration at every step, rather than leaving you to come up with things yourself - ensuring zero writer's block!

WE WILL COVER THE TEN MOST COMMON GENRES

- Fantasy
- Science Fiction
- Romance
- Crime
- Psychological
- Horror
- Historical Fiction
- Young Adult
- Contemporary/Women's/Domestic
- Paranormal

INTRODUCTION

WHAT OUR SHORT STORY WRITING PROCESS INCLUDES

Zero-fluff. Only actionable steps that take you straight to the outcome you want. No messing around.

We even provide an example of a short story we produced on the fly using our strategy (and it took minutes to create the plot with how we do it).

Your story will have peaks and troughs like so:

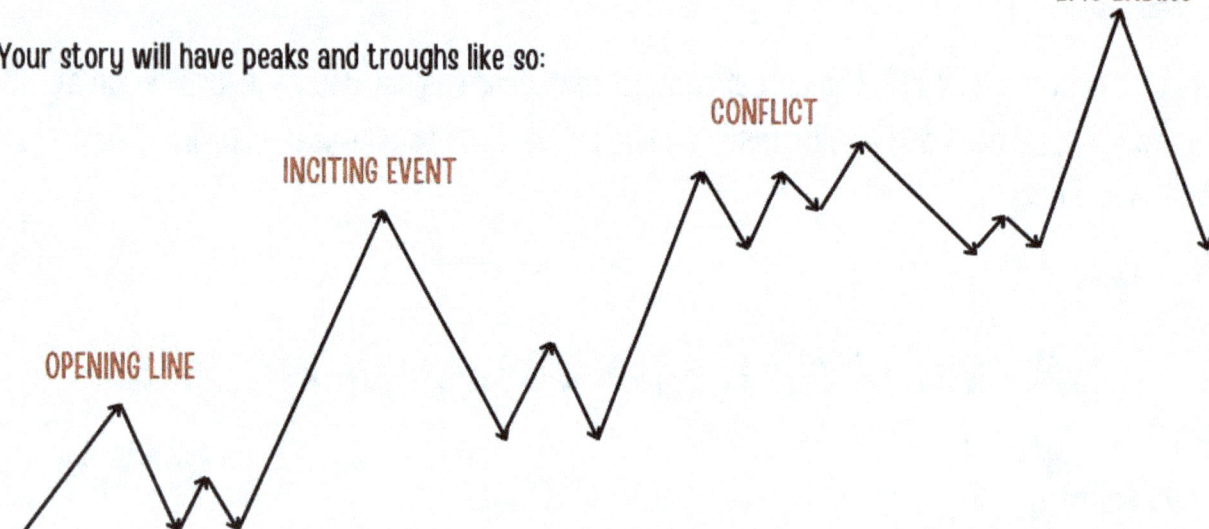

THESE ARE THE VITAL ELEMENTS FOR YOUR SHORT STORY:

- Characters - Are they interesting? Will your readers enjoy reading about them?
- Settings - Where does your story take place? In the city? Space? In the country
- Plot - The sequence of events in your story to drive it forward.
- Goal - What does your main character want/need to achieve and why?
- Conflict - What/Who stands in your main characters' way of getting what they want?
- Consequences - What happens if your main character doesn't get what they want?

INTRODUCTION

IF YOU ONLY REMEMBER THREE THINGS BY THE END OF THIS PROCESS

- Your reader comes first – always. Make sure you create a story that keeps your readers guessing, but one that's not too complicated. They are investing time, energy and sometimes money reading your work. Don't worry – we've got you covered with EVERYTHING! Just follow the steps.

- Once you write short stories, you can write a novel. Yes! You really can. How do we know? We've done it ourselves.

- Follow the roadmap we give you, but don't be afraid to create your own tracks as well. We personally advise outlining your stories – it really helps with writer's block – but when you are confident with the plot/scenes etc. don't be afraid to follow your inspiration.

OUR MOTTO FOR AVOIDING WRITER'S BLOCK

IF YOU CAN...

Use your imagination: Think of an awesome character from your imagination.

IF YOU CAN'T...

Use your observation: Think of a character you have read in a book or seen in the movies.

IF YOU NEED...

Resources: Use the resources section at the back of this workbook for inspiration.

> USE THIS MOTTO TO KEEP YOU ON TRACK

WHO ARE WE?

Claire Hackney is a former teacher turned full-time novelist and publisher, from Cheshire. Her background in English, Drama, and Media Studies fuels her storytelling passion.

Claire's intrigue for history finds a home in her work, particularly her 1950s-inspired novels (Meet Me at 10 etc.). Beyond this, she's set to embark on an exciting path, including finishing the upcoming DI Rachel Morrison crime thriller series.

Follow us and say hi!

TWITTER: @ClaireHac
INSTAGRAM: @clairehackneyauthor

Vicky Jones is from Essex, England. She joined the Royal Navy at 20 but felt something was missing. So, she made a bold list of 300 things to do, and her life transformed, especially after attending a writing group to help write a novel which went on to become a bestseller.

Vicky has written songs for iTunes and YouTube. One of her songs, "House of Cards," is centred around the theme of bullying. She also co-wrote a book called 'Meet Me at 10' that deals with controversial societal issues.

She loves to travel and has been to around 50 countries. She has also gained a psychology and criminology degree from The Open University.

Although now living in Cheshire, Vicky keeps ties with her Essex roots. Her journey is about being creative, brave, and discovering herself.

TWITTER: @VickyJones7
INSTAGRAM: @vickytjones

OUR WRITING JOURNEY

WE HAVE WRITTEN FICTION AND NON-FICTION BOOKS!

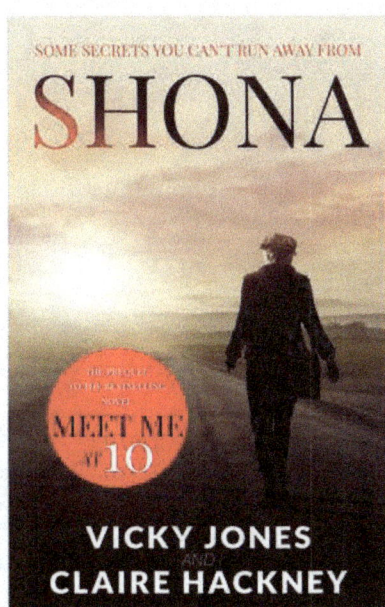
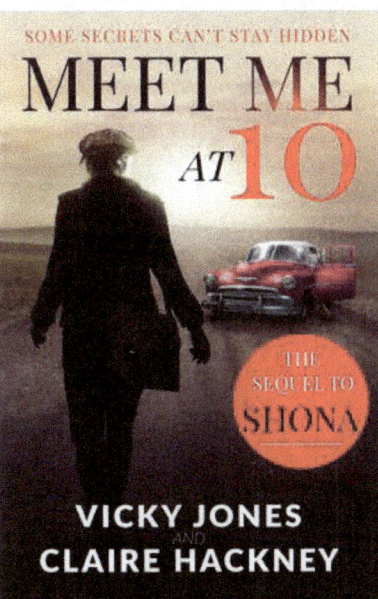
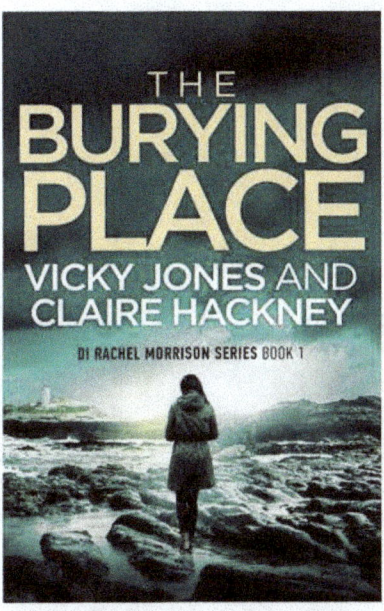

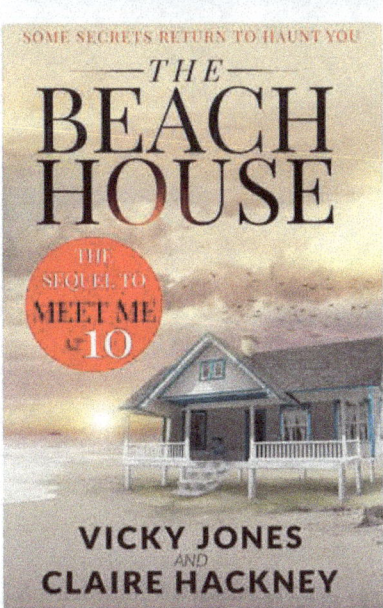
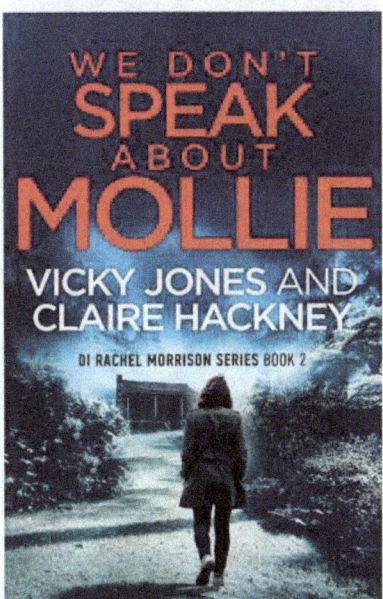

MYTH BUSTING

BLAST THROUGH WRITING MYTHS AND UNLOCK YOUR TRUE POTENTIAL

MYTH BUSTING

MYTH	TRUTH
Writing short stories is easy.	Crafting impactful short stories takes practice. Writing concisely while conveying emotions and themes can be challenging.
You need to be a naturally talented writer to succeed.	Writing is a skill that can be learned with practice. Successful authors started from scratch.
Only published authors are "real" writers.	If you write, you're a writer. Publication isn't the only measure of success.
Writing short stories has no impact.	Short stories can evoke emotions, explore themes, and leave lasting impressions.
You need to follow strict rules and formulas.	No strict rules. Find your unique style and voice.
Rejection means you're a bad writer.	Rejections are normal. Learn from them to improve.
Writing short stories is not "serious" writing.	Short stories are respected literature. They pack a punch.
You need a degree in writing to be good at it.	Passion and willingness to learn matter more.
Writing is a solitary endeavour.	It doesn't have to be! Seek support from other writers for growth. Join a local writing group like we did.
You must be original in every aspect.	Uniqueness comes from your perspective and voice.

Remember: Writing is a journey. Embrace your love for writing, be persistent, and trust in your ability to create meaningful stories.

WHAT HAS STOPPED YOU BEFORE?

There is a reason why you are here. Something has stopped you from either starting your story or writing 'The End,' right?

It is useful to know what those reasons are so you can progress.

Here are the most common reasons writers struggle. We will help you solve them all:

- Self-doubt:
    - Issue: Many new writers grapple with self-doubt, questioning their abilities and fearing that their writing won't meet their own or others' expectations.
    - Impact: This can lead to hesitation, perfectionism, and a reluctance to begin or complete a story.

- Overwhelm:
    - Issue: The sheer scope of writing a story, with its characters, plot, and settings, can be overwhelming for new writers.
    - Impact: Feeling overwhelmed can result in procrastination and a sense of being unable to navigate the complexities of storytelling.

- Lack of structure or planning:
    - Issue: Some new writers may dive into writing without a clear plan or structure, leading to uncertainty and difficulty in maintaining a coherent narrative.
    - Impact: Without a roadmap, writers may get lost or discouraged during the writing process.

- Fear of failure or criticism:
    - Issue: The fear of failure or criticism can be paralyzing for new writers. The thought of negative feedback or rejection can hinder creative expression.
    - Impact: Writers may be hesitant to take risks, experiment with their writing, or submit their work for fear of judgment.

WHAT HAS STOPPED YOU BEFORE?

- Time management challenges:

    - Issue: Balancing writing with other responsibilities, such as work or studies, can be challenging for new writers.
    - Impact: Limited time may result in sporadic writing habits, making it difficult to maintain momentum and complete a story.

- The blank page:

    - Issue: Confronting a blank page can be intimidating, and the pressure to start with the perfect sentence can be paralysing.
    - Impact: The blank page challenge can stifle creativity and prevent writers from taking the initial steps in their storytelling journey.

- Confidence:

    - Issue: A lack of confidence in one's writing abilities can hinder the creative process, making it difficult to express ideas with conviction.
    - Impact: Low confidence may lead to second-guessing, self-censorship, and reluctance to share one's writing with others. Building confidence is crucial for a writer's growth.

Put simply...

- You won't write a whole story, you will a scene, then another and then another.

- You will join them together and they just happen to create a gripping story!

- We take all the stress and overwhelm out of the process, so relax and enjoy!

GENERATING IDEAS

WHERE IT ALL BEGINS...!

MIND MAP

Mind mapping is a visual representation of information that organises thoughts, ideas, and concepts around a central theme or topic. It is a creative and structured method for brainstorming, planning, and organising information. In a mind map, the central idea is placed in the centre, and related ideas radiate outwards in a branching, hierarchical fashion.

Here is an example mind map for a crime story:

At a crime scene, the detective is shocked to find he knows the victim. It looks like a mistaken identity, no murder weapon is found but there are footprints in the blood stains.

Was the detective the intended target?

MIND MAP

Have a go yourself at generating a mind map for a topic that interests you. What kinds of ideas does this topic generate? Add these to the arrows with as much detail as possible. Then write out your complete idea below.

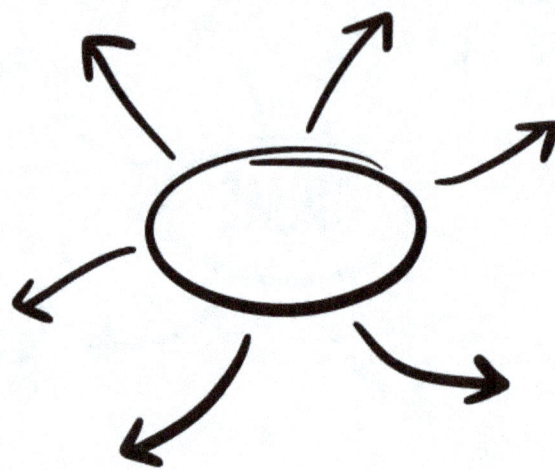

Your idea:

....
....
....
....

14

THE FICTION SQUARE

The Fiction Square is a fun way of writing down lots of individual ideas for a story, then picking one from each category completely at random to then stitch together to make an intriguing plot for a story.

Below is an example of a fiction square - can you see how many different ideas it can generate? The possibilities are endless!

CHARACTER	SETTING	GOAL	CONFLICT	CONSEQUENCE
DETECTIVE	FOREST	SUCCESS	RACE AGAINST TIME	DEATH
WARRIOR	CASTLE	FAME	SURVIVAL AGAINST ELEMENTS	EXTICTION
DOCTOR	SPACE	HEALTH	STRUGGLE AGAINST TECHNOLOGY	JOB LOSS
EXPLORER	VILLAGE	DISCOVERY	FACING OLD ENEMY	IMPRISONMENT
SPY	MOUNTAIN	SURVIVAL	CHALLENGE SOCIETAL NORMS	DISGRACE
MUSICIAN	BEACH	JUSTICE	PROTECTING LOVED ONES AGAINST CRIME	FAILURE
ASTRONAUT	ISLAND	LOVE	CAN'T ESCAPE	DEVASTATION

THE FICTION SQUARE

WE CHOSE THESE

IDEA 1	WARRIOR	VILLAGE	SURVIVAL	FACING OLD ENEMY	DEATH
	In a secluded village, a skilled warrior must ensure the survival of the people by facing an old enemy, risking everything to prevent inevitable death.					

WHY?	Why is the warrior facing the old enemy now?
WHAT IF...?	The old enemy can't be killed as he has the answer to an important question that ensures survival.
AND THEN...?	The warrior and old enemy discover there is a bigger force after them both...

AND THESE

IDEA 2	DOCTOR	VILLAGE	RACE AGAINST TIME	SURVIVAL	DEVASTATION
	In a remote village, a resourceful doctor races against time to ensure the survival of the community striving to prevent devastation.					

WHY?	Why does the doctor care so much about this particular community?
WHAT IF...?	He can't find the necessary tools or resources to make an impact?
AND THEN...?	He has to make an immoral decision when he is offered a way of procuring the resources.

THE FICTION SQUARE: YOUR CHOICES

From the fiction square, pick one thing from each column.

You should have: A character, setting, goal, conflict and consequence

IDEA 3					
WHY?					
WHAT IF...?					
AND THEN...?					

You should have: A character, setting, goal, conflict and consequence

IDEA 4					
WHY?					
WHAT IF...?					
AND THEN...?					

GENRE

FIND YOUR PLAYGROUND!

GENRE

YOUR ROADMAP TO CREATIVE WRITING EXPLORATION

Genre refers to different categories or types of artistic works, like books, movies, or music, that share similar themes, styles, or characteristics. It helps classify and identify the specific style or content of a creative piece.

PROBLEM

Selecting the right genre can be confusing, leaving you unsure about where to begin and how to shape your tale. Like having a puzzle with missing pieces.

COMMON MISTAKE

Choosing the wrong genre can leave your story feeling disjointed, unsatisfying, and like a song without a melody.

GENRE

WHAT YOU NEED TO KNOW BEFORE YOU WRITE YOUR STORY

- Familiarise yourself with genres

HERE ARE TEN OF THE MOST COMMON GENRES OF FICTION:

1. Fantasy: Involves magical or supernatural elements, often set in imaginary worlds or alternate realities.

2. Science Fiction: Set in futuristic or speculative worlds, exploring scientific and technological advancements.

3. Romance: Focuses on romantic relationships, emotions, and the development of love between characters.

4. Crime: Involves solving a puzzle or uncovering secrets, often with a detective or amateur sleuth as the protagonist.

5. Psychological: Builds suspense and tension, with a focus on internal personality conflicts and behaviours.

6. Horror: A genre of fiction designed to disturb, frighten or scare. It usually includes murder, blood and gore.

7. Historical Fiction: Takes place in the past and incorporates real historical events and characters.

8. Young Adult (YA): Targets a teenage audience, dealing with themes of coming-of-age, identity, and growth.

9. Contemporary Fiction: Portrays realistic and current settings, exploring relatable characters and issues.

10. Paranormal: Includes supernatural creatures such as demons, ghosts, spirits, elves and witches. The storylines include events that defy logic and scientific explanation.

GENRE

WHAT YOU NEED TO KNOW BEFORE YOU WRITE YOUR STORY

- Identify your genre

Determine which genre suits your story's theme, characters, and plot.

- Study successful examples of your chosen genre

Dive into books of your chosen genre and study how accomplished authors weave their narratives.

WHY IS GENRE RELEVANT?

- Audience connection

When you pick the right genre, you're inviting the most appropriate audience to enjoy your creative masterpiece.

- Reader expectations

Readers approach a story with a list of expectations. Fulfil those expectations by using correct genre conventions, and keep your readers captivated and eager for more.

- Marketing and promotion

Genre helps readers find your work easily, aiding in marketing and promotion endeavours.

GENRE

Here are a selection of front covers in specific genres:

CRIME

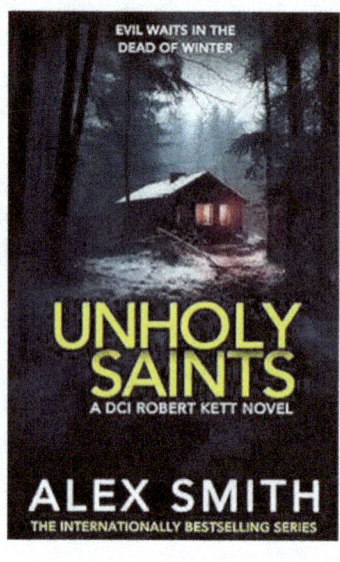
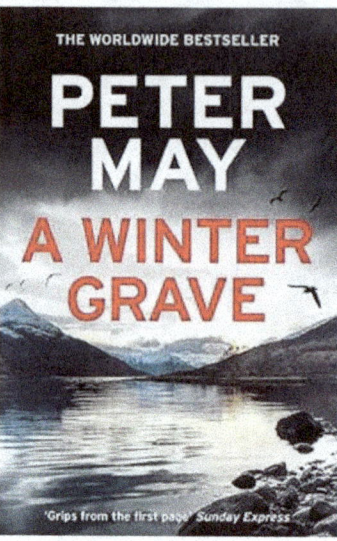
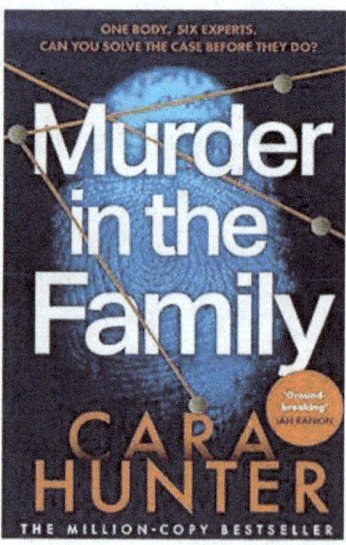

HISTORICAL

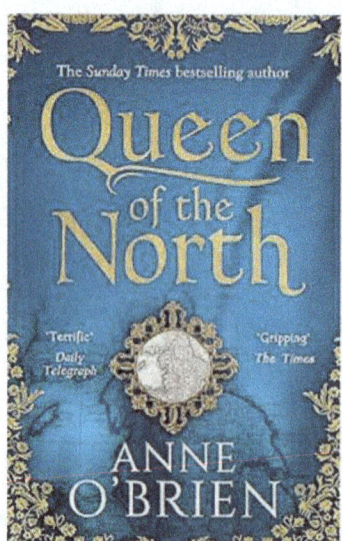

GENRE

Here are a selection of front covers in specific genres:

SCIENCE FICTION

FANTASY

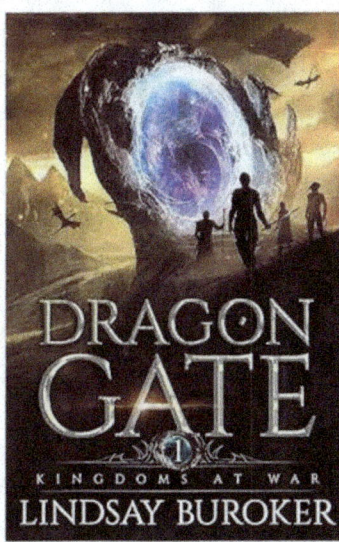
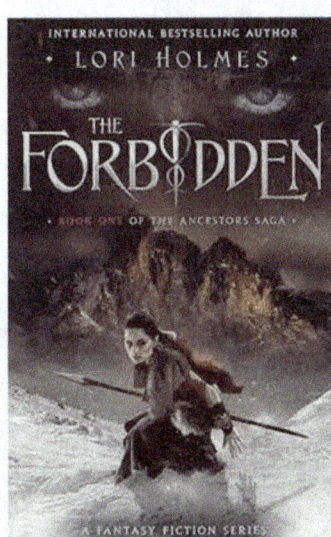
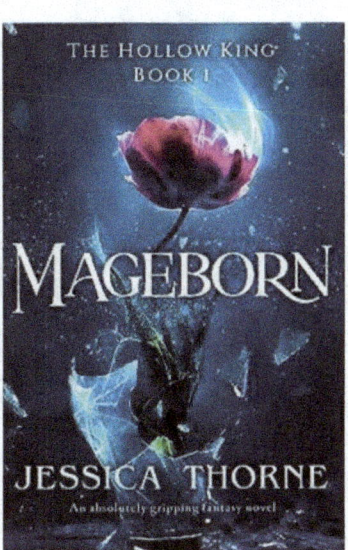

GENRE

Here are a selection of front covers in specific genres:

ROMANCE

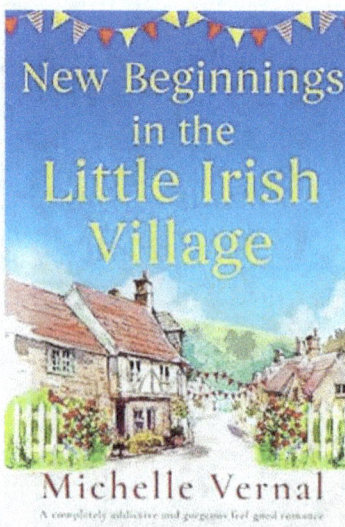

PSYCHOLOGICAL

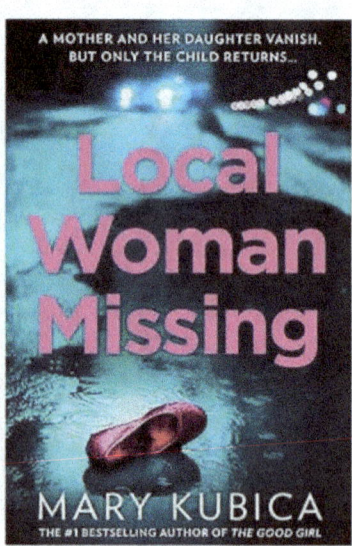

GENRE

Here are a selection of front covers in specific genres:

WOMEN'S/DOMESTIC

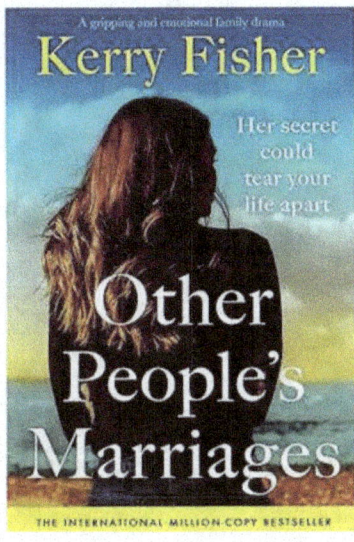

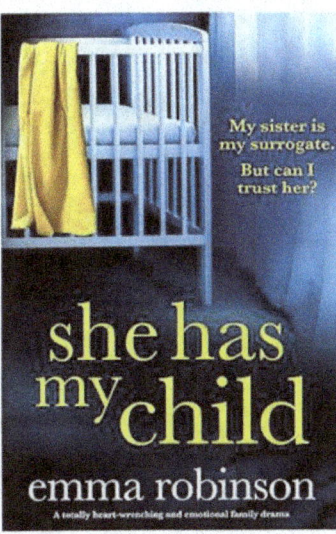

HORROR

GENRE

Here are a selection of front covers in specific genres:

PARANORMAL

YOUNG ADULT

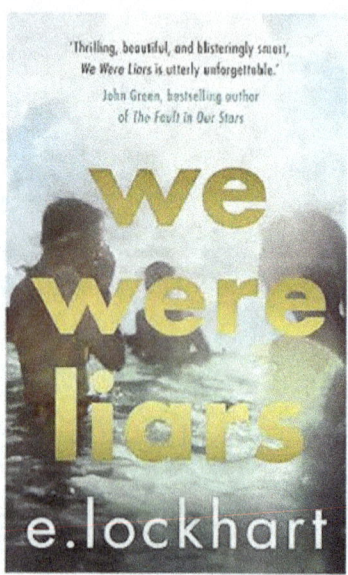

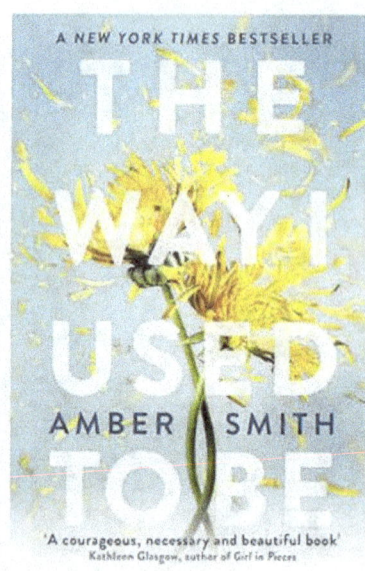

WHICH GENRE CAUGHT YOUR EYE THE MOST? WHY?

GENRE

OUR RECOMMENDED APPROACH:
WHAT WE DO AND HOW

When we plan our stories we engage in brainstorming activities, writing exercises, and genre analysis. We then research our chosen genre thoroughly, looking at famous examples of genre-specific writing, and then ensure we fit our story themes, settings and characters into these conventions. Finally, we ensure our book cover includes suitable imagery and fonts so our readers recognise our book as fitting into their genre of choice.

Mastering genre selection means you'll craft stories that not only entertain but also resonate deeply. This ability empowers you to create narratives that leave a lasting impact on both you and your readers.

QUICK TASK

List your 5 favourite books and movies and start seeing if there is a common genre – which one is it?

	BOOK OR MOVIE	GENRE
1		
2		
3		
4		
5		

CHOOSING YOUR SHORT STORY GENRE

From the list of 10 genres, choose one that you like the sound of the most.

My chosen genre is:

....

Write a few sentences about why you chose that genre and what initial thoughts and ideas you have about writing in this genre.

I chose this genre because:

....
....
....
....
....
....
....
....
....
....
....
....
....
....
....

SETTINGS

**PAINTING WORLDS WITH WORDS:
THE ART OF CAPTIVATING SETTINGS**

SETTINGS

CRAFTING THE PERFECT STAGE FOR YOUR STORY

Settings are the background or the place where a story happens. It's where the characters live, events unfold, and everything takes place. Settings create the environment for your story to come to life.

WHAT YOU NEED TO KNOW BEFORE YOU WRITE YOUR STORY

- Research and familiarise

Before you write, think about your story's settings. Whether real, fictional, or historical, knowing them well brings your tale to life. Watch movies, read, and use tools like Google Maps for inspiration, just like we did for our novels.

- Setting's impact on the story

Think about how each setting element affects the plot, characters, and overall vibe of your story. A carefully chosen setting can give your narrative richness and depth.

- Create a vivid imagery

Use descriptive language to paint vivid pictures of your settings. Transport your readers to these worlds you've created and immerse them in your tale.

> IF YOU WANT GENRE-SPECIFIC IDEAS, HEAD TO YOUR GENRE TOOLKIT AND YOU'LL FIND LOTS OF IDEAS THERE!

SETTINGS

WHY IS SETTING RELEVANT?

- Setting establishes atmosphere

Setting shapes the mood and emotional tone for your readers as they travel through your narrative.

- Character development

Settings can mould your characters. The places they inhabit influence their beliefs, actions, and even their personalities, making them more relatable and genuine.

- Plot and conflict

A well-chosen setting can offer opportunities for drama and challenges that your characters must face, propelling your plot forward with every step.

- World-building

In genres like fantasy and science fiction, settings aren't just backdrops; they're the very foundations of your world. Craft them meticulously to create captivating and unique universes.

SETTINGS

COMMON MISTAKES TO AVOID

- Lack of research

Inaccuracies can chip away at your story's believability. Make sure you know your chosen settings well through thorough research.

- Overwhelming descriptions

Less is more. Balance your descriptions. Let them complement, not overpower, your narrative.

- Inconsistent setting

Keep your setting consistent to avoid losing your reader's attention.

- Using setting as a crutch

Your setting should enhance, not overshadow your story. Characters and plot remain the key ingredients.

- Ignoring the impact of an interesting setting

Each setting choice should serve a purpose.

PATHETIC FALLACY

Pathetic fallacy is when the feelings of a character match the weather or surroundings in a story. It's like saying nature acts the same way a character feels, using it to show emotions in a symbolic way.

For example, if a character is sad, the weather might be rainy to match their mood.

WEATHER = RAINING

WEATHER = SUNNY

CHARACTER = SAD

CHARACTER = HAPPY

PATHETIC FALLACY

EMOTION	WEATHER	WEATHER EFFECT
ANGER	THUNDERSTORM	The character's rage shown in thunder and lightning, echoing their inner storm.
HAPPY	SUNNY DAY	Joy mirrored in warm sunshine, creating a bright and cheerful atmosphere.
SAD	RAINY DAY	The character's sadness reflected in gentle rain, as if the sky sheds tears with them.
EXCITED	CLEAR BLUE SKY	Thrill and excitement mirrored in a cloudless sky, symbolizing boundless possibilities.
FEARFUL	DARK AND STORMY NIGHT	Fear embodied in a night of ominous clouds, echoing inner turmoil.
ROMANTIC	GENTLE BREEZE AND BLOOMING FLOWERS	Romantic emotions mirrored in a gentle breeze with the scent of blooming flowers.
ANXIOUS	WINDY AND UNSETTLED WEATHER	Anxiety conveyed through unsettled and gusty winds, reflecting inner restlessness.
HOPEFUL	CLEAR SUNRISE	Hope and optimism are reflected in the soft hues of a clear sunrise, symbolising a new day's promise.

Famous movie example:

"Forrest Gump" (1994):

- **Scene:** In the scene where Jenny passes away, it starts raining heavily. The rain reflects the emotional weight of the moment, providing a poignant backdrop to Forrest's grief and loss.

CHOOSING YOUR SHORT STORY SETTING

Take a moment to choose a setting that resonates most with your story. Whether it's a bustling city, a tranquil village, or a distant planet, let your imagination run free and set the stage for your masterpiece.

My chosen setting is:

....

Write a few sentences about why you chose that setting for your short story and what initial thoughts and ideas you have about the significance of this setting.

I chose this setting because:

....
....
....
....
....
....
....
....
....
....

CHARACTERS

LET THEM LEAP OFF THE PAGE!

CHARACTERS

THE SOUL OF YOUR STORY

Characters are the heart and soul of your story. They're the people or beings who experience the events and drive the plot forward. Their thoughts, feelings, and actions make the story come alive.

PROBLEM

Creating characters can be like navigating a labyrinth without a map, leaving you puzzled and unsure of where to start. It's sometimes hard to know where to start visualising them.

COMMON MISTAKE

One common mistake is crafting characters without depth, resulting in a story that falls flat and fails to connect with your readers.

CHARACTERS

WHAT YOU NEED TO KNOW BEFORE YOU WRITE YOUR STORY

- Character profiles

Before you begin, spend time getting to know your characters intimately. Create detailed profiles (we provide you with these later in this workbook) that reveal their past, motivations, and unique personalities. This foundation will ensure they come alive on the page.

- Roles and arcs

Characters are like actors in a play. Before you begin to write, you must understand the roles your characters will play in your story. They will change and grow as the tale unfolds.

- Relationships

Explore how your characters interact, clash, or bond with each other. Well-crafted relationships add layers of complexity.

CHARACTERS

WHY ARE CHARACTERS RELEVANT?

- Readers' connection

Characters are the bridge between your story and your readers' hearts. Crafting strong, relatable characters invites readers to step into your world.

- Driving the plot

Characters propel your story forward. Their choices and actions create ripples that drive the plot, keeping readers engaged throughout.

- Emotional impact

Characters have the power to evoke strong emotions. Readers laugh, cry, and cheer alongside them, forging a bond that lingers beyond the final page.

- Themes and messages

Characters promote your story's themes, carrying messages that resonate deeply with your audience.

CHARACTERS

COMMON MISTAKES TO AVOID

- Stereotyping

Imagine meeting someone who's just a stereotype. Characters deserve more! Avoid painting them with broad strokes; delve into their complexities.

- Inconsistent behaviour

Characters should remain consistent, behaving in ways that align with their personalities and motivations.

- Overwhelming cast

Like a party where everyone talks at once, too many characters can overwhelm. Focus on a core cast, allowing you to develop each character meaningfully.

- Neglecting supporting characters

Even supporting actors have their own stories to tell. Develop their purpose and arcs too.

- Unrealistic perfection

Flaws add depth to characters. Embrace their imperfections. Flawed characters are more relatable and endearing.

CHARACTERS

DIFFERENT TYPES OF CHARACTER

- **Protagonist:** The main character of the story, often the hero or heroine, whose actions drive the plot forward.

- **Antagonist:** The primary character or force that opposes the protagonist, creating conflict and obstacles. The 'baddie.'

- **Ally:** A character who supports and helps the protagonist in their journey, providing assistance and friendship.

- **Sidekick:** A close companion to the protagonist, often offering comic relief or additional support.

QUICK TASK

List your 5 favourite books and movies and write down the most memorable character – think about WHY they are memorable

	BOOK OR MOVIE	FAVOURITE CHARACTER AND WHY
1		
2		
3		
4		
5		

CHOOSING YOUR MAIN CHARACTER

Choose a main character for your story and begin crafting their detailed profile. Explore their past, motivations, and personality traits to lay a strong foundation. Think of your favourite characters from books, TV programmes or movies.

My main character is:

....

Write a short character profile for your main character. Detail things about their personality, appearance, accent, height, build etc...

....
....
....
....
....
....
....
....
....
....
....
....
....
....

VILLAINS

EMBRACE YOUR DARK SIDE AND CRAFT COMPELLING ANTAGONISTS

43

VILLAINS

CRAFTING COMPLEX ANTAGONISTS

A villain (the antagonist) is a character in a story who opposes/is against the main character (protagonist). The villain engages in actions that cause conflict, harm and obstacles for the main character.

Villains can be people, creatures, or even powerful forces. Crafting well-developed villains adds depth and excitement to your story.

PROBLEM

Creating a lacklustre villain leaves your story dull and uninspiring. Create complex villains, with good traits and bad, to ensure your narrative is nuanced with conflict.

COMMON MISTAKE

Crafting one-dimensional villains reduces your story to a flat and boring tale. Poorly thought-out villains take away your opportunity to create true tension in your story and engagement with your readers.

VILLAINS

WHAT YOU NEED TO KNOW BEFORE YOU WRITE YOUR STORY

- **Motivations and backstory**

Before you write, peel back your villain's layers. Understand what fuels their actions. What events led them down this path? This depth transforms them from caricatures into captivating characters.

- **Conflict with the protagonist**

Villains challenge your protagonists at every turn. Understand how their goals clash, driving your narrative forward with a thrilling sense of conflict.

- **Complexity and flaws**

Villains aren't simply cardboard cutouts of evil. Give them complexities, virtues, and vulnerabilities that make them fascinating and relatable. Never make them all bad. Give them some good qualities too.

VILLAINS

WHY ARE VILLAINS RELEVANT?

- Source of conflict

The opposition of heroes and villains fuels conflict, creating obstacles that your characters must navigate, ensuring your story remains gripping and unpredictable.

- Character development

Villains force the protagonist's growth. Interactions with them encourage your heroes to evolve, learn, and adapt, adding layers of emotional depth to their journey.

- Audience engagement

Crafting an enigmatic and captivating villain keeps readers invested, turning each page with eager anticipation.

VILLAINS

COMMON MISTAKES TO AVOID

- Stereotypes and clichés

Avoid the pitfall of creating villains based on tired clichés or generic moulds. Forge a path of originality and surprise.

- Lack of motivation

A villain without clear motivations feels disjointed and hollow. Unravel their reasons for action to give them depth and authenticity.

- Weak villain

Consider villains as worthy opponents in a high-stakes duel. Ensure they pose a genuine threat, challenging your protagonist's skills, morals, and determination.

- Monologuing

While a villain's monologue can be powerful, too much talk can dull the impact. Balance their speeches with action and interaction to keep the narrative engaging.

- Villain's defeat

Craft a climax where the villain's defeat is earned, resonating deeply with the story's themes and resolutions.

CHOOSING YOUR VILLAIN

Choose a villain from your story and delve into their backstory. What events shaped them into who they are today? How do these experiences fuel their actions?

The key features of my main villain:

ALLY

"YOU'VE GOT A FRIEND IN ME..."

ALLY

THE KEY HELPER IN YOUR MAIN CHARACTER'S TASK

The ally to your main character is the person who offers them a wise ear, piece of crucial advice, or can even act as the love interest to your main character.

PROBLEM

Creating a strong, relatable and relevant ally takes a keen insight as to what your main character's key weakness is. If your main character is disorganised, your ally should be diligent. If your main character is emotional, the ally needs to be cold and analytical. If your main character is prone to impulsive decisions, your ally must be the voice of calm reason.

COMMON MISTAKE

One common mistake is crafting allies that are mere background decoration for the main character's narrative. They must be integral to the plot, not just there to make up the numbers.

ALLY

WHY IS THE ALLY RELEVANT?

- Adding in the solution to the problem faced by the main character

That key piece of information? That motivational speech? The rallying of the troops on behalf of the hero? This is your ally's main job in the story.

- Driving the plot

Allies propel your story forward. Their support, advice, and sometimes even their sacrifice, creates emotional engagement in the reader, keeping them engaged and invested in the story throughout.

- Emotional impact

Allies have the power to pull at the heartstrings, especially if there is a sacrifice to be made at the end so the main character can complete their mission.

- Themes and messages

Allies promote your story's themes, carrying messages that resonate deeply with your audience, especially if the theme is the true meaning of friendship.

ALLY

COMMON MISTAKES TO AVOID

- Background filler

Not giving your ally a sufficient role in the story makes them almost surplus to requirements. There is no point in having them in the story if they don't "advance the mission" in some way.

- Inconsistent behaviour

Allies should remain consistent, behaving in ways that align with the vows of friendship they have sworn with the main character.

- Overwhelming cast

Like a party where everyone talks at once, too many allies can overwhelm. Develop your main ally's goal meaningfully, and, if the story requires it, have a wider group of helpers in the background that aren't as fleshed out.

CHOOSING YOUR ALLY

Choose an ally from your story and delve into their backstory. What events shaped them into who they are today? How do these experiences fuel their actions?

The key features of my main ally:

GOALS

BUILD THEIR BOLD AMBITIONS

GOALS

Character goals are the desires and ambitions that drive your character's actions and decision-making forward. These are things they want to achieve, like winning a competition, finding love, or solving a mystery. Goals are like destinations your characters aim for in their journey.

HOW TO KEEP READERS READING? GOALS
"Will the hero succeed in his quest? I must find out..."

HOW TO GET READERS TO CARE ABOUT MY CHARACTER? GOALS
"I really hope the hero succeeds, he's been through so much already..."

HOW TO KEEP MY CHARACTER MOVING FORWARD? GOALS
"I hope he gets out of this situation (obstacle) so he can achieve his goal."

PROBLEM

Creating characters without clear goals leaves your story lacking direction and purpose. Creating character profiles is a great way to avoid this common pitfall.

COMMON MISTAKE

Characters without goals are pointless and very frustrating to readers. There is no conflict or obstacle for them to overcome hence leaving the reader wondering what the point of them is. They drift through your narrative without making a meaningful impact, leaving readers disconnected and unengaged.

GOALS

WHAT YOU NEED TO KNOW BEFORE YOU WRITE YOUR STORY

- Character motivations

Before you start writing, delve into your main character's motivations. What fuels their passion? What keeps them awake at night? These inner drives fuel their goals.

- External vs. internal goals

Differentiate between external goals, which are visible and tangible (like saving a village), and internal goals, which are emotional and psychological (like finding self-acceptance). Both layers shape your character's journey.

- Stakes and consequences

Every goal comes with stakes and consequences. Whether it's gaining the treasure or losing a loved one, these stakes add tension, drama, and urgency to your character's path.

GOALS

WHY ARE GOALS RELEVANT?

- Plot focus

Character goals are incredibly important. They guide the plot's trajectory, steering your narrative towards a destination, and ensuring it doesn't lose its way.

- Character development

Character goals should be treated like milestones in the narrative. As characters pursue their goals, they evolve, learn, and transform. This evolution is the heart of character development.

- Reader engagement

Readers root for characters to conquer challenges and achieve their goals. The journey becomes a shared experience that captivates and binds your audience.

- Theme reinforcement

Goals reflect and reinforce the story's themes, deepening its impact and resonating with readers.

GOALS

COMMON MISTAKES TO AVOID

- Lack of goals

Characters without clear goals lead to a plot without purpose. Define their aims to give your story a compelling direction.

- Unrealistic goals

Setting goals as unattainable will affect your story's credibility. Make goals challenging yet attainable within your story's context.

- Inconsistent goals

Ensure goals remain consistent unless it's part of the character's growth.

- Overemphasising external goals

External goals are the visible tip of the iceberg, but internal goals are the submerged part. Balance both for well-rounded characters with emotional depth.

- Neglecting stakes

Characters need stakes — the risks and rewards that amplify the importance of their goals and make readers care deeply.

CHOOSING GOALS AND MOTIVATIONS

Choose your main character and jot down their key motivations and potential goals. How do these desires drive their actions? What are the stakes involved?

The key motivations and goals of my main character:

....
....
....
....
....
....
....
....
....
....
....
....
....
....
....
....
....
....
....

OBSTACLES

HELP YOUR CHARACTERS NAVIGATE THEIR JOURNEY

OBSTACLES

FORGING PATHWAYS OF CHALLENGE

An obstacle in a story is a challenge or problem that characters must overcome to achieve their goals, adding complexity and interest to the plot.

Obstacles create tension and make the story interesting. Obstacles can be anything from physical barriers to emotional struggles. They shape the journey your characters take.

PROBLEM

Writing a story without obstacles leaves your narrative on a straight and dull road. You must ensure your characters' journeys are as captivating as they are challenging.

COMMON MISTAKE

An obstacle-free story lacks the pulse-pounding excitement that keeps readers hooked.

OBSTACLES

WHAT YOU NEED TO KNOW BEFORE YOU WRITE YOUR STORY

- Character goals

Before you begin, pinpoint your characters' specific goals — what they're striving for. Obstacles should be roadblocks that directly challenge these ambitions.

- Types of obstacles

Obstacles come in various forms. There are external hurdles (like climbing a treacherous mountain) and internal ones (like battling self-doubt). A mix of both adds depth and authenticity to your characters' struggles.

- Obstacle Placement

Place obstacles at just the right moments. Strategically position obstacles to maintain a rhythm that keeps readers engaged and eagerly turning pages.

OBSTACLES

WHY ARE OBSTACLES RELEVANT?

- Conflict and tension

Obstacles are the unexpected twists that keep readers guessing and invested in your characters' journey.

- Character growth

Overcoming challenges forces characters to evolve, revealing their true potential and inner resilience.

- Plot development

Obstacles shape the narrative's blueprint, guiding characters to make crucial choices and driving the story forward toward its climax.

OBSTACLES

COMMON MISTAKES TO AVOID

- Insufficient obstacles

Ensure your characters face meaningful challenges that fuel their development and keep readers engaged.

- Unrelated obstacles

Make sure each hurdle is directly tied to the characters' goals and the central conflict, creating a seamless and purposeful narrative.

- Overwhelming characters

Too many obstacles can overwhelm your characters and the readers. Balance is key: choose obstacles that naturally arise from the story's context.

- Easily resolved obstacles

Obstacles should be formidable foes, presenting characters with genuine struggles that demand ingenuity and effort.

- Neglecting emotional obstacles

Emotions are essential. Don't forget emotional obstacles that delve into characters' inner struggles, adding layers of depth and relatability.

OBSTACLES

BETRAYAL	CONFLICT	DECEPTION
CORRUPTION	SOLITUDE	VENGEANCE
TRAGEDY	ABDUCTION	DEPENDENCY
CALAMITY	CALAMITY	ALIEN INCURSION
SUPERNATURAL PRESENCE	MUTATION	ECOLOGICAL CRISIS
CONSPIRACIES	ESPIONAGE	TECHNICAL MALFUNCTION
SHAPE-SHIFTING	POWER DYNAMICS	POLITICAL UNREST
VIRTUAL REALMS	FORBIDDEN EMOTIONS	SURVIVAL CHALLENGE
INFORMATION MANIPULATION	MIND MANIPULATION	IDENTITY CHALLENGE
REBELLION	UNSTABLE PARTNERSHIPS	PROPHETIC EVENTS
ECONOMIC COLLAPSE	REALITY DISTORTION	TIME CONSTRAINT
MISINFORMATION	LOST CIVILIZATIONS	FAMILY DISCORD
TEMPORAL RIFT	ANCESTRAL HEX	CIVIL UNREST
CURSED OBJECT	ROGUE TECHNOLOGY	FEAR

OBSTACLES

LET'S SEE 'OBSTACLES' IN ACTION

Let's pick three common obstacles:

Betrayal, Conflict, and Survival Challenge.

- Betrayal:

    - Example: In a thriller novel, the protagonist discovers that their closest ally, who was thought to be working towards a common goal, has been secretly working for the antagonist all along. This betrayal puts the protagonist's life and mission at risk, forcing them to reevaluate their trust in others.

- Conflict:

    - Example: In a family drama, two siblings inherit a family business but have conflicting visions for its future. The clash of ideas and values leads to intense conflicts between them, jeopardising not only the business but also the family bonds. The main character must navigate these conflicts to find a resolution that preserves both the business and their relationship.

- Survival Challenge:

    - Example: In a post-apocalyptic setting, the main character and a group of survivors are stranded in a harsh environment with limited resources. As tensions rise and external threats loom, the group must make tough decisions to ensure their survival. The main character takes on the role of a leader, facing the challenge of balancing the needs of the group while dealing with internal strife and external dangers.

CHOOSING OBSTACLES

Select a character and jot down their goals. Then brainstorm obstacles that could stand in their way — both external and internal challenges that will test their determination.

	GOAL	OBSTACLE
1		INTERNAL:
		EXTERNAL:
2		INTERNAL:
		EXTERNAL:
3		INTERNAL:
		EXTERNAL:
4		INTERNAL:
		EXTERNAL:
5		INTERNAL:
		EXTERNAL:

THEMES

DISCOVERING THE HEART OF YOUR STORY

THEMES

UNVEILING DEEPER MEANINGS

A theme is the main idea or message that a story wants to share. It's like the big lesson or important thought that the story teaches us.

Themes are the hidden messages in your story. They give your story depth and make readers think. Themes can be about friendship, courage, or even the meaning of life. Unveiling these deeper meanings adds richness to your story, making it more intriguing and thought-provoking.

PROBLEM

A story without themes lacks the profound layers that captivate and linger in readers' minds.

COMMON MISTAKE

A themeless story robs your narrative of emotional depth and leaves readers yearning for substance.

THEMES

WHAT YOU NEED TO KNOW BEFORE YOU WRITE YOUR STORY

- Central message

Before you put pen to paper, unravel the central message or concepts you want to explore. Themes are the undercurrents that enrich your story.

- Character journeys

Consider how themes will influence your characters' growth, choices, and transformations, giving your narrative an emotional heartbeat.

- Symbolism and imagery

Use symbolism and vivid imagery to reinforce your story's themes, creating a multi-dimensional experience that lingers in readers' minds.

THEMES

WHY ARE THEMES RELEVANT?

- Deeper meaning

Themes infuse your narrative with layers of meaning, encouraging readers to ponder the bigger questions.

- Emotional resonance

Themes connect readers to characters and events on a profound level, leaving a lasting emotional impact.

- Coherence and unity

Themes provide a sense of coherence, making your story a well-crafted masterpiece.

THEMES

COMMON MISTAKES TO AVOID

- Forced themes

Avoid forcing themes into your narrative; let them arise organically, weaving seamlessly into the fabric of your story.

- Overly explicit

Allow readers to unearth your themes rather than spoon-feeding every nuance. Subtlety invites exploration.

- Conflicting themes

Ensure your themes work together harmoniously, enhancing rather than conflicting with each other.

- Neglecting themes

Even if not overt, themes provide the texture that transforms a story from ordinary to extraordinary.

- Heavy-handedness

Balance is key; themes should be felt. Avoid heavy-handed approaches that overshadow your narrative's beauty.

THEMES

HERE ARE TEN OF THE MOST COMMON THEMES IN FICTION

1. Love and sacrifice: The selflessness and sacrifices people make for those they care about.

2. Good vs. evil: The eternal struggle between moral righteousness and malevolence.

3. Identity and self-discovery: Characters find their true selves and embrace their uniqueness.

4. Power and corruption: The corrupting influence of power and the consequences of unchecked authority.

5. Coming of age: The journey of growth and maturation as characters transition from adolescence to adulthood.

6. Redemption and forgiveness: Characters seek redemption for past mistakes and learn to forgive themselves and others.

7. Isolation and connection: The impact of loneliness and the significance of meaningful connections with others.

8. Survival and resilience: The strength and determination required to overcome life-threatening challenges.

9. Justice and injustice: The pursuit of fairness and the consequences of inequality or injustice.

10. Family and belonging: The importance of family bonds and the search for a sense of belonging.

CHOOSING THEMES

Select a theme you want to explore in your story. Brainstorm ways to subtly incorporate it into various scenes and character interactions.

The key theme I have chosen to explore in my story is:

TITLES

PIQUE YOUR READER'S CURIOSITY...!

TITLES

"WHAT SHALL I CALL MY STORY?"

A story/book title is designed to capture the essence of the content, evoke interest, and provide a glimpse into the themes, tone, or central idea of the story or book.

SOME COMMON QUESTIONS ABOUT TITLES

- How important is the title?

  - The title is highly important as it serves as the first point of contact between your story and potential readers. A compelling title can grab attention, convey the essence of the story, and contribute to its overall appeal.

- When should I create the title?

  - There's flexibility in when you create the title. Some writers prefer to have a working title from the start, while others find inspiration during or after completing the story. Experiment and choose a time that feels most comfortable for you.

- How long should a title be?

  - The length of a title can vary. Generally, it's good to aim for a title that is concise, memorable, and relevant to the story. Short titles can be impactful, but longer titles can work if they effectively capture the essence of the narrative.

- What if I can't think of a good title?

  - If you're struggling with a title, don't worry. It's a common challenge. Experiment with brainstorming sessions, involve others for input or even revisit your story once it's complete to find elements that could inspire a fitting title. Be patient and open to revisions as your story evolves.

TITLES

WAYS TO COME UP WITH INTRIGUING STORY TITLES:

- Theme:
  - Reflect on a central theme or emotion from your story, such as "Whispers of Betrayal" or "Eternal Hope."

- Location:
  - Highlight the setting or a significant location in your story, like "Midnight in Paris" or "Island of Shadows."

- Phrases used in the story:
  - Pull a powerful or intriguing phrase directly from your story, such as "Silent Echoes" or "Dancing with Shadows."

- Character Name:
  - Feature the name of a key character, emphasising their importance or the story's focus, like "Elena's Awakening" or "The Mystery of Captain Black."

- Symbolic imagery:
  - Use symbolic imagery that represents a key aspect of your story, for example, "The Crimson Rose" or "Wings of Destiny."

TITLES

WAYS TO COME UP WITH INTRIGUING STORY TITLES:

- Genre elements:
  - Incorporate elements specific to your genre, like "Whispers of the Supernatural" or "Noir Nights."

- Key event:
  - Focus on a pivotal event in your story, creating intrigue, such as "The Vanishing Act" or "Beneath the Moonlit Bridge."

- Mood or tone:
  - Convey the mood or tone of your story, whether it's mysterious, romantic, or adventurous, like "Whispers of the Enchanted Forest" or "Shattered Dreams."

- Alliteration:
  - Play with words that start with the same letter or sound, providing a rhythmic quality to the title, for example, "Secrets in the Shadows" or "Echoes of Eternity."

- Contrast:
  - Create a title with contrasting elements that capture the essence of your story, like "Whispers in the Storm" or "The Lighthouse's Darkness."

IF YOU WANT GENRE-SPECIFIC IDEAS, HEAD TO YOUR GENRE TOOLKIT AND YOU'LL FIND LOTS OF IDEAS THERE!

LOGLINES

HOOK, LINE AND SINKER: CAPTIVATING READERS WITH LOGLINES

LOGLINES

A logline is a brief, one-sentence summary that captures the essence of a story, conveying its main character, goal, conflict, and sometimes its unique twist or hook.

Loglines are the keys that unlock curiosity and encourage readers to embark on a thrilling literary journey!

Think of your logline as a trailer for your story - a short preview that captures the excitement, essence, and intrigue of your entire narrative in just a few seconds, leaving the audience eager to experience the full

PROBLEM

Creating a logline-less story leaves readers puzzled and unmoved. Understanding loglines prevents this and creates intrigue in your story from the outset.

COMMON MISTAKE

A lacklustre logline can have the same effect as a movie trailer that reveals the whole plot. It spoils the excitement for the reader.

LOGLINES

WHAT YOU NEED TO KNOW BEFORE YOU CREATE YOUR LOGLINE

- Central focus

Before you begin writing your logline, grasp your story's core — genre, main characters, and the burning conflict that propels the narrative.

- Hooking element

Identify the unique aspect that sets your narrative apart, the hook that will leave readers craving more.

- Simplicity and clarity

Keep your logline brief, crystal-clear, and free of clutter, encapsulating your entire tale in a few simple sentences.

LOGLINES

WHY ARE LOGLINES RELEVANT?

- **Attention grabber**

A well-constructed logline hooks curiosity, making readers eager to explore further.

- **Pitching tool**

Agents, publishers, and curious minds can quickly grasp your story's essence from your logline, opening doors to exciting opportunities.

- **Story essence**

Loglines encapsulate your story's key elements – the characters, conflict, and tone – in a tantalising nutshell.

LOGLINES

COMMON MISTAKES TO AVOID

- Vagueness

A vague logline lacks the punch to intrigue. Ensure your logline is a clear, crisp image that entices readers to carry on reading.

- Revealing too much

Avoid plot spoilers in your writing. Keep major twists and surprises under wraps, inviting readers to savour every discovery.

- Ambiguity

Your logline should be clear and outline the central conflict and stakes.

- Complexity

Craft your logline clearly. Complex sentence structures can cloud the message you're trying to convey.

- Omitting main characters

Include key characters in the logline. This will forge an immediate connection to them with the readers.

LOGLINES

HERE ARE SOME GENRE-SPECIFIC LOGLINES

1. **Adventure/fantasy:** A young farm boy discovers he is the heir to a powerful kingdom and must embark on a perilous quest to defeat an ancient evil and restore peace to the realm.

2. **Romantic comedy:** When a workaholic executive and a free-spirited artist cross paths in a quirky small town, they find themselves on an unexpected journey of love, self-discovery, and hilarious mishaps.

3. **Mystery/thriller:** A brilliant detective races against time to catch a serial killer who leaves cryptic clues at crime scenes, but as the body count rises, the detective realises the killer is someone from their past.

4. **Science fiction:** In a future where emotions are outlawed, a rebel group fights to restore humanity's ability to feel, and a young woman must choose between loyalty to the cause and her forbidden love for an emotionless soldier.

5. **Drama:** A struggling musician navigates fame, addiction, and the complexities of love as he rises to stardom in the music industry, ultimately discovering the true cost of his dreams.

CREATING YOUR LOGLINE

HERE WE GO!
LET'S GET CATCHY!

CREATING YOUR LOGLINE

STEP 1:
HOW TO WRITE A BASIC LOGLINE

Writing a compelling logline is crucial for capturing the essence of your story concisely and intriguingly. The following framework will help you to craft your logline.

1. **Genre:** Start by identifying the genre of your story. This sets the overall tone and helps readers understand the type of story they can expect.

2. **Setting:** Introduce the setting or the world in which your story takes place. This helps create a visual backdrop for your logline.

3. **Main character:** Introduce the main character or protagonist. Mention their name (if relevant) and provide a concise description of who they are and their role in the story.

4. **Goal:** State the main character's primary goal or what they are striving to achieve throughout the story. This is the driving force behind the plot.

5. **Obstacle:** Identify the main obstacle or challenge the protagonist must overcome to achieve their goal. This creates conflict and raises stakes in the logline.

CREATING YOUR LOGLINE

STEP 1:
HOW TO WRITE A BASIC LOGLINE

6. **Love Interest/villain/supporting characters:** If applicable, include any key supporting characters, love interests, or antagonists that play a significant role in the story.

7. **Consequences:** Mention the consequences or risks involved if the main character fails to achieve their goal. This adds tension and urgency to the logline.

8. **Theme:** If possible, subtly hint at the theme or underlying message of your story. This adds depth and intrigue to the logline.

9. **Length:** Keep the logline concise and to the point. Aim for one to two sentences, ideally not exceeding 25-30 words.

10. **Edit and revise:** Craft several versions of the logline, experimenting with different word choices and arrangements. Edit and revise until you have a logline that is clear, engaging, and piques the readers' curiosity.

Remember, the logline should provide a snapshot of your story's core elements and entice the reader to want more.

CREATING YOUR LOGLINE

EXAMPLE

GENRE: Romance

SETTING: City

MAIN CHARACTER: Reluctant Banker

GOAL: To realise his dream of becoming an artist

OTHER CHARACTERS: His love interest, Grace

OBSTACLE: He wants to leave the family business, but can't

CONSEQUENCES: If the banker leaves his job (family business), his family will disown him

THEME: Love over everything.

LOGLINE:

In a *bustling city*, a *reluctant banker* longs to pursue his passion for art and become an *artist*, but when he falls for *Grace*, he *risks disownment by his family if he follows his heart*, in this heartfelt *romance*, where *love defies expectations and empowers dreams*.

- SETTING: bustling city
- MAIN CHARACTER AND THEIR NAME: reluctant banker
- GOAL: for art and become an artist
- LOVE INTEREST: Grace
- OBSTACLE: he risks disownment by his family if he follows his heart
- GENRE: romance
- THEME: love defies expectations and empowers dreams
- CONSEQUENCES: disownment by his family

CREATING YOUR LOGLINE

STEP 2:
HOW TO INCLUDE MORE DETAIL IN YOUR LOGLINE

Let's expand upon this logline, including more detail, a plot twist and an ending.

GENRE: Romance

SETTING: City of London

TIME PERIOD: Modern day

MAIN CHARACTER: Reluctant banker named Ethan Roberts

GOAL: To realise his dream of becoming an artist

OTHER CHARACTERS: His love interest, Grace who is an artist

VILLAIN: Another banker called Eric Winters

OBSTACLE: He wants to leave the family business, but can't

CONSEQUENCES + WHY: If Ethan leaves his job (the family business, Roberts Banking and Co.), his family will disown him and disinherit him and it will bring shame on generations of wealthy and successful family members.

THEME: Love over everything.

CREATING YOUR LOGLINE

OUR NEW, IMPROVED LOGLINE

In the <u>modern-day City of London</u> [SETTING / TIME PERIOD], <u>Ethan Roberts, a reluctant banker</u> [MAIN CHARACTER AND THEIR NAME] at Roberts Banking and Co., <u>dreams of becoming an artist</u> [GOAL], but his aspirations clash with family expectations. When he meets <u>Grace, a talented artist</u> [LOVE INTEREST], love blossoms, but the <u>sinister banker Eric Winters</u> [VILLAIN] becomes an obstacle, <u>risking disinheritance and shame from generations of wealth</u> [CONSEQUENCES] if Ethan follows his heart, in this <u>heart-warming romance</u> [GENRE] where <u>love triumphs</u> [THEME] over societal pressures.

PLANNING YOUR LOGLINE

Follow the prompts, and inspiration from the three examples in this workbook, and think of the logline for your short story idea.

GENRE: ....

SETTING: ....

MAIN CHARACTER: ....

GOAL: ....

OTHER CHARACTERS: ....

OBSTACLE: ....

CONSEQUENCES: ....

THEME: ....

LOGLINE:

....

....

....

....

....

....

....

....

CHARACTER ARCS

CREATING MEMORABLE CHARACTER JOURNEYS

CHARACTER ARCS

WHAT IS A CHARACTER ARC?

A character arc is like a journey of change and growth for a character in a story. It's how the character learns and evolves as they face challenges and experiences.

We need character arcs in stories because they make the characters more interesting and relatable. When we see a character overcome struggles and develop throughout the story, we feel more connected to them emotionally. It also helps the story feel complete and meaningful as we see the characters learn important lessons and become better versions of themselves.

HOW CHARACTER ARCS WORK IN THE THREE-ACT STRUCTURE

Here is an example of Russell Crowe's character in Gladiator:

Act 1 (Beginning): Maximus is a loyal and respected Roman general, devoted to the Emperor, Marcus Aurelius. He dreams of returning to his farm and family after serving Rome.

Act 2 (Middle): (Something happened to change him) Betrayed and sentenced to death by Commodus, Maximus becomes a gladiator. He gains fame and respect, fighting for justice and freedom, becoming known as "The Spaniard."

Act 3 (End): Maximus seeks revenge against Commodus and fights to restore Rome's greatness. He confronts Commodus in the Colosseum, defeating him in a final showdown. Maximus sacrifices himself to ensure Rome's legacy and the Senate's rule are upheld.

So Maximus went from a simple man wanting to get back to his farm (Act 1) to seeking revenge against high-powered people (Act 3).

CHARACTER DESCRIPTIONS

CHARACTER DESCRIPTIONS

Using the following lists, writers can mix and match descriptions to create well-rounded and visually descriptive characters that resonate with readers. Remember to use vivid language to bring the characters to life and evoke clear mental images in the minds of your audience.

BUILD/PHYSIQUE

SLENDER	CURVY	CHUBBY	HEAVYSET
ATHLETIC	LANKY	WELL-BUILT	TONED
MUSCULAR	STOCKY	THIN	FIT
STOUT	VOLUPTUOUS	BROAD-SHOULDERED	TRIM
PETITE	LEAN	SVELTE	GAUNT

HEIGHT

TALL	SHORT	AVERAGE	TOWERING
PETITE	STATUESQUE	LANKY	COMPACT
STATURED	STUNTED	VERTICALLY-CHALLENGED	DIMINUTIVE

95

CHARACTER DESCRIPTIONS

HAIR

STRAIGHT	SILKY	CURLY	SHAGGY
SPIKY	SLEEK	MESSY	FRIZZY
LONG	SHORT	SHOULDER-LENGTH	BALD
THICK	THIN	FLOWING	TOUSLED

EYES

DEEP-SET	ALMOND-SHAPED	ROUND	NARROW
SPARKLING	INTENSE	DREAMY	PIERCING
SOULFUL	DOE-EYED	BRIGHT	HOODED
DULL	MISCHIEVOUS	EXPRESSIVE	SLANTED

CHARACTER DESCRIPTIONS

SKIN

FAIR	TANNED	OLIVE-SKINNED	DARK-SKINNED
PALE	ROSY	FLAWLESS	FRECKLED
SCARRED	WRINKLED	SMOOTH	SUN-KISSED
POCKMARKED	SALLOW	BLEMISHED	FRESH

FACIAL FEATURES/DISTINGUISHING MARKS

HIGH CHEECKBONES	STRONG JAWLINE	CHISELED FEATURES	DIMPLES
FULL LIPS	THIN LIPS	BUTTON NOSE	ROMAN NOSE
CLEFT CHIN	SHARP NOSE	CROOKED TEETH	DASHING SMILE
SUNKEN CHEEKS	PROMINENT BROW	DEFINED CHIN	MOLEY COMPLEXION
BIRTHMARK	TATTOO	SCARS	FRECKLES
BEAUTY SPOT	CROSS-EYED	PIERCINGS	EYEBROW SLIT
HARELIP	MISSING LIMB	FACIAL HAIR	GAP-TOOTHED

POSITIVE CHARACTER TRAITS

POSITIVE CHARACTER TRAITS

COMPASSIONATE	A character stops to help a homeless person on a cold night, offering them food and warm clothing.
COURAGEOUS	Despite facing their own fears, a character stands up to a bully, defending a friend from harm.
HONEST	In a difficult situation, a character admits their mistake to their boss, even though it could have serious consequences.
EMPATHETIC	A character listens attentively to a friend going through a tough time, offering support and understanding without judgment.
LOYAL	In the face of adversity, a character remains steadfastly loyal to their family, standing by them through thick and thin.
WISE	An elderly character shares valuable life lessons with a young protagonist, guiding them on their journey.
OPTIMISTIC	Despite setbacks, a character maintains a positive attitude, believing that things will improve in the future.
CHARISMATIC	During a public speech, a character captivates the audience with their charm and charisma, winning their hearts.
DETERMINED	In pursuit of their dream, a character tirelessly perseveres, never giving up on their goal.
CREATIVE	A character uses their artistic talents to create unique and beautiful works of art, inspiring others with their creativity.

POSITIVE CHARACTER TRAITS

RESILIENT	After facing a major setback, a character bounces back and rebuilds their life with renewed strength and determination.
GENEROUS	A character selflessly donates their time and resources to help those in need, without expecting anything in return.
PATIENT	A character remains calm and understanding while teaching a difficult concept to someone, offering guidance at their own pace.
HUMBLE	Despite their success, a character remains modest and does not boast about their achievements.
RELIABLE	A character always keeps their promises and is there to support their friends in times of need.
CONFIDENT	In a challenging situation, a character shows self-assurance and belief in their abilities, inspiring others around them.
KIND	A character shows kindness to animals, feeding a stray cat and providing shelter during a storm.
INDEPENDENT	A character takes charge of their own life decisions, not relying on others for approval or validation.
RESOURCEFUL	In a survival situation, a character cleverly uses the available resources to overcome obstacles and find a way out.
OPEN-MINDED	A character respects and considers different perspectives, engaging in thoughtful discussions without prejudice.

NEGATIVE CHARACTER TRAITS

NEGATIVE CHARACTER TRAITS

AGGRESSIVE	A character starts a physical altercation over a minor disagreement, resorting to violence to resolve the issue.
ARROGANT	A character constantly brags about their achievements, belittling others and believing they are superior.
MANIPULATIVE	A character uses charm and deceit to manipulate others into doing what they want, even if it's against their best interests.
DISHONEST	A character lies about their actions to avoid taking responsibility for their mistakes.
GREEDY	A character is obsessed with accumulating wealth and will do anything, even unethical acts, to acquire more.
JEALOUSLY	A character becomes envious and resentful of a friend's success, leading to strained relationships.
STUBBORN	A character refuses to change their mind or consider alternative viewpoints, leading to conflicts and misunderstandings.
SELF-CENTRED	A character only cares about their own needs and desires, disregarding others' feelings and priorities.
IMPULSIVE	A character makes hasty decisions without considering the consequences, often leading to trouble.
PESSIMISTIC	A character always expects the worst outcome in any situation and lacks hope for positive outcomes.

NEGATIVE CHARACTER TRAITS

MOODY	A character's emotions fluctuate dramatically, making them unpredictable and challenging to interact with.
VENGEFUL	A character seeks revenge against someone who has wronged them, planning and executing harmful actions.
RUDE	A character consistently uses offensive language and behavior towards others, showing a lack of manners.
RECKLESS	A character takes unnecessary risks without considering the potential dangers or consequences.
INSECURE	A character is constantly doubting their abilities and seeking validation from others.
CYNICAL	A character has a negative and distrustful attitude towards people's motives and the world in general.
NARCISSISTIC	A character is obsessed with their appearance and achievements, lacking empathy for others.
SARCASTIC	A character uses sarcasm to mock and belittle others, often causing hurt feelings.
JUDGEMENTAL	A character quickly forms negative opinions about others based on superficial characteristics.
CONDESCENDING	A character talks down to others, believing they are superior in knowledge or status.

BACKGROUND IDEAS

BACKGROUND IDEAS

- Grew up in a large city or small town
- Raised in a close-knit family or an orphan
- Experienced a significant loss or tragedy
- Faced financial struggles or grew up wealthy
- Had a challenging childhood with abusive parents
- Overcame a serious illness or disability
- Grew up in a strict religious household
- Moved frequently due to a parent's job
- Faced discrimination or prejudice based on their race, gender, or identity
- Was a rebellious teenager who clashed with authority figures
- Excelled in academics or struggled with school
- Developed a strong passion for a specific hobby or talent

- Experienced a life-changing event that shaped their future decisions
- Had a mentor or role model who influenced their life choices
- Pursued a dream or goal despite societal or family pressures
- Lived through a natural disaster or a war
- Immigrated to a new country and experienced culture shock
- Had a troubled past involving criminal activities or addiction
- Overcame a fear or phobia that affected their life choices
- Struggled with mental health issues and sought therapy or treatment
- Faced discrimination or challenges in their career or profession
- Served in the military and experienced combat
- Formed deep friendships or severed ties with old friends due to conflicts
- Had a childhood friend who became an enemy or rival

INTERNAL STRUGGLES/ CONFLICTS

INTERNAL STRUGGLES/CONFLICTS

SELF-DOUBT AND INSECURITY	Feeling uncertain about one's abilities, worth, or appearance, which can hinder personal growth and confidence.
FEAR OF FAILURE	Being afraid of not succeeding or falling short of expectations, leading to avoidance or reluctance to take risks.
DESIRE FOR ACCEPTANCE VS. AUTHENTICITY	Struggling to balance the need for social acceptance with staying true to one's authentic self.
REGRET AND GUILT	Feeling remorseful about past actions or decisions and finding it difficult to forgive oneself.
NEED FOR CONTROL VS. GOING WITH THE FLOW	Battling the urge to control every aspect of life versus learning to accept uncertainty and relinquish control when necessary.
BALANCING WORK-LIFE PRIORITIES	Striving to find a harmonious balance between professional responsibilities and personal life.
MANAGING EXPECTATIONS	Coping with the pressure of meeting others' expectations or societal norms while maintaining individual aspirations.
HANDLING CHANGE AND UNCERTAINTY	Dealing with the discomfort of unpredictable situations or major life changes.
CONFLICT BETWEEN REASON AND EMOTION	Struggling to align logical reasoning with emotional impulses, leading to inner turmoil.
IMPOSTER SYNDROME	Feeling like a fraud or unworthy of success despite evidence of competence or achievement.

INTERNAL STRUGGLES/CONFLICTS

LONELINESS AND ISOLATION	Experiencing feelings of disconnectedness or isolation, even when surrounded by others.
OVERCOMING A TRAUMATIC EXPERIENCE	Working through the aftermath of a traumatic event and finding ways to heal and move forward.
BODY IMAGE AND SELF-ESTEEM	Struggling with body image issues and negative self-perception.
FEAR OF REJECTION	Being hesitant to express oneself or form close relationships due to the fear of rejection.
DEALING WITH LOSS AND GRIEF	Coping with the emotional impact of losing a loved one or experiencing other significant losses.
MANAGING ANGER AND RESENTMENT	Finding healthy ways to deal with feelings of anger or resentment towards others.
FINDING PURPOSE AND MEANING	Seeking a sense of purpose and direction in life, and grappling with existential questions.
DEPENDENCY VS. INDEPENDENCE	Balancing the desire for independence with the need for support and connection from others.
BALANCING PERSONAL NEEDS AND OTHERS' EXPECTATIONS	Striving to meet personal needs and goals while also fulfilling obligations to others.
OVERCOMING PERFECTIONISM	Dealing with the constant need to achieve perfection and the associated anxiety of not meeting impossibly high standards.

External Struggles/ Conflicts

EXTERNAL STRUGGLES/CONFLICTS

INTERPERSONAL CONFLICT	Struggles within relationships with family members, friends, colleagues, or romantic partners.
WORKPLACE CONFLICT	Challenges and disagreements with co-workers, supervisors, or the work environment.
SOCIAL PRESSURES AND EXPECTATIONS	Dealing with societal norms and expectations that may conflict with personal values or choices.
FINANCIAL STRUGGLES	Coping with financial difficulties, debt, or economic hardships.
ENVIRONMENTAL OR NATURAL DISASTERS	Facing challenges posed by natural calamities like hurricanes, earthquakes, or floods.
HEALTH ISSUES AND MEDICAL CRISES	Dealing with physical or mental health problems, chronic illnesses, or medical emergencies.
LEGAL ISSUES AND DISPUTES	Coping with legal challenges, lawsuits, or conflicts with the law.
CULTURAL OR ETHNIC CONFLICTS	Struggles arising from cultural or ethnic differences, discrimination, or prejudice.
TECHNOLOGICAL CHALLENGES	Dealing with issues related to technology, such as cyber threats, data breaches, or digital privacy concerns.
COMPETING LIFE PRIORITIES	Juggling multiple responsibilities and obligations, such as family, career, education, and personal pursuits.

EXTERNAL STRUGGLES/CONFLICTS

CONFLICT WITH AUTHORITIES	Facing challenges with government agencies, law enforcement, or institutional authorities.
WAR AND ARMED CONFLICTS	Coping with the impact of war, violence, or political unrest in one's country or region.
BULLYING OR HARASSMENT	Dealing with aggressive or harmful behaviour from others.
NAVIGATING MAJOR LIFE TRANSITIONS	Coping with significant life changes like moving to a new city, starting college, or getting married.
FAMILY DISPUTES OR ESTRANGEMENT	Struggling with conflicts or disconnect within one's family, including sibling rivalry or parental issues.
WORK-LIFE BALANCE	Balancing the demands of work and personal life, such as long work hours affecting family time.
DEALING WITH LOSS OF PROPERTY OR POSSESSIONS	Coping with the aftermath of theft, accidents, or natural disasters that result in property loss.
SOCIAL ISOLATION OR EXCLUSION	Feeling excluded or isolated from social groups or communities.
SURVIVING IN HOSTILE ENVIRONMENTS	Coping with challenging conditions in extreme climates or dangerous locations.
GLOBAL CRISES	Facing widespread issues like pandemics, economic downturns, or political upheavals that affect societies on a global scale.

MOTIVATIONS AND GOALS

MOTIVATIONS AND GOALS

ACHIEVEMENT AND SUCCESS

MOTIVATION	SHORT-TERM GOALS	LONG-TERM GOALS
The character is driven by the desire to achieve greatness, reach their full potential, and excel in their chosen field or endeavour.	To complete specific tasks, win competitions, or receive recognition for their efforts.	To become a respected leader, reach the pinnacle of success in their career, or leave a lasting legacy.

LOVE AND CONNECTION

MOTIVATION	SHORT-TERM GOALS	LONG-TERM GOALS
The character is motivated by the need for love, belonging, and meaningful relationships with others.	To establish new connections, strengthen existing relationships, or mend broken bonds.	To build a close-knit family, find a life partner, or cultivate a supportive and loving social circle.

MOTIVATIONS AND GOALS

DISCOVERY AND KNOWLEDGE

MOTIVATION	SHORT-TERM GOALS	LONG-TERM GOALS
The character is driven by a thirst for knowledge, understanding, and exploration of the world around them.	To unravel mysteries, acquire new skills, or explore uncharted territories.	To become an expert in their field, make groundbreaking discoveries, or contribute significantly to human knowledge.

JUSTICE AND ADVOCACY

MOTIVATION	SHORT-TERM GOALS	LONG-TERM GOALS
The character is motivated by a strong sense of justice, fairness, and the desire to help those in need.	To right wrongs, protect the vulnerable, or stand up against injustice.	To bring about meaningful change, fight for equal rights, or create a more just and compassionate society.

OCCUPATIONS

OCCUPATIONS

DOCTOR	TEACHER	DETECTIVE	CHEF
MUSICIAN	SCIENTIST	POLICE OFFICER	ACTOR/ACTRESS
FIREFIGHTER	JOURNALIST	ENGINEER	LAWYER
ARCHAEOLOGIST	PHOTOGRAPHER	FARMER	PILOT
ATHLETE	PSYCHOLOGIST	ARTIST	ARCHITECT
FASHION DESIGNER	SOCIAL WORKER	VETERINARIAN	ASTRONAUT
CHEF	MECHANIC	PERSONAL TRAINER	ENVIRONMENTALIST
PARAMEDIC	NURSE	ENTREPRENEUR	ECONOMIST
GEOLOGIST	MARKETING EXECUTIVE	LIBRARIAN	ELECTRICIAN
FILM DIRECTOR	SOFTWARE DEVELOPER	ZOOLOGIST	PROFESSOR
DANCER	CARPENTER	FLIGHT ATTENDANT	ECONOMIST
MARINE BIOLOGIST	TRANSLATOR	POOL ATTENDANT	GRAPHIC DESIGNER
MEDICAL ILLUSTRATOR	SPEECHWRITER	ANIMAL TRAINER	BILINGUAL INTERPRETER

OCCUPATIONS

FINANCIAL ANALYST	CARTOGRAPHER (MAPMAKER)	GAME DEVELOPER	BOTANIST
POLICE DETECTIVE	NEWS REPORTER	BIOMEDICAL ENGINEER	MAGICIAN/ILLUSIONIST
ARCHAEOLOGIST	ENVIRONMENTAL SCIENTIST	ARCHAEOLOGIST	CRIME SCENE INVESTIGATOR
WEDDING PLANNER	PARK RANGER	PHYSICAL THERAPIST	GENETICIST
HUMAN RESOURCES MANAGER	EVENT PLANNER	HISTORIAN	PROFESSIONAL ATHLETE
LIFE COACH	SPEECH THERAPIST	INVESTMENT BANKER	AIR TRAFFIC CONTROLLER
METEOROLOGIST	SOCIAL MEDIA MANAGER	WILDERNESS GUIDE	GENETIC COUNSELLOR
CRYPTOGRAPHER	WEDDING PHOTOGRAPHER	FITNESS INSTRUCTOR	MARKET RESEARCH ANALYST
MAGISTRATE	ETHICAL HACKER	RADIO HOST	INTERIOR DESIGNER
FOOD CRITIC	COURT REPORTER	TRAVEL WRITER	GAME TESTER
LANDSCAPE ARCHITECT	PRIVATE INVESTIGATOR	POLITICAL ANALYST	SPORTS COACH
MUSIC PRODUCER	URBAN PLANNER	HUMANITARIAN AID WORKER	FOREIGN CORRESPONDENT

CHARACTER PROFILES

CREATING UNFORGETTABLE CHARACTERS

CHARACTER PROFILES

WHY DO WE BUILD DETAILED PROFILES FOR OUR CHARACTERS?

When you create your character profile, have this in mind.

You want your characters to go through an element of growth and change so reflect this when you write how they behave in Act 1, 2 and 3.

OUR PRO TIP FOR CREATING DETAILED CHARACTER PROFILES

What we do is think about how our characters behave at the very end of the story then make them act the COMPLETE OPPOSITE in ACT 1.

ACT 2 sees them change and their character arc develops. ACT 3 shows that change in more detail, and the end result – this makes our characters much more 3D and the story much more interesting to read.

Let's build our characters from LOGLINE EXAMPLE and make them come alive!

MAIN CHARACTER (PROTAGONIST)

CREATING UNFORGETTABLE CHARACTERS

CHARACTER PROFILES

MAIN CHARACTER (PROTAGONIST)

BASIC INFORMATION

Name: Ethan Roberts

Age: 30

Gender: Male

Occupation: Reluctant banker at Roberts Banking and Co.

Build/Physical Description: Tall and lean, with tousled brown hair and expressive blue eyes.

Which movie actor do they look like?: A young Tom Hanks

What accent do they have?: London

What actor do they sound like?: Christian Bale

What is their average daily routine?: Gets up at 8 am, showers and has a bagel and cream cheese for breakfast. He plays football after work with some old friends from college.

Childhood dream and why: To become a world-famous artist as this is his secret passion.

Life plan BEFORE the inciting event: Works for his father in the family banking empire.

PERSONALITY TRAITS

Positive Traits

Trait 1: Artistic and creative

Trait 2: Compassionate and caring

Trait 3: Determined and passionate about his dreams

Negative Traits

Trait 1: Indecisive and conflicted

Trait 2: Reserved and introverted

Trait 3: Prone to self-doubt and easily influenced by family expectations

CHARACTER PROFILES

MAIN CHARACTER (PROTAGONIST)

EMOTION	HOW THEY WOULD ACT IF THEY FELT THIS
HAPPINESS	Grins and bounces around hugging everyone
SADNESS	Retreats into himself
ANGER	A quite rage takes him over. Not violent
FEAR	Goes pale and retreats
SURPRISE	Ethan isn't jumpy but gets a cold shiver when someone surprises him
DISGUST	The edges of his mouth turn out and he looks down
LOVE	Becomes a jibbering wreck, finds it hard to make eye contact – not confident
EXCITEMENT	Fidgets and talks rapidly, wears a bright smile, and eagerly shares his news or enthusiasm with others
BOREDOM	Yawns and looks around for stimulation
GUILT	Wrings his hands and looks down at his shoes

CHARACTER PROFILES

MAIN CHARACTER (PROTAGONIST)

BACKGROUND AND HISTORY

Brief background story and key life events that shaped the character:

Ethan grew up in a wealthy and prestigious family, expected to follow in the footsteps of his successful banker father. However, he always had a deep love for art and secretly painted in his spare time. His family's expectations weighed heavily on him, leading him to reluctantly join the family business as a banker. Despite his success in the corporate world, he feels unfulfilled and longs to pursue his true passion for art.

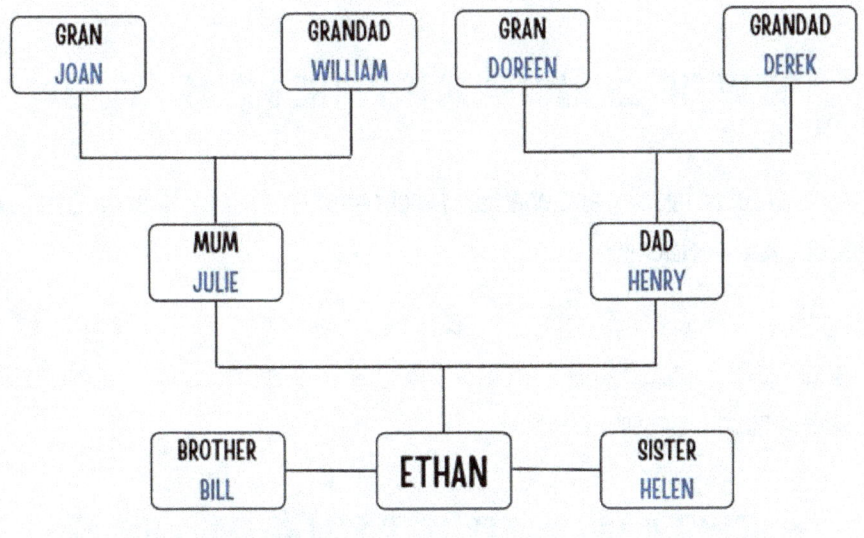

MOTIVATIONS AND GOALS

What drives the character? What are their short-term and long-term goals?:

Ethan's main motivation is to break free from the constraints of his family's expectations and pursue his dream of becoming a successful artist. His short-term goal is to find the courage to follow his heart and be with Grace, the love of his life, despite the consequences. His long-term goal is to establish himself as an accomplished artist and make a name for himself in the art world.

CHARACTER PROFILES

MAIN CHARACTER (PROTAGONIST)

HOW THE CHARACTER ACTS AT THE BEGINNING: (ACT 1)

Describe the character's initial demeanour, attitudes, and behaviours at the start of the story:

At the beginning of the story, Ethan appears reserved and conflicted, torn between his desire to be an artist and his duty to the family business. He keeps his artistic talent a secret from his family and presents himself as the reluctant banker they expect him to be.

HOW THE CHARACTER ACTS IN THE MIDDLE: (ACT 2)

Describe how the character evolves and changes throughout the story. How do their experiences impact their actions and decisions?:

As Ethan's relationship with Grace deepens, he starts to gain confidence in his artistic abilities and becomes more assertive in pursuing his dreams. He begins to challenge his family's expectations and becomes more open about his passion for art.

HOW THE CHARACTER ACTS AT THE END: (ACT 3)

Describe the character's behaviour and mindset at the conclusion of the story. How have they grown or transformed?:

At the end of the story, Ethan undergoes a significant transformation. He becomes more self-assured and decides to prioritise love and passion over societal pressures. He takes a leap of faith to be with Grace and fully embraces his identity as an artist.

CHARACTER PROFILES

MAIN CHARACTER (PROTAGONIST)

RELATIONSHIPS

How does the character interact with other key characters in the story? Describe their relationships.

Ethan's relationship with Grace is deep and profound. They share a strong emotional connection, and she becomes his biggest supporter in pursuing his dreams. His relationship with his family is strained as he navigates the conflict between his desires and their expectations. His interactions with Eric Winters, the sinister banker and villain, are filled with tension and conflict.

STRENGTHS AND WEAKNESSES

What are the character's strengths that help them overcome obstacles? What weaknesses might hinder their progress?

Ethan's strengths lie in his artistic talent and creativity, which allow him to express himself authentically. His compassionate nature and determination help him navigate challenges. However, his indecisiveness and vulnerability to family pressure are weaknesses that hinder his progress.

INNER CONFLICTS

What internal struggles does the character face? How do these conflicts affect their choices and development?

Ethan's internal struggle is the conflict between following his heart and satisfying his family's expectations. He grapples with feelings of guilt and fear of disappointing his family, while also longing to pursue his true passion for art. This inner conflict shapes his choices and development throughout the story.

EXTERNAL CONFLICTS

Describe the external challenges or conflicts the character encounters in the story.

Ethan faces external conflicts such as the pressure from his family to remain in the banking business and the obstacle of Eric Winters, the rival banker who stands in his way. The consequences of leaving the family business and the risk of disinheritance add to the external challenges he must confront.

CHARACTER PROFILES

MAIN CHARACTER
(PROTAGONIST)

BASIC INFORMATION

Name: ....

Age: ....

Gender: ....

Occupation: ....

Build/Physical Description: ....

Which movie actor do they look like?: ....

What accent do they have?: ....

What actor do they sound like?: ....

What is their average daily routine?: ....

Childhood dream and why: ....

Life plan BEFORE the inciting event: ....

PERSONALITY TRAITS

Positive Traits

Trait 1: Artistic and creative

Trait 2: Compassionate and caring

Trait 3: Determined and passionate about his dreams

Negative Traits

Trait 1: Indecisive and conflicted

Trait 2: Reserved and introverted

Trait 3: Prone to self-doubt and easily influenced by family expectations

CHARACTER PROFILES

MAIN CHARACTER
(PROTAGONIST)

EMOTION	HOW THEY WOULD ACT IF THEY FELT THIS

CHARACTER PROFILES

MAIN CHARACTER (PROTAGONIST)

BACKGROUND AND HISTORY

Brief background story and key life events that shaped the character:

....

....

....

```
  GRAN      GRANDAD        GRAN      GRANDAD
   |_____|              |_____|
        |                         |
       MUM                       DAD
        |_____|
                    |
   BROTHER ————— [     ] ————— SISTER
```

MOTIVATIONS AND GOALS

What drives the character? What are their short-term and long-term goals?:

....

....

....

CHARACTER PROFILES

MAIN CHARACTER (PROTAGONIST)

HOW THE CHARACTER ACTS AT THE BEGINNING: (ACT 1)

Describe the character's initial demeanour, attitudes, and behaviours at the start of the story:

....

....

....

HOW THE CHARACTER ACTS IN THE MIDDLE: (ACT 2)

Describe how the character evolves and changes throughout the story. How do their experiences impact their actions and decisions?:

....

....

....

HOW THE CHARACTER ACTS AT THE END: (ACT 3)

Describe the character's behaviour and mindset at the conclusion of the story. How have they grown or transformed?:

....

....

....

....

CHARACTER PROFILES

MAIN CHARACTER (PROTAGONIST)

RELATIONSHIPS

How does the character interact with other key characters in the story? Describe their relationships:

....
....
....
....

STRENGTHS AND WEAKNESSES

What are the character's strengths that help them overcome obstacles? What weaknesses might hinder their progress?:

....
....
....
....

INNER CONFLICTS

What internal struggles does the character face? How do these conflicts affect their choices and development?:

....
....
....
....

EXTERNAL CONFLICTS

Describe the external challenges or conflicts the character encounters in the story:

....
....
....
....

THE VILLAIN

CREATING UNFORGETTABLE CHARACTERS

CHARACTER PROFILES

THE VILLAIN

BASIC INFORMATION

Name: Eric Winters

Age: 35

Gender: Male

Occupation: Banker and Businessman

Build/Physical Description: Eric has a commanding presence, with a tall and imposing figure. He exudes an air of confidence and sophistication, with sharp features and piercing blue eyes.

Which movie actor do they look like?: A young Bradley Cooper

What accent do they have?: Home Counties (posh)

What actor do they sound like?: Tom Hardy

What is their average daily routine?: Gets up at 6 am, goes for a run, and lifts weights at the gym. He goes out to dinner most nights.

Childhood dream and why: To be rich and powerful as he comes from a poor background where he felt powerless.

Life plan BEFORE the inciting event: Be a middle-of-the-road banker as it would have been Ethan who would have inherited the company.

PERSONALITY TRAITS

Positive Traits

Trait 1: Ambitious and driven

Trait 2: Intelligent and strategic

Trait 3: Charismatic and persuasive

Negative Traits

Trait 1: Ruthless and manipulative

Trait 2: Greedy and power-hungry

Trait 3: Disregards others' emotions and feelings for personal gain

CHARACTER PROFILES

THE VILLAIN

EMOTION	HOW THEY WOULD ACT IF THEY FELT THIS
HAPPINESS	Quiet smugness
SADNESS	Would never allow himself to show this to anyone
ANGER	Boiling rage, shouts at anyone near him
FEAR	Eric would not react at all. He would be cold, still.
SURPRISE	Never allows himself to be surprised. Pretends he hasn't noticed
DISGUST	The edges of his mouth turn out and he looks sick
LOVE	Overpower her with charm
EXCITEMENT	Shouts louder, barks orders
BOREDOM	Yawns and looks around for stimulation
GUILT	Laughs and tries to pass it off as an accident

CHARACTER PROFILES

THE VILLAIN

BACKGROUND AND HISTORY

Brief background story and key life events that shaped the character:

Eric comes from a modest background, but his ambition and desire for success led him to rise through the ranks of the banking industry. He is determined to make a name for himself and is not afraid to use manipulation and cunning to achieve his goals.

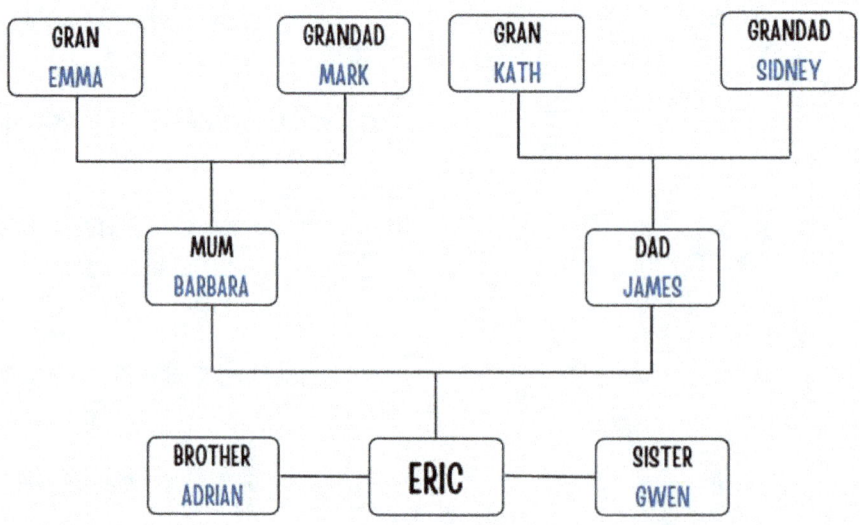

MOTIVATIONS AND GOALS

What drives the character? What are their short-term and long-term goals?:

Eric's main motivation is to gain control and power within the banking industry. His short-term goal is to eliminate Ethan as competition and take over Roberts Banking and Co. His long-term goal is to secure his position as a top banker and be recognised as a formidable force in the financial world.

CHARACTER PROFILES

THE VILLAIN

HOW THE CHARACTER ACTS AT THE BEGINNING: (ACT 1)

Describe the character's initial demeanour, attitudes, and behaviours at the start of the story:

At the beginning of the story, Eric presents himself as a charming and influential figure. He tries to win Ethan's trust but secretly harbours sinister intentions to further his own agenda.

HOW THE CHARACTER ACTS IN THE MIDDLE: (ACT 2)

Describe how the character evolves and changes throughout the story. How do their experiences impact their actions and decisions?:

As the story progresses, Eric's manipulative nature becomes more apparent as he takes advantage of Ethan's vulnerabilities and tries to exploit their romantic relationship for his gain. His desire for control intensifies, leading him to orchestrate events that put Ethan in a compromising position.

HOW THE CHARACTER ACTS AT THE END: (ACT 3)

Describe the character's behaviour and mindset at the conclusion of the story. How have they grown or transformed?:

Towards the end of the story, Eric's character arc reveals a layer of complexity. While he remains driven and ambitious, a hint of regret and longing for something more genuine emerges. He starts to question his ruthless methods and realises that love and relationships may have a place in his life, but he is still reluctant to change his ways entirely.

CHARACTER PROFILES

THE VILLAIN

RELATIONSHIPS

How does the character interact with other key characters in the story? Describe their relationships:

Eric's relationship with Ethan is a facade of friendship and mentorship, but behind the scenes, he is driven by envy and a desire to gain control over Ethan's position in the company. His interactions with Grace are manipulative as he attempts to sow doubt and mistrust in her relationship with Ethan.

STRENGTHS AND WEAKNESSES

What are the character's strengths that help them overcome obstacles? What weaknesses might hinder their progress?:

Eric's strengths lie in his intelligence and ability to strategise, which make him a formidable opponent. He is also skilled at manipulating others to further his agenda. However, his arrogance and disregard for others' feelings make him vulnerable to underestimating the power of genuine love and emotions.

INNER CONFLICTS

What internal struggles does the character face? How do these conflicts affect their choices and development?:

Eric wrestles with his desire for power and control versus the possibility of finding genuine connection and love. He battles with his own ambition and the realisation that love may be the one thing he has been missing in his quest for success.

EXTERNAL CONFLICTS

Describe the external challenges or conflicts the character encounters in the story:

Eric faces external conflicts such as competition with Ethan for control of the banking company and the consequences of his manipulative actions. The revelation of the valuable locket and its impact on the relationship dynamics adds to the external conflicts he must navigate.

CHARACTER PROFILES

THE VILLAIN

BASIC INFORMATION

Name: ....

Age: ....

Gender: ....

Occupation: ....

Build/Physical Description: ....

Which movie actor do they look like?: ....

What accent do they have?: ....

What actor do they sound like?: ....

What is their average daily routine?: ....

Childhood dream and why: ....

Life plan BEFORE the inciting event: ....

PERSONALITY TRAITS

Positive Traits

Trait 1: Artistic and creative

Trait 2: Compassionate and caring

Trait 3: Determined and passionate about his dreams

Negative Traits

Trait 1: Indecisive and conflicted

Trait 2: Reserved and introverted

Trait 3: Prone to self-doubt and easily influenced by family expectations

CHARACTER PROFILES

THE VILLAIN

EMOTION	HOW THEY WOULD ACT IF THEY FELT THIS

CHARACTER PROFILES

THE VILLAIN

BACKGROUND AND HISTORY

Brief background story and key life events that shaped the character:

....
....
....

```
  [GRAN]      [GRANDAD]      [GRAN]      [GRANDAD]
     |_____|              |_____|
           |                          |
         [MUM]                      [DAD]
           |_____|
                        |
        [BROTHER]——[        ]——[SISTER]
```

MOTIVATIONS AND GOALS

What drives the character? What are their short-term and long-term goals?:

....
....
....

CHARACTER PROFILES

THE VILLAIN

HOW THE CHARACTER ACTS AT THE BEGINNING: (ACT 1)

Describe the character's initial demeanour, attitudes, and behaviours at the start of the story:

....

....

HOW THE CHARACTER ACTS IN THE MIDDLE: (ACT 2)

Describe how the character evolves and changes throughout the story. How do their experiences impact their actions and decisions?:

....

....

HOW THE CHARACTER ACTS AT THE END: (ACT 3)

Describe the character's behaviour and mindset at the conclusion of the story. How have they grown or transformed?:

....

....

....

CHARACTER PROFILES

THE VILLAIN

RELATIONSHIPS

How does the character interact with other key characters in the story? Describe their relationships:

....
....
....

STRENGTHS AND WEAKNESSES

What are the character's strengths that help them overcome obstacles? What weaknesses might hinder their progress?:

....
....
....

INNER CONFLICTS

What internal struggles does the character face? How do these conflicts affect their choices and development?:

....
....
....

EXTERNAL CONFLICTS

Describe the external challenges or conflicts the character encounters in the story:

....
....
....

THE ALLY

CREATING UNFORGETTABLE CHARACTERS

CHARACTER PROFILES
THE ALLY
BASIC INFORMATION

Name: Grace Williams

Age: 28

Gender: Female

Occupation: Talented artist

Build/Physical Description: Grace has an elegant and slender figure with flowing auburn hair that cascades down her shoulders. Her warm hazel eyes are filled with creativity and passion.

Which movie actor do they look like?: A young Julia Roberts

What accent do they have?: London

What actor do they sound like?: Kate Winslet

What is their average daily routine?: Grace gets up at 10 am after having spent a late night at the studio getting ready for her next exhibition. She walks to the coffee shop at the end of her toad every morning for a double espresso and croissant.

Childhood dream and why: To become respected in the art world and succeed.

Life plan BEFORE the inciting event: Be a struggling artist, fighting her insecurities and never hitting the big time.

PERSONALITY TRAITS

Positive Traits

Trait 1: Artistic and passionate about her craft

Trait 2: Supportive and caring

Trait 3: Independent and determined

Negative Traits

Trait 1: Guarded and hesitant to trust others

Trait 2: Fearful of being judged for her background

Trait 3: Prone to self-doubt about her abilities

CHARACTER PROFILES

THE ALLY

EMOTION	HOW THEY WOULD ACT IF THEY FELT THIS
HAPPINESS	Goes giddy and claps her hands
SADNESS	Cries and throws head in cushion
ANGER	Her face goes read and her eyes blaze
FEAR	She faces it head on
SURPRISE	Acts surprised but usually susses things out quite quickly
DISGUST	Turns her nose up
LOVE	Enjoys the hearts and flowers, but also treating her partner too
EXCITEMENT	Can't hold it in, skips about and smiles
BOREDOM	Rests head on palm and gets restless
GUILT	Feels terrible, tries to make amends quickly

CHARACTER PROFILES

THE ALLY

BACKGROUND AND HISTORY

Brief background story and key life events that shaped the character:

Grace grew up in a humble background, raised by a single mother who worked tirelessly to provide for her. Despite facing financial challenges, Grace discovered her passion for art at a young age. She attended art school and honed her talent, but the fear of being judged or underestimated because of her background made her hesitant to pursue her dreams fully.

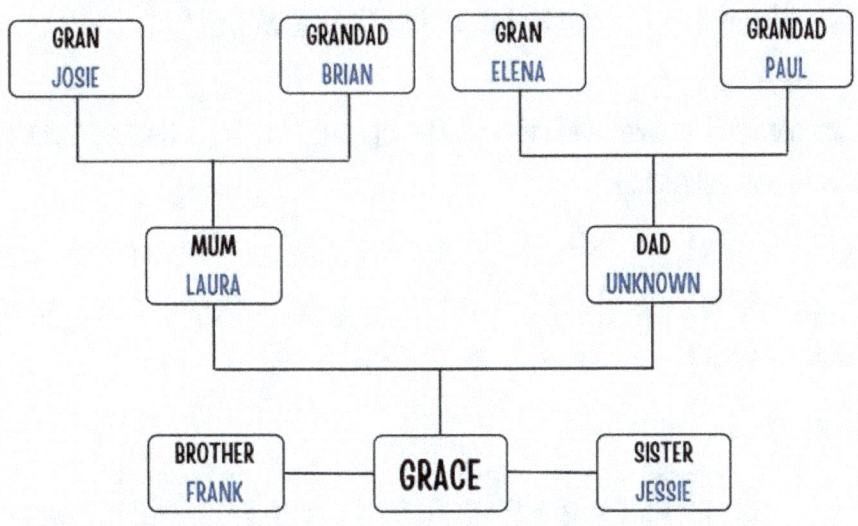

MOTIVATIONS AND GOALS

What drives the character? What are their short-term and long-term goals?:

Grace's main motivation is to excel in her art and establish herself as a respected artist. Her short-term goal is to build her art gallery and showcase her work to the world. Her long-term goal is to overcome her insecurities and be with Ethan, the man she loves, even if it means facing societal pressures.

CHARACTER PROFILES

THE ALLY

HOW THE CHARACTER ACTS AT THE BEGINNING: (ACT 1)

Describe the character's initial demeanour, attitudes, and behaviours at the start of the story:

At the beginning of the story, Grace is somewhat guarded and keeps her personal struggles hidden. She is focused on her art and doesn't let anyone get too close to her emotionally.

HOW THE CHARACTER ACTS IN THE MIDDLE: (ACT 2)

Describe how the character evolves and changes throughout the story. How do their experiences impact their actions and decisions?:

As Grace's relationship with Ethan deepens, she starts to open up about her background and insecurities. She becomes more willing to take risks, both in her art and in her personal life, especially in pursuing a relationship with Ethan despite the challenges they face.

HOW THE CHARACTER ACTS AT THE END: (ACT 3)

Describe the character's behaviour and mindset at the conclusion of the story. How have they grown or transformed?:

At the end of the story, Grace undergoes a significant transformation. She becomes more confident in her art and in expressing her feelings for Ethan. She learns to trust others and let go of her fear of judgment, embracing her identity and the love she shares with Ethan.

CHARACTER PROFILES

THE ALLY

RELATIONSHIPS

How does the character interact with other key characters in the story? Describe their relationships:

Grace's relationship with Ethan is passionate and supportive. She becomes his biggest advocate in pursuing his dreams and offers unwavering love and encouragement. Her interactions with Eric Winters, the sinister banker and villain, are tense and filled with suspicion.

STRENGTHS AND WEAKNESSES

What are the character's strengths that help them overcome obstacles? What weaknesses might hinder their progress?:

Grace's strengths lie in her artistic talent and determination, which drive her to succeed as an artist. Her caring and supportive nature helps Ethan navigate his challenges. However, her guardedness and fear of judgment are weaknesses that hinder her progress in fully embracing her feelings for Ethan.

INNER CONFLICTS

What internal struggles does the character face? How do these conflicts affect their choices and development?:

Grace grapples with insecurities about her background and talent. She battles with the fear of judgment from others, especially in the competitive art world. These internal conflicts impact her choices and hold her back from fully embracing her relationship with Ethan.

EXTERNAL CONFLICTS

Describe the external challenges or conflicts the character encounters in the story:

Grace faces external challenges such as societal pressure and the risk of disinheritance if she chooses to be with Ethan. The revelation of the valuable locket and the misunderstanding it causes add to the external conflicts she must navigate.

CHARACTER PROFILES

THE ALLY

BASIC INFORMATION

Name: ....

Age: ....

Gender: ....

Occupation: ....

Build/Physical Description: ....

Which movie actor do they look like?: ....

What accent do they have?: ....

What actor do they sound like?: ....

What is their average daily routine?: ....

Childhood dream and why: ....

Life plan BEFORE the inciting event: ....

PERSONALITY TRAITS

Positive Traits

Trait 1: Artistic and creative

Trait 2: Compassionate and caring

Trait 3: Determined and passionate about his dreams

Negative Traits

Trait 1: Indecisive and conflicted

Trait 2: Reserved and introverted

Trait 3: Prone to self-doubt and easily influenced by family expectations

CHARACTER PROFILES

THE ALLY

EMOTION	HOW THEY WOULD ACT IF THEY FELT THIS

CHARACTER PROFILES

THE ALLY

BACKGROUND AND HISTORY

Brief background story and key life events that shaped the character:

....
....
....

```
  [GRAN]   [GRANDAD]     [GRAN]   [GRANDAD]
      \___/                   \___/
        |                       |
      [MUM]                   [DAD]
         _____/
                    |
     [BROTHER]---[    ]---[SISTER]
```

MOTIVATIONS AND GOALS

What drives the character? What are their short-term and long-term goals?:

....
....
....

CHARACTER PROFILES

THE ALLY

HOW THE CHARACTER ACTS AT THE BEGINNING: (ACT 1)

Describe the character's initial demeanour, attitudes, and behaviours at the start of the story:

....

....

....

HOW THE CHARACTER ACTS IN THE MIDDLE: (ACT 2)

Describe how the character evolves and changes throughout the story. How do their experiences impact their actions and decisions?:

....

....

....

HOW THE CHARACTER ACTS AT THE END: (ACT 3)

Describe the character's behaviour and mindset at the conclusion of the story. How have they grown or transformed?:

....

....

....

....

CHARACTER PROFILES

THE ALLY

RELATIONSHIPS

How does the character interact with other key characters in the story? Describe their relationships:

....
....
....
....

STRENGTHS AND WEAKNESSES

What are the character's strengths that help them overcome obstacles? What weaknesses might hinder their progress?:

....
....
....
....

INNER CONFLICTS

What internal struggles does the character face? How do these conflicts affect their choices and development?:

....
....
....
....

EXTERNAL CONFLICTS

Describe the external challenges or conflicts the character encounters in the story:

....
....
....
....

PLOT TWISTS AND ENDINGS

KEEPING READERS ON THEIR TOES AND CRAFTING UNFORGETTABLE ENDINGS

PLOT TWISTS

WHAT IS A PLOT TWIST?

A plot twist is like a surprise in a story. It's when something unexpected happens that changes the direction of the plot. It's like a sudden turn or twist that makes you go, "Wow, I didn't see that coming!"

Plot twists make you think differently about what might happen next. Just when you're sure of the rules, they change, adding excitement and making the story more interesting.

Here are some famous plot twists in movies:

- The Sixth Sense (1999): The revelation about the true nature of the main character's relationships leaves audiences in shock.

- Fight Club (1999): The unexpected connection between the two main characters changes the entire perspective of the story.

- The Usual Suspects (1995): The identity of the mysterious criminal mastermind is a major plot twist that redefines the entire narrative.

- Psycho (1960): The revelation about Norman Bates and his mother takes the story in a completely unexpected direction.

- The Empire Strikes Back (1980): The revelation of the true parentage of a key character is a pivotal and iconic plot twist in the Star Wars saga.

PLOT TWISTS

- How can I make the plot twist surprising?

Misdirect the audience's attention by setting up false expectations or introducing red herrings.

- Should the audience see it coming, or should the plot twist be truly unexpected?

Balance foreshadowing with unpredictability. Provide subtle hints without giving away the twist.

- Should I foreshadow the plot twist heavily, or is it better to catch the audience completely off guard?

Strike a balance. Foreshadow enough to make the twist plausible, but avoid making it too obvious. Surprise while remaining logically connected.

PLOT TWISTS

HOW DO I ACTUALLY CREATE AN EPIC PLOT TWIST?

Creating a plot twist involves careful planning and execution. Here's a step-by-step guide:

Understand your story:

- Know your characters, their motivations, and the overall plot.
- Identify key moments or turning points in your narrative.

Identify assumptions:

- Pinpoint assumptions readers might make about the story or characters.
- Consider common tropes or expectations for your genre.

Choose a strategic point:

- Decide where in the story you want the twist. Midpoint, climax, or resolution can be effective.
- Ensure it aligns with the overall pacing of your narrative.

Build foreshadowing:

- Introduce subtle hints or details related to the twist earlier in the story.
- Foreshadowing creates a sense of inevitability without giving away the surprise.

Create misdirection:

- Include misleading elements or events to divert attention from the true twist.
- Keep readers guessing by presenting alternative possibilities.

PLOT TWISTS

Character motivations:

- Ensure the twist is rooted in the motivations and characteristics of your characters.
- The twist should make sense in the context of their actions and development.

Test the twist:

- Share your draft with beta readers and gauge their reactions to the twist.
- Identify confusion or predictability and refine accordingly.

Reveal and impact:

- Execute the twist with a clear revelation that challenges assumptions.
- Consider the emotional and practical impact on the characters and the story.

Address loose ends:

- Review your story for consistency post-twist.
- Adjust details or narrative elements that may be affected.

Evaluate reader response:

- Consider feedback from beta readers or early reviews.
- Assess whether the twist resonates and serves the narrative effectively.

It's all about the planning

PLOT TWISTS

ADDING PLOT TWISTS TO OUR LOGLINE

IF YOU CAN...

Use your Imagination: Think of an idea from your imagination

- What would be a good twist in the tale for the main character to experience?

Eric Winters, the villain, buys Ethan out of the company.

IF YOU CAN'T...

Use your observation: Think of something the reader would hope to happen in the story but not in the way they thought

- What would be something the reader would hope to happen but not in the way they thought?

Grace is secretive about her finances, Ethan's friend thinks she may be taking him for a ride – but she is a millionaire instead!

IF YOU NEED...

Resources: Use the resources provided by us

Ethan finds the locket Grace has dropped and he sees it's worth a fortune. He starts questioning her and thinks he doesn't initially think she is telling him the truth about being poor.

FORESHADOWING

Foreshadowing in a story is like dropping small hints or clues early on that give a heads-up about important surprises or twists later in the plot, making the revelation more impactful.

FAMOUS EXAMPLE OF FORESHADOWING IN A MOVIE:

In "The Shawshank Redemption," Andy Dufresne talks about hope and dreams, hinting at his escape plan. When he later asks for rock-carving tools to shape his dreams, it foreshadows his meticulous escape. This subtle setup makes the ultimate revelation of his escape a powerful and well-foreshadowed plot twist.

'NOTHING' SCENES

A 'nothing scene'...

You may hear us talk about writing 'nothing scenes'. These are essentially the foreshadowing scenes that appear to be 'nothing' at the time but will play a part later on - foreshadowing.

Therefore, Andy asking for rock-carving tools in a conversation could seem like a 'nothing scene', but it will play an almost central role in the plot twist/ending of his escape.

FORESHADOWING

HOW DO YOU KNOW WHAT TO FORESHADOW?

Firstly, you create your plot twist using our method (unless you already have your own).

Then you would say to yourself, 'What would my audience need to have happen for the plot twist to be believable or make sense?"

For instance, in Shawshank Redemption, for Andy to escape by carving a tunnel out of prison, he would need tools. Otherwise, when the tunnel appears, the audience would switch off and say how unbelievable that would be.

But, if he has shown that he is 'responsible, trusted' etc. and asks for tools that seemingly would do no harm, in a 'nothing scene,' when the tunnel is exposed the audience has a 'wow!' moment, realising how long it would have taken him, and how pre-meditated it was. But it all becomes believable now as he has done it using the tools that we saw Andy use/ask for.

For you – if your plot twist is that your main character's best friend is actually the 'betrayer,' you could foreshadow this with 'nothing scenes' of them taking calls and leaving the room, or meeting people in secret – things that appear to be totally innocent. At first.

ENDINGS

ADDING ENDINGS TO OUR LOGLINE

IF YOU CAN...

Use your Imagination: **Think of an idea from your imagination**

- What would be the <u>WORST</u> thing to happen to the main character and why?

Ethan loses Grace (at first) because he picks family over love, he is heartbroken and lost and then gives up his job anyway (and finds Grace a month after travelling and finding himself again).

IF YOU CAN'T...

Use your observation: **Think of something the reader would hope to happen in the story but not in the way they thought**

- What would be something the reader would hope to happen but not in the way they thought?

Grace speaks to the head of the family in a 'showdown' to tell him how much she loves Ethan and gives them some home truths. They realise they may lose Ethan and give them both their blessing.

IF YOU NEED...

Resources: **Use the resources provided by us**

When the pressure gets too much, Ethan calls off the relationship and it's heartbreaking for both. Grace understands but is devastated and has to move away from work. She gives Ethan a teddy bear as a gift with her perfume on it.

One night Ethan cries and throws the bear against the wall in desperation. The bear has an audio recording of Grace's voice message inside and the bang against the wall triggered it. The voice recording tells Ethan that his paintings were a hit at her gallery and that she has saved the money (which is a small fortune) for when/if he was ever ready to make the leap (and he gets disinherited). Ethan immediately calls her, but no answer, so he flies to meet her, and tells his dad to employ Eric Winters. Ethan thinks he will care more about the business than he will.

When Ethan first goes to see his dad in his office, Ethan sees a canvas on his dad's office wall – of Ethan's. Grace gave it to him before she left and his dad didn't realise how good he was and then gave his blessing for them to be together and he will still be in the family.

HOW OUR LOGLINE LOOKS NOW

LOGLINE

In the modern-day City of London, Ethan Roberts, a reluctant banker at Roberts Banking and Co., dreams of becoming an artist, but his aspirations clash with family expectations. When he meets Grace, a talented artist, love blossoms, but the sinister banker Eric Winters becomes an obstacle, risking disinheritance and shame from generations of wealth if Ethan follows his heart, in this heart-warming romance where love triumphs over societal pressures.

PLOT TWIST/S

Ethan finds the locket Grace has dropped and he sees it's worth a fortune. He starts questioning her and thinks he doesn't initially think she is telling him the truth about being poor.

Eric Winters buys Ethan out of the company.

ENDING

When the pressure gets too much, Ethan calls off the relationship and it's heartbreaking for both. Grace understands but is devastated and has to move away from work. She gives Ethan a Teddy Bear as a gift with her perfume on it.

One night Ethan cries and throws the bear against the wall in desperation. The bear has an audio recording of Grace's voice message inside and the bang against the wall triggered it. The voice recording tells Ethan that his paintings were a hit at her gallery and that she has saved the money (which is a small fortune) for when/if he was ever ready to make the leap (and he gets disinherited). Ethan immediately calls her, but no answer, so he flies to meet her, and tells his dad to employ Eric Winters. Ethan thinks he will care more about the business than he will.

When Ethan first goes to see his dad in his office, Ethan sees a canvas on his dad's office wall – of Ethan's. Grace gave it to him before she left and his dad didn't realise how good he was and then gave his blessing for them to be together and he will still be in the family.

CAN YOU SEE HOW IT'S ALL COMING TOGETHER?

WRITING YOUR LOGLINE

Now, write your complete logline and add in a possible plot twist and ending.

LOGLINE

....
....
....
....
....

PLOT TWIST/S

....
....
....
....
....

ENDING

....
....
....
....
....
....
....

ACTS 1,2 AND 3

YOUR STORY'S LIVING, BREATHING SOUL

ACTS 1,2 AND 3

THE THREE-ACT STRUCTURE

In a story, the 'acts' are big sections that split up the whole story. Each act has a specific purpose:

- **Act 1 (Beginning):** This is where the story starts. We meet the characters and learn about the setting. Something happens that sets the main problem in motion. By the end of Act 1, the main character decides what they want to achieve.

- **Act 2 (Middle):** This is the longest part of the story. The main character faces challenges and obstacles while trying to reach their goal. There's a big moment in the middle where things change. The main character keeps struggling and adapting to the increasing problems.

- **Act 3 (End):** This is where the big showdown happens. The tension reaches its highest point, and the main character confronts the main problem. They make important decisions that affect the outcome. Then, the story wraps up and shows what happens after the big conflict.

Dividing the story into acts makes it more exciting and helps us follow the main character's journey from the beginning to the end.

SHOW NOT TELL AND DIALOGUE

MAKING YOUR CHARACTERS SPEAK AND UNLEASH THEIR POWER!

SHOW NOT TELL

"Show not tell' is a writing technique where authors use descriptive language, actions, and sensory details to help readers experience the story's events, emotions, and characters, rather than simply telling them what's happening.

WHAT YOU NEED TO KNOW BEFORE YOU WRITE YOUR STORY

- **Emotional impact**

Understand that "show not tell" is a technique that engages readers' emotions and immerses them in the story.

- **Descriptive language**

Use vivid and sensory-rich descriptions to paint a clear picture in readers' minds.

- **Character actions**

Focus on characters' actions, expressions, and body language to convey emotions and thoughts.

SHOW NOT TELL

WHY IS "SHOW NOT TELL" RELEVANT?

- Reader connection

It creates a deeper emotional connection between readers and characters, making the story more engaging.

- Visual experience

Readers can visualise the scenes, events, and emotions, making the story come alive.

- Subtley and inference

It allows readers to draw their own conclusions and be active participants in the story.

SHOW NOT TELL

COMMON MISTAKES TO AVOID

- Over explanations

Avoid excessive explanations of characters' feelings or emotions, as it can feel heavy-handed.

- Lack of descriptions

Providing too little detail may leave readers disconnected from the story.

- Telling instead of showing

Be cautious of simply stating emotions or events without illustrating them through actions or descriptions.

- Ignoring dialogue

Dialogue is a powerful tool for showing characters' emotions and relationships.

- Omitting inner thoughts

Including characters' inner thoughts and reflections helps readers understand their motivations.

DIALOGUE

Dialogue is the conversation between characters in a story. It's the spoken or written communication that reveals personality, advances the plot, and provides insight into the characters' thoughts, feelings, and relationships.

WHAT YOU NEED TO KNOW BEFORE YOU WRITE YOUR STORY

- Character voice

Understand each character's unique voice, personality, and speech patterns.

- Purposeful dialogue

Ensure that every line of dialogue serves a specific purpose in advancing the plot, revealing character traits, or conveying emotions.

- Natural flow

Write dialogue that sounds authentic and flows naturally in conversation.

DIALOGUE

WHY IS DIALOGUE RELEVANT?

- Characterisation

Dialogue provides insight into characters' personalities, beliefs, and relationships.

- Engaging narrative

Well-crafted dialogue adds depth and energy to the story, captivating readers.

- Exposition and subtext

Dialogue can reveal important information without resorting to direct exposition.

DIALOGUE

COMMON MISTAKES TO AVOID

- Info-dumping

Aim to avoid using dialogue solely to dump information; integrate it seamlessly into the conversation.

- Lack of variation

Give each character a distinct voice to avoid monotony in the dialogue.

- Overusing tags

Use dialogue tags (e.g., "said," "asked") sparingly; rely on context and actions to identify speakers.

- Unrealistic dialogue

While dialogue should flow naturally, avoid excessive filler words or overly formal language.

- Ignoring pacing

Use dialogue to control the story's pacing, balancing action, description, and conversation.

SHOW NOT TELL IN ACTION

SOME EXAMPLES OF SHOW NOT TELL TO HELP YOU

WHEN A CHARACTER IS ANGRY

Telling: Sarah was very angry and yelled at John.

Showing: Sarah clenched her fists, her face turning red. "How could you do this?" she shouted, her voice trembling with fury.

WHEN A CHARACTER IS SAD

Telling: Jake felt sad after his pet ran away.

Showing: Jake's eyes welled up with tears as he searched the empty backyard, calling for his beloved pet who had vanished.

WHEN A CHARACTER IS UPSET

Telling: Emily was upset when she failed the exam.

Showing: Emily's shoulders slumped, and her hands trembled as she received the test results. Her eyes glistened with unshed tears, and she struggled to hold back her disappointment.

WHEN A CHARACTER IS HAPPY

Telling: Alex was very happy when he got the promotion.

Showing: Alex's face lit up with a wide grin, and he jumped up and down, unable to contain his excitement as he shared the news with his friends.

WHEN A CHARACTER IS CONTENT

Telling: Maria was content sitting by the fireplace.

Showing: Maria leaned back with a soft sigh, a gentle smile on her face, enjoying the warmth of the crackling fireplace, and feeling at peace with the world.

YOUR OPENING LINE

START OFF WITH A BANG!

174

YOUR OPENING LINE

'DIRTY WATER'

Ed Sheeran once said in an interview that he writes hundreds of songs that are rubbish, to create a hit.

He likened this process to running the 'dirty water' until he eventually got the 'clean water' where the gems were (i.e. the hits).

How does this apply to me...?

When you are creating things as important as your opening line, don't just settle.

Run the tap (write lots of 'dirty water') until the good stuff starts flowing (the 'clean water').

'CLEAN WATER'

YOUR OPENING LINE

So, with your opening line write something. Anything!

Don't edit. Just write what you would like to say. Just get it out of your head and onto the page.

Write a long paragraph of fluff if you have to. Then dig for the gold.

Can't find the gold?

Write some more…

It really is as simple as that.

WHAT WE DID

In our novel 'The Burying Place,' our first line is: 'Don't mess this up, Rachel!'

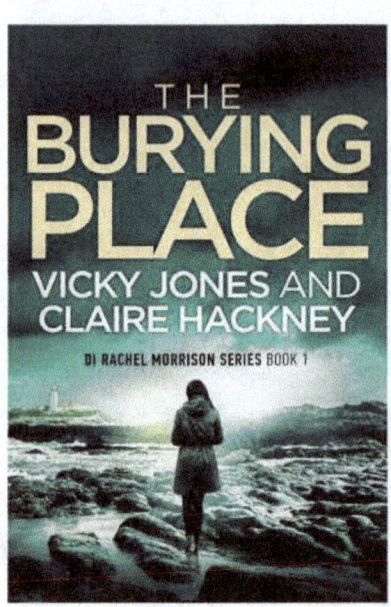

It throws the reader straight into a scene (that happens to be a missing persons press conference).

A lot is riding on it for the main character, Rachel, so rather than us dilly-dallying around describing the scene, and the clothes, we throw the reader right in, where they will immediately 'ask' questions of the story.

'Who's Rachel? Mess what up? Who's telling her not to mess it up?'

The reader finds these all out but has to read on…

YOUR OPENING LINE

WHAT WE COULD HAVE STARTED WITH

THE 'DIRTY WATER'

The room buzzed with anticipation as a diverse crowd filled the space, each person eager for news about the missing individual. A series of microphones stood poised on a professional-looking podium at the front.

Detective Rachel Morrison, surrounded by her colleagues, focused on the unfolding scene.

A commanding police officer approached Rachel with a stern reminder, "Don't mess this up, Rachel!"

The atmosphere conveyed a gravity that hinted at the significance of the occasion.

Standard professional attire adorned the attendees, and the ambient lighting subtly accentuated the mood. Beyond the doors, the routine facade of the setting concealed the potential for an ordinary day to unravel into something much more intricate and demanding.

Ok, this isn't terrible, but it could maybe come afterwards, once we have hooked our readers. Right?

Once we have written our 'dirty water', we go hunting for a gem – 'Don't mess this up, Rachel!' It tells us in one sentence the gravity of the situation.

"DON'T MESS THIS UP, RACHEL!"

'CLEAN WATER'

OUTLINES

PLOTTING YOUR COURSE TO SUCCESS!

OUTLINES

YOUR STORY'S BLUEPRINT

Unveil the secret to a well-structured and engaging story that stands strong.

PROBLEM

Writing without an outline is like wandering in a maze without a map. Lost in a sea of ideas, you risk losing sight of your story's destination.

COMMON MISTAKE

Think of an outline-less story as a puzzle missing crucial pieces. It lacks direction, coherence, and the power to captivate.

OUTLINES

WHAT YOU NEED TO KNOW BEFORE YOU WRITE YOUR STORY

- Story structure

Imagine the outline as a skeleton that supports your narrative's body. Before you begin, grasp the story's basic structure – the beginning, the journey, and the fulfilling end.

- Plot points

It is crucial when mapping out your story that you identify the milestones that drive your narrative forward.

- Character arcs

Outline your character's journeys, and how they change, learn, and transform throughout the narrative.

OUTLINES

WHY ARE OUTLINES RELEVANT?

- Roadmap

Outlines keep you on track throughout your writing and prevent detours into writer's block.

- Plot development

An outline serves as a panoramic view of your story's landscape. It helps you visualise the plot points, ensuring a captivating and well-paced narrative.

- Character consistency

Consider the outline preserving your characters' essence and ensuring they remain true to themselves from start to finish.

OUTLINES

COMMON MISTAKES TO AVOID

- Overcomplicating

An outline should resemble a clear path, not a labyrinth. Avoid overwhelming details; keep it streamlined for effortless navigation.

- Lack of flexibility

Imagine your outline as a flexible guide, not a rigid master. Be open to creative detours as your story takes unexpected turns.

- Rigid structure

While the outline is a scaffold, don't hesitate to stray if inspiration beckons. Flexibility can lead to surprising discoveries.

- Neglecting subplots

Consider subplots as vital veins pumping life into your story. Integrate them into the outline, weaving them seamlessly into the narrative.

- Insufficient detail

Provide enough detail to keep your creative compass on course.

WRITING YOUR OUTLINE

TIME TO GET CREATIVE!

WRITING YOUR OUTLINE

GENRE

SETTING

THEME

MAIN CHARACTER

GOAL

OBSTACLE

ALLY

VILLAIN

CONSEQUENCES

LOGLINE

....
....
....

MY CHARACTER ARC

In Act 1, my main character will act like: ....

In Act 2, my main character will act like: ....

In Act 3, my main character will act like: ....

My character will go from: .... To: ....

WRITING YOUR OUTLINE

MAIN CHARACTER: ....

STORY GOAL: ....

LIFE GOAL: ....

STORY ENDING

	STORY GOAL	LIFE GOAL
WHAT DOES YOUR GOAL ACHIEVED LOOK LIKE?		
WHAT WOULD THE OPPOSITE OF THIS BE?		
WHAT WOULD A DEVASTATING, CATASTROPHIC END TO THE GOAL BE?		
WHAT WOULD BE A DREAM OUTCOME?		
WHAT WOULD BE AN UNUSUAL END TO THIS GOAL?		

Pick different combinations of story goals and life goals for an ending to your story - Write below:

1. STORY GOAL: .... LIFE GOAL: ....

2. STORY GOAL: .... LIFE GOAL: ....

YOUR STORY ENDING
Pick your favourite combination:

....
....
....
....

WRITING YOUR OUTLINE

VILLAIN: ....

STORY GOAL: ....

LIFE GOAL: ....

STORY ENDING

	STORY GOAL	LIFE GOAL
WHAT DOES YOUR GOAL ACHIEVED LOOK LIKE?		
WHAT WOULD THE OPPOSITE OF THIS BE?		
WHAT WOULD A DEVASTATING, CATASTROPHIC END TO THE GOAL BE?		
WHAT WOULD BE A DREAM OUTCOME?		
WHAT WOULD BE AN UNUSUAL END TO THIS GOAL?		

Pick different combinations of story goals and life goals for an ending to your story – Write below:

1. STORY GOAL: .... LIFE GOAL: ....

2. STORY GOAL: .... LIFE GOAL: ....

YOUR STORY ENDING
Pick your favourite combination:

....

....

....

WRITING YOUR OUTLINE

ALLY: ....

STORY GOAL: ....

LIFE GOAL: ....

STORY ENDING

	STORY GOAL	LIFE GOAL
WHAT DOES YOUR GOAL ACHIEVED LOOK LIKE?		
WHAT WOULD THE OPPOSITE OF THIS BE?		
WHAT WOULD A DEVASTATING, CATASTROPHIC END TO THE GOAL BE?		
WHAT WOULD BE A DREAM OUTCOME?		
WHAT WOULD BE AN UNUSUAL END TO THIS GOAL?		

Pick different combinations of story goals and life goals for an ending to your story – Write below:

1. STORY GOAL: .... LIFE GOAL: ....

2. STORY GOAL: .... LIFE GOAL: ....

YOUR STORY ENDING
Pick your favourite combination:

....
....
....
....

THE ENDING: LOCKED IN

MAIN CHARACTER: ....
....

VILLAIN: ....
....

ALLY: ....
....

FORESHADOWING IDEAS

Write down scene headings/ideas you'd like to include, or need to include, in order to achieve this story ending:

SCENE IDEA/HEADING	IN WHICH ACT WILL THIS SCENE APPEAR?

STEPS TO THE ENDING: GOALS

MAIN CHARACTER

Now we know their ending, write the LOGICAL STEPS they would need to take to get there, starting from the 'inciting event.'

STEP	STORY GOAL	CHARACTER ARC (HOW THEY WILL ACT)	LIFE GOAL	WHEN WILL THIS APPEAR?
1	OBSTACLE TO THIS GOAL:		OBSTACLE TO THIS GOAL:	ACT 1
2	OBSTACLE TO THIS GOAL:		OBSTACLE TO THIS GOAL:	ACT 2
3	OBSTACLE TO THIS GOAL:		OBSTACLE TO THIS GOAL:	ACT 2
4	OBSTACLE TO THIS GOAL:		OBSTACLE TO THIS GOAL:	ACT 3
5	OBSTACLE TO THIS GOAL:		OBSTACLE TO THIS GOAL:	ACT 3
	STORY GOAL ENDING:		LIFE GOAL ENDING:	ACT 3

STEPS TO THE ENDING: GOALS

VILLAIN

Now we know their ending, write the LOGICAL STEPS they would need to take to get there, starting from the 'inciting event.'

STEP	STORY GOAL	CHARACTER ARC (HOW THEY WILL ACT)	LIFE GOAL	WHEN WILL THIS APPEAR?
1	OBSTACLE TO THIS GOAL:		OBSTACLE TO THIS GOAL:	ACT 1
2	OBSTACLE TO THIS GOAL:		OBSTACLE TO THIS GOAL:	ACT 2
3	OBSTACLE TO THIS GOAL:		OBSTACLE TO THIS GOAL:	ACT 2
4	OBSTACLE TO THIS GOAL:		OBSTACLE TO THIS GOAL:	ACT 3
5	OBSTACLE TO THIS GOAL:		OBSTACLE TO THIS GOAL:	ACT 3
	STORY GOAL ENDING:		LIFE GOAL ENDING:	ACT 3

STEPS TO THE ENDING: GOALS

ALLY

Now we know their ending, write the LOGICAL STEPS they would need to take to get there, starting from the 'inciting event.'

STEP	STORY GOAL	CHARACTER ARC (HOW THEY WILL ACT)	LIFE GOAL	WHEN WILL THIS APPEAR?
1	OBSTACLE TO THIS GOAL:		OBSTACLE TO THIS GOAL:	ACT 1
2	OBSTACLE TO THIS GOAL:		OBSTACLE TO THIS GOAL:	ACT 2
3	OBSTACLE TO THIS GOAL:		OBSTACLE TO THIS GOAL:	ACT 2
4	OBSTACLE TO THIS GOAL:		OBSTACLE TO THIS GOAL:	ACT 3
5	OBSTACLE TO THIS GOAL:		OBSTACLE TO THIS GOAL:	ACT 3
STORY GOAL ENDING:			LIFE GOAL ENDING:	ACT 3

THE JUICY BITS!

MAIN CHARACTER

Fill in the blanks for ideas - you probably won't use them all.

	STORY	LIFE
WHAT WOULD BE THE WORST THING TO HAPPEN ALONG THE WAY?		
WHAT WOULD SOMETHING FUNNY BE?		
WHAT WOULD A FEAR COMING TRUE BE?		
WHAT WOULD MAKE YOUR CHARACTER FURIOUS?		
WHAT WOULD SOMETHING SHOCKING BE?		
WHAT WOULD BE A BIT OF GOOD LUCK?		
WHAT WOULD BE SOMETHING SCARY?		
WHAT WOULD BE SOMETHING OUT OF THE BLUE?		
WHAT WOULD BE SOMETHING SAD?		
WHAT WOULD BE SOMETHING INSPIRING?		

PLOT TWIST

Pick 2 MASSIVE scenes from the list on the previous page for a plot twist (or use your own ideas):

1. ....
2. ....

eg. 'worst....', 'shocking....', 'scary....', 'out of the blue....', 'sad...,' are good ideas to use here.

YOUR PLOT TWIST - LOCKED IN

....
....
....

FORESHADOWING SCENES - WHAT NEEDS TO HAPPEN BEFORE

1. ....
2. ....

AFTER THE PLOT TWIST

Once the plot twist has happened, what does each character have to do in order to achieve their ending/how are they affected/acting?

MAIN CHARACTER NEEDS TO:

1. ....
2. ....

VILLAIN NEEDS TO:

1. ....
2. ....

ALLY NEEDS TO:

1. ....
2. ....

SPRINKLE SOME SCENES

Go back over 'The Juicy Bits.' Pick some scenes that would make interesting reading and what you want to include in your story.

1. ....
2. ....
3. ....
4. ....
5. ....
6. ....
7. ....
8. ....
9. ....
10. ....
11. ....
12. ....
13. ....
14. ....
15. ....

SCENE DUMP!

Go back over EVERY SCENE you want to include in your story. Then, once you have done that, go back over each scene and decide if they should appear in the beginning, middle or end of each act. For example, 'scene..... act 1, beginning,' or 'scene.... act 2, middle.'

CHARACTER INVOLVED IN THIS SCENE	ACT 1	HOW DOES THIS MAKE THEM ACT/ BEHAVE?	BEGINNING? MIDDLE? END?

SCENE DUMP!

Go back over EVERY SCENE you want to include in your story. Then, once you have done that, go back over each scene and decide if they should appear in the beginning, middle or end of each act. For example, 'scene..... act 1, beginning,' or 'scene.... act 2, middle.'

CHARACTER INVOLVED IN THIS SCENE	ACT 2	HOW DOES THIS MAKE THEM ACT/ BEHAVE?	BEGINNING? MIDDLE? END?

SCENE DUMP!

Go back over EVERY SCENE you want to include in your story. Then, once you have done that, go back over each scene and decide if they should appear in the beginning, middle or end of each act. For example, 'scene..... act 1, beginning,' or 'scene.... act 2, middle.'

CHARACTER INVOLVED IN THIS SCENE	ACT 3	HOW DOES THIS MAKE THEM ACT/ BEHAVE?	BEGINNING? MIDDLE? END?

LET'S PUT YOUR STORY IN ORDER

TIME TO GET CREATIVE!

WRITING YOUR OUTLINE
ACT 1

STORY TITLE

OPENING LINE

EVERYDAY LIFE

SOMETHING CHANGING

INCITING EVENT: WHAT STARTS THE ACTION OFF?

STATE THE MAIN CHARACTER'S GOAL

STATE THE MAIN OBSTACLE

STATE THE 'TICKING CLOCK'

STATE THE CONSEQUENCES OF FAILURE

STATE THE STEPS/WHAT NEEDS TO BE DONE TO ACHIEVE THE GOAL

My main character will act like: ....

My villain will act like: ....

My ally will act like: ....

LET'S GET TO THE GOOD BIT!
ACT 1

This is where we put all your scenes together, eg. all the 'act 1 beginnings' together, all the 'act 1 middles' together etc. but now in a logical and entertaining order.

As you list them, vary who is appearing in each scene, e.g. 'main character act 1, beginning,' then 'villain act 1, beginning.'

ALL THE 'BEGINNINGS'

ACT 1

LET'S GET TO THE GOOD BIT!
ACT 1

ALL THE 'MIDDLES'

ACT 1

LET'S GET TO THE GOOD BIT!
ACT 1

ALL THE 'ENDS'

ACT 1

LET'S GET TO THE GOOD BIT!
ACT 2

ALL THE 'BEGINNINGS'

ACT 2

LET'S GET TO THE GOOD BIT!
ACT 2

ALL THE 'MIDDLES'

ACT 2

LET'S GET TO THE GOOD BIT!
ACT 2

ALL THE 'ENDS'

ACT 2

LET'S GET TO THE GOOD BIT!
ACT 3

ALL THE 'BEGINNINGS'

ACT 3

LET'S GET TO THE GOOD BIT!
ACT 3

ALL THE 'MIDDLES'

ACT 3

LET'S GET TO THE GOOD BIT!
ACT 3

ALL THE 'ENDS'

ACT 3

WRITING YOUR OUTLINE

THE ENDING

THE FALLOUT FROM THE ENDING (INCLUDING REFERENCE TO THE MAIN THEME)

OUTLINE COMPLETE

NOW YOUR STORY SCENES ARE IN ORDER –

IT'S TIME TO GET WRITING!

Start by writing all your 'beginning' scenes out in full, then your 'middles,' then your 'ends.'

HAPPY WRITING!

YOUR SHORT STORY CHECKLIST

HAVE YOU INCLUDED EVERYTHING?

YOUR SHORT STORY CHECKLIST

ELEMENT	DONE?
Am I excited to write my story?	
Have I created a logline?	
Have I picked my MAIN genre?	
Have I read the 'what to do/what not to do' pages in the workbook for my genre?	
Have I picked an interesting main character?	
Have I picked a theme for my story?	
Have I picked an ally?	
Have I picked a villain?	
Have I picked a sequence of obstacles for my main character to overcome?	
Have I created consequences for my character NOT achieving their goal?	
Have I included a plot twist?	
Have I included a gripping ending?	
Have I included a hooky opening line?	
Have I included a big inciting event?	
Have I written a clear character arc for my main character?	
Have I included 1-3 locations in my story?	

YOUR SHORT STORY CHECKLIST

ELEMENT   DONE?

Have I given my story an intriguing title?

Does my character's use of dialogue match their personality and traits?

Have I included 'show, not tell' where appropriate in my writing?

Have I made sure my character's names are distinguishable from each other (not John, Jan and Jim)

EDITING MY SHORT STORY

ELEMENT   DONE?

Have I done a spell check?

Have I done a grammar check?

Have I deleted all the "fluff" – (if it doesn't add to the scene, it goes!)

Does my story clearly flow?

FOR EVERY SCENE, MAKE SURE YOU THINK ABOUT...

- LOCATION
- TIME OF DAY
- WEATHER
- WHERE IS THE CHARACTER IN THEIR ARC? SHOW THIS!
- MAKE SURE THE SCENE COUNTS TOWARDS THE GOAL

- THE 5 SENSES: (SEE/HEAR/TOUCH/TASTE/SMELL)
- WHICH CHARACTERS ARE IN THE SCENE AND WHY?
- DESCRIPTIONS (BUT NOT TOO MANY)
- DIALOGUE
- WHAT IS THE POINT OF THIS SCENE – THE WHY?

SETTING TARGETS

OUT OF YOUR HEAD AND ONTO THE PAGE!

SETTING TARGETS

You've planned out your story.

Firstly, a massive well done to you! You've already achieved something not many people do and you've probably come further than you have before.

Not let's get writing...

You've done all the hard work, now it's like joining the dots (joining the scenes together).

Our advice is, to break it down and make it easier on yourself.

You can either divide it by scene or word count (up to you)

SCENES

If you say have 30 scenes to write and you want to get your story done in a month (4 weeks).

Let's say you commit to writing 5 times a week.

That's 20 writing sessions for the month = 1.5 scenes per writing session.

That seems a lot more manageable now, right?

WORD COUNT

If you commit to writing 500 words per writing session (not too overwhelming, right?) and you write 5 times a week, you will hit 10,000 words in a month.

MY COMMITMENT

My target completion date = ...

I will to writing .... times a week.

The best time for me to write is ....

The place where I will be more productive in writing is: ....
....
....

My target word count/scenes per session = ...

EDITING YOUR SHORT STORY

SCRAP THE CHAFF, KEEP THE WHEAT!

EDITING YOUR SHORT STORY

Editing a short story means fixing mistakes, making sentences sound better, and improving the overall writing to tell the story clearly and neatly.

DIFFERENT TYPES OF EDITING

- Developmental Editing:

    - Definition: Developmental editing involves big-picture improvements to the manuscript. It focuses on the overall structure, organisation, and coherence of the content.

    - Use: It helps refine the storyline, character development, and major plot elements, ensuring a solid foundation for the entire work.

- Structural (or "Evaluation") Editing:

    - Definition: Structural editing assesses the manuscript's framework and narrative flow. It addresses issues related to pacing, plot progression, and the logical arrangement of ideas.

    - Use: It provides insights into the story's effectiveness, identifying areas that require restructuring for better readability and engagement.

- Content Editing:

    - Definition: Content editing involves a detailed examination of the narrative elements. It aims to enhance clarity, coherence, and the overall impact of the story.

    - Use: This editing stage focuses on refining characters, dialogue, and themes, ensuring a compelling and well-developed narrative.

EDITING YOUR SHORT STORY

- Line Editing:

  - Definition: Line editing concentrates on refining the prose at the sentence and paragraph levels. It involves improving language use, style, and overall readability.

  - Use: Line editing enhances the narrative's flow, addressing issues like word choice, and sentence structure, and ensuring a smooth reading experience.

- Copy Editing:

  - Definition: Copy editing is a meticulous review of the manuscript for grammar, punctuation, spelling, and consistency in style. It aims to eliminate errors and improve overall language usage.

  - Use: Copy editing ensures a polished and error-free manuscript, focusing on the technical aspects of writing to enhance professionalism.

- Proofreading:

  - Definition: Proofreading is the final stage of editing, focusing on catching typographical errors, misspellings, and formatting issues.

  - Use: Proofreading ensures the manuscript is error-free before publication, providing a last check for any overlooked mistakes.

YOU CAN PAY AN EDITOR TO DO EACH OF THESE FOR YOU

EDITING YOUR SHORT STORY

WHERE CAN I FIND AN EDITOR?

FREELANCE WEBSITES	Such as: Upwork, Fiverr, and Freelancer
LITERARY MAGAZINES AND JOURNALS	Many literary magazines offer editorial services
WRITING COMMUNITIES AND FORUMS	Such as: writing groups on Reddit and Absolute Write
SOCIAL MEDIA PLATFORMS	Such as: Twitter/ 'X', LinkedIn, and Facebook groups
LOCAL WRITING CENTRES OR WORKSHOPS	Such as: community writing centres, and writing workshops.
PERSONAL NETWORK	Such as: friends, colleagues, and writing peers.
ONLINE WRITING COMMUNITIES	Such as: Wattpad, and critique groups on Goodreads
WORD OF MOUTH	Recommendations from other authors
BOOKS LIKE THE 'WRITERS AN ARTISTS YEARBOOK'	

SCAN HERE

EDITING YOUR SHORT STORY

SELF-EDITING - HOW TO DO IT

- Take a break:

    - What to do: Put your story aside for a little while to gain fresh eyes.
    - What to look for: Notice any parts that feel confusing or unclear when you return.

- Read aloud:

    - What to do: Read your story out loud.
    - What to look for: Listen for awkward-sounding sentences or areas where the flow seems off.

- Check for clarity:

    - What to do: Ensure your ideas are clear and your sentences make sense.
    - What to look for: Identify any confusing or vague parts that might need clarification.

- Look for repetition:

    - What to do: Check for repeated words or ideas.
    - What to look for: Eliminate unnecessary repetition to keep your writing fresh.

- Evaluate dialogue:

    - What to do: Review your characters' dialogue.
    - What to look for: Ensure it sounds natural and fits the character, and check for clarity in conversations.

EDITING YOUR SHORT STORY

SELF-EDITING - HOW TO DO IT

- Check pacing:

  - What to do: Assess the speed of your story.
  - What to look for: Make sure there's a good balance between action scenes and slower, descriptive moments.

- Eliminate unnecessary words:

  - What to do: Trim down your sentences.
  - What to look for: Remove words that don't contribute to the meaning or flow of the sentence.

- Verify consistency:

  - What to do: Ensure details are consistent throughout.
  - What to look for: Check character names, settings, and plot details to avoid contradictions.

- Watch for grammar and spelling:

  - What to do: Go through your story for grammar and spelling mistakes.
  - What to look for: Correct any errors to improve the professionalism of your writing.

- Get Feedback:

  - What to do: Share your story with others for feedback.
  - What to look for: Consider the comments and suggestions, and make adjustments as needed.

EDITING YOUR SHORT STORY

SELF-EDITING SOFTWARE
(FREE AND PAID)

GRAMMARLY	Grammar and spelling checks, style suggestions and tone analysis
PROWRITING AID	Grammar and style checking, readability analysis and writing reports
HEMINGWAY EDITOR	Highlights complex sentences, identifies common errors and provides suggestions for readability improvement
AUTOCRIT	Manuscript editing for fiction and identifies overused words and phrases
SCRIVENER	Writing and editing tool, organisational features and is ideal for long-form writing
REEDSY BOOK EDITOR	Formatting and editing tool. Exports to various formats
SLICK WRITE	Grammar and style checking. Analyses structure and flow
GINGER	Grammar and spell checking, sentence rephrasing and translation
PAPERRATER	Grammar and plagiarism checking. Writing suggestions
WHITESMOKE	Grammar and style checking, language translation

EDITING YOUR SHORT STORY

IF YOU DON'T EDIT YOUR STORY

- Poor clarity and coherence:

    - Without editing, your ideas may lack clarity, and the overall structure of your story might be confusing to readers.

- Grammatical and spelling errors:

    - Unedited writing is more likely to contain grammatical and spelling mistakes, which can distract readers and diminish the professionalism of your work.

- Inconsistent plot and characters:

    - Lack of editing may result in inconsistencies in the plot, character development, or other story elements, leading to a disjointed reading experience.

- Weak flow and pacing:

    - Editing helps refine the flow of your narrative. Without it, your story may have awkward transitions, poor pacing, or repetitive elements that affect the overall reading experience.

- Reduced engagement:

    - Readers may disengage from a story that is poorly edited, finding it difficult to connect with the characters or follow the plot.

EDITING YOUR SHORT STORY

IF YOU DON'T EDIT YOUR STORY

- Missed opportunities for improvement:

    - Editing provides an opportunity to enhance your writing, refine your style, and strengthen your storytelling. Without it, you may miss chances to make your story more impactful.

- Reduced professionalism:

    - A lack of editing can make your work appear less professional. Agents, publishers, or readers may be less likely to take your writing seriously if it contains errors and inconsistencies.

- Negative reviews and feedback:

    - Readers and critics are likely to provide negative reviews if your story is riddled with errors and lacks polish, potentially harming your reputation as a writer.

- Difficulty in conveying ideas:

    - Your intended message or theme may not come across effectively without careful editing, leading to misunderstandings or misinterpretations.

- Missed publishing opportunities:

    - Publishers and literary agents often expect manuscripts to be well-edited before considering them for publication. Neglecting editing may result in missed opportunities for your work to be accepted.

GENRE TOOLKITS

WHERE TO FIND YOUR TOOLKIT

FANTASY	228-253
SCIENCE FICTION	254-277
ROMANCE	278-308
CRIME	309-340
PSYCHOLOGICAL	341-368
HORROR	369-394
HISTORICAL FICTION	395-416
YOUNG ADULT	417-439
CONTEMPORARY/WOMEN'S/DOMESTIC	440-466
PARANORMAL	467-494

FANTASY

FICTION SQUARE

CHARACTER	SETTING	GOAL	CONFLICT	CONSEQUENCE
THE CHOSEN ONE	FOREST	PREVENT TRAGEDY	TIME	DEATH
EXPLORER	GARDEN	UNCOVER TRUTH	LACK OF KNOWLEDGE	DARK POWERS TAKING OVER
MAGICIAN	CITY	KEEP TRUTH HIDDEN	SELF-DOUBT	CHAOS
DRAGON RIDER	KINGDOM	FIND PEACE	TECHNOLOGY	CURSED
SORCERER	MYTHICAL LAND	TO BOND	SCEPTICISM	LOSS
TIME TRAVELLER	DUNGEON	NAVIGATE THE LAND	ENEMY	FADING MEMORIES
MONARCH	MAZE	TO FIND THE END OF THE MAP	BETRAYAL	POWERS LOST

	TIME TRAVELLER	CITY	PREVENT TRAGEDY	SCEPTICISM	DEATH
IDEA 1	A city-dwelling time traveller, determined to prevent a tragedy that unfolded years ago, battles massive scepticism from the populace. As the clock ticks, the consequence of disbelief looms larger—not just one death, but the potential loss of many lives hangs in the balance if the time traveller fails to alter the course of the past.					
WHY?	Haunted by a personal connection to the tragic event that unfolded in the past, the time traveller is driven by a deep sense of responsibility and the desire to rewrite history for the better.				
WHAT IF…?	However, the city's inhabitants, sceptical of the fantastical notion of time travel, dismiss the warnings, leaving the time traveller isolated in their quest.				
AND THEN…?	As the impending tragedy approaches, the time traveler must find a way to bridge the gap between disbelief and reality, racing against time to convince the city's residents and rewrite the course of history before the devastating events unfold once again.				

FICTION SQUARE

You should have: A character, setting, goal, conflict and consequence

IDEA 2					
WHY?					
WHAT IF...?					
AND THEN...?					

You should have: A character, setting, goal, conflict and consequence

IDEA 3					
WHY?					
WHAT IF...?					
AND THEN...?					

WHAT TO DO

CRAFT AN ENCHANTING FANTASY STORY

Creating a captivating fantasy story means building a unique and immersive world. Develop its history, geography, cultures, and magic. Think about creatures, societies, and the rules of magic. A well-crafted fantasy world transports readers into a new reality.

HOW TO DO IT

START WITH BASICS	Define the world's core elements like geography and history. What are its notable features? Is it divided into regions? Major events matter.
INVENT CULTURES AND PEOPLE	Make your world distinct with diverse cultures. Think about customs, beliefs, and species interactions. This adds depth.
ESTABLISH MAGIC AND WONDERS	Magic is crucial. Set its rules, sources, and limits. Enrich with mythical creatures, legendary places, and more.

WHAT TO DO

CREATE UNFORGETTABLE CHARACTERS

Engaging characters make your story shine. Develop protagonists with strengths, weaknesses, and goals. Relatable villains and secondary characters add depth. Their interactions drive the tale.

HOW TO DO IT

BUILD REAL PROTAGONISTS	Craft real characters with personalities and goals. Add challenges. Make them relatable for emotional connection.
SHAPE INTRIGUING ANTAGONISTS	Villains with motives and complexities challenge your heroes. Their clash drives growth.
ENRICH WITH SECONDARY CHARACTERS	Supporting roles with distinct traits and roles deepen your story. Don't overcrowd; quality matters.
SHOW CHARACTER GROWTH	Characters evolving from experiences enrich your tale. Transform their beliefs, skills, and relationships.

WHAT TO DO

WEAVE AN EXCITING PLOT

A compelling plot keeps readers engaged. Define a central conflict or quest. Introduce twists, obstacles, and tension. High stakes drive characters' growth.

HOW TO DO IT

START WITH A QUEST	Define a clear mission – save, retrieve, defeat. Keep this central. Subplots should support it.
ADD CHALLENGES AND SURPRISES	Test characters with obstacles and surprises. Keep readers guessing. Tension propels the story.
RAISE THE STAKES	Make outcomes impactful. Success and failure must matter. This keeps readers invested.
THEMES FROM FANTASY ELEMENTS	Use fantasy elements to explore real themes metaphorically. Friendship, love, good vs. evil – bring depth.

WHAT TO AVOID DOING

AVOID OVERLOADING READERS
Don't overwhelm readers with too much world-building information all at once. Instead, reveal details naturally through dialogue, character interactions, and plot progression. Trust readers to pick up on subtle cues and understand your fantastical setting over time.

STEER CLEAR OF CLICHÉS AND TROPES
Resist relying solely on familiar fantasy clichés. Add your own twist to classic elements to create a fresh and unique story. Strive for originality to set your fantasy world apart and keep readers engaged.

DON'T UNDERPLAY CHARACTER DEVELOPMENT
Avoid sacrificing character depth for fantasy elements. Well-developed characters are essential. Let them grow, face challenges, and respond to the plot's events. This adds emotional resonance to your storytelling.

PLOT STRUCTURE MATTERS
Don't disregard proper plot structure in pursuit of world-building. Have a clear beginning, middle, and end with defined conflicts and resolutions. A well-structured plot keeps readers invested and eager to follow the story.

REMEMBER THE HUMAN TOUCH
Even in a magical world, infuse relatable human emotions, desires, and relationships into your story. Explore universal themes like love, friendship, and personal growth. This adds depth and connection for readers.

TAKE TIME FOR EDITING
Don't rush editing. Revise and polish your work after the first draft. Editing ensures a coherent and error-free story.

COMMON FANTASY SETTINGS

MEDIEVAL-INSPIRED REALMS	Frequent in fantasy, these worlds resemble medieval times with castles, villages, knights, and magic. Kings and queens rule amidst mythical creatures and lush landscapes like forests and mountains.
MYTHICAL ANCIENT LANDS	Drawing from real-world myths, these settings host gods, ancient artefacts, and epic quests. Rich with legends, they're perfect for heroic journeys.
POST-APOCALYPTIC FANTASY	Beyond sci-fi, these worlds faced disaster, mixing magic and survival. Characters navigate ruins and supernatural challenges, seeking hope.
PARALLEL WORLDS AND PORTALS	Characters journey between dimensions, exploring diverse cultures, magical systems, and encounters with fantastical beings through portals or gateways.
MODERN MAGIC IN URBAN SETTINGS	Urban fantasy blends the modern world with magic, where hidden societies and supernatural events coexist, adding intrigue to city life.
EPIC KINGDOMS OF HIGH-FANTASY	Grand and intricate, these kingdoms host epic battles, quests, and the struggle for power among diverse realms, cultures, and histories.

Remember, while these settings are common, your creativity is limitless. Blend, twist, and reimagine to craft your own captivating world. Mix imaginative elements, compelling characters, and a well-crafted plot to create an enchanting fantasy journey for readers.

FANTASY TIME PERIODS/ERAS

MEDIEVAL CHARM	Drawing from the Middle Ages, this era features knights, castles, and epic quests. Kings and queens rule with magic and mythical creatures.
ANCIENT MYSTERIES	Set in civilisations like ancient Egypt or Greece, gods and ancient artefacts create a backdrop for characters on epic quests.
RENAISSANCE WONDERS	Blending art and alchemy, this era mixes medieval and modern elements. Secret societies and magical discoveries add intrigue.
ELEGANT STEAMPUNK	Victorian or Edwardian eras merge with steam-powered technology, offering historical charm and futuristic fantasy.
SURVIVAL AND HOPE	Post-apocalyptic or dystopian settings combine catastrophe with magic or creatures, as characters fight for survival and hope.

KEY CHARACTER ROLES IN FANTASY

THE PROTAGONIST (HERO/HEROINE)	At the heart of the story, the protagonist embarks on a quest, facing challenges and growing as they pursue their goals.
THE ANTAGONIST (VILLAIN)	The main opponent who creates obstacles and conflict for the protagonist, is often driven by personal motivations or opposing beliefs.
THE MENTOR/GUIDE	Wise and experienced, they offer guidance, knowledge, and skills to aid the protagonist on their journey.
THE SIDEKICK/COMPANION	Loyal and skilled, they accompany the protagonist, providing assistance, humour, and support.
THE LOVE INTEREST	Adding depth, they share a romantic connection with the protagonist, influencing their actions and emotions.
THE CHOSEN ONE	Destined for greatness, they hold a unique power or purpose vital to the story's resolution.
THE WISE ELDER	Imparting wisdom and guidance, they hold ancient knowledge crucial to the quest's success.
THE SHADOW SELF	Representing inner conflicts, they challenge the protagonist's fears and doubts on a psychological level.

CHARACTER NAMES

MALE CHARACTERS		FEMALE CHARACTERS	
HELTHORN	GREGOR	SWINDOM	AWTHEN
RELCHED	FINDOL	PLYOL	SLEA
TYGOR	DRILENT	ELARA	SERAPHINA
VINTEX	LOMPET	IBRIEQ	AURORA
ALISTAIR	ROLAND	MYRROLD	ROSALIND
LUCIAN	ADRIOLE	YOMAE	GWYR
CREALOR	WELTHIM	ISANORA	LYRA

Keep in mind that this is not an exhaustive list (and some have already been used in very famous novels, but are included here so you get the idea and can adapt them), and the names used in fantasy fiction can vary widely depending on the author's imagination and the world they've created. Additionally, some names may be more common in specific subgenres of fantasy or influenced by cultural inspirations.

As a writer, feel free to create unique names that fit the tone and setting of your fantasy world, and let your creativity soar!

MOST COMMON OCCUPATIONS

KNIGHT/WARRIOR	Brave and skilled in combat, knights and warriors are often protectors of the realm, serving their king or queen and fighting against enemies and mythical creatures.
WIZARD/MAGE	Masters of arcane arts, wizards and mages wield powerful magic and often play pivotal roles in shaping the course of the story.
RANGER	Rangers are skilled trackers and hunters who navigate the wilderness and protect the land from threats. They are adept at survival and often have a deep connection with nature.
THIEF/ROGUE	Stealthy and nimble, thieves and rogues excel at stealth, lockpicking, and deception. They may work as spies, spies, or treasure hunters.
PRIEST/HEALER	Devoted to serving the gods or divine forces, priests and healers possess healing abilities and may provide spiritual guidance to characters.
BARD/MINSTREL	Bards and minstrels are talented musicians and storytellers, using their arts to entertain, inspire, and spread knowledge.
MERCHANT/TRADER	Merchants and traders facilitate commerce in the fantasy world, dealing with rare magical items, artefacts, or exotic goods.

MOST COMMON OCCUPATIONS

BLACKSMITH	Blacksmiths forge weapons, armour, and magical artefacts. They may also have knowledge of enchanting and imbuing items with magical properties.
INNKEEPER	Innkeepers run taverns and inns, offering shelter, food, and information to travellers and adventurers.
ALCHEMIST	Alchemists dabble in potion-making, transmutation, and experimental magic. They seek to unlock the secrets of magical substances.
SEER/ORACLE	Seers and oracles have the gift of foresight, providing cryptic visions and prophecies that guide the characters' actions.
SORCERER/SORCERESS	Sorcerers and sorceresses possess innate magical abilities, often drawing their powers from bloodlines or mystical origins.
GUARD/SOLDIER	Guards and soldiers protect cities, fortresses, and important figures from threats both mundane and magical.
ADVENTURER	Adventurers are free-spirited characters who roam the lands in search of quests, treasures, or opportunities for heroism.
SCHOLAR/LIBRARIAN	Scholars and librarians are keepers of knowledge, often found in grand libraries or ancient archives, seeking answers in dusty tomes.

CHALLENGES AND CONFLICTS

QUEST FOR MAGIC	Characters journey for a potent artefact, facing puzzles and foes to save their realm.
BATTLE DARK FORCES	The protagonist confronts a menacing antagonist, leading to an ultimate clash of good and evil.
DARING RESCUES	A loved one's rescue unfolds, with risks and obstacles against powerful adversaries.
MASTERY OF MAGIC	Characters unlock their magical might or fulfil a prophecy, braving doubts and training.
POLITICAL INTRIGUE	Navigating treacherous politics, characters strive in a world of schemes and power struggles.
ESCAPE AND RETURN	Trapped or captive, the path home means escaping dangerous lands or foes.
POST-APOCALYPTIC SURVIVAL	Characters endure a world of scarcity and danger, facing ruthless factions.
BREAKING CURSES	Protagonist battles curses, seeking remedies through challenges and rare magic.
INNER STRUGGLES	Characters wrestle with inner demons, dark temptations, or conflicting desires.
UNRAVEL MYSTERIES	Characters solve complex puzzles, unveil secrets, and discover hidden treasures.
DEFENDING AGAINST INVASION	Heroes rally allies against invading forces or monstrous hordes.
DEADLY TOURNAMENT	Characters engage in life-threatening contests, where only one can emerge victorious.

HIGH STAKES IN FANTASY

WORLD'S FATE HANGS	The world or kingdom's survival hinges on the protagonist's success, determining its destiny.
LIFE OR DEATH	Characters face choices with life-or-death consequences, impacting their own lives and others'.
BALANCE OF LIGHT AND DARK	The battle of good versus evil decides the realm's balance, shaping its destiny.
LOSS OF LOVED ONES	Personal stakes involve risking loved ones' safety, adding urgency to the mission.
ANCIENT EVIL UNLEASHED	Characters prevent chaos by stopping a malevolent force from wreaking havoc.
PROPHECY'S FATE	The fulfilment or failure of a prophecy shapes characters' paths and world outcomes.
ARTEFACT'S PROTECTION	Safeguarding a sacred artefact from misuse prevents dire consequences.
MAGIC'S LAST STAND	Characters defend fading magic, preventing a world-altering shift.
HIDDEN TRUTH UNVEILED	Discovery of a secret alters characters' lives and world history.
CHARACTER'S REDEMPTION	A flawed character's redemption is on the line, guiding them toward light or darkness.
TIME AND REALITY UNRAVEL	Consequences involve unraveling time or reality, with unpredictable outcomes.
FREEDOM FROM TYRANNY	Characters seek liberation from oppressors, igniting revolutions and rebellions.

HEROIC GOALS IN FANTASY

SAVE THE REALM	The protagonist's mission is to save the world or kingdom from impending doom, battling evil forces.
RECLAIM LOST HERITAGE	Seeking justice, the protagonist strives to regain a stolen throne or rightful birthright.
MASTER MAGICAL ABILITIES	The protagonist embarks on a journey to master unique powers, pivotal for defeating darkness.
RETRIEVE LEGENDARY ARTEFACT	Questing for a fabled artefact, the protagonist aims to reshape the fantasy world's destiny.
RESCUE LOVED ONES	The mission is to rescue a captive loved one, friend, or comrade facing grave danger.
DEFEAT THE DARK	Confronting an evil force or villain, the protagonist fights to safeguard the realm's well-being.

HEROIC GOALS IN FANTASY

UNEARTH HIDDEN TRUTHS	The goal is to uncover ancient truths, prophecies, or lost knowledge, unravelling mysteries.
FIND PERSONAL REDEMPTION	Seeking redemption, the protagonist confronts past errors and embarks on a path of growth.
DEFY CHOSEN FATE	Rebelling against destiny, the protagonist shapes their own future, defying prophecies.
RESTORE WORLD'S BALANCE	Striving to restore harmony, the protagonist combats chaos caused by cataclysmic events.
FORGE ALLIANCES	Building unity among factions, the protagonist rallies diverse races against a shared threat.
CONQUER PERSONAL DEMONS	Overcoming flaws and fears, the protagonist grows and reaches their true potential.

NOTORIOUS VILLAINS IN FANTASY

THE DARK CONQUEROR	A malevolent ruler aims to dominate and enforce their will through dark magic and fear.
SINISTER SORCERER/SORCERESS	Masters of forbidden magic, they sow chaos or lust for ultimate power.
CORRUPTED CHAMPION	A fallen hero from the past, now an adversary, twisted by tragedy or manipulation.
JEALOUS ADVERSARY	Envious of the protagonist's status or achievements, they scheme to seize it for themselves.
MONSTROUS TERROR	Fearsome beasts or creatures, driven by malevolence or curses, threaten all in their path.
CULT LEADER OF DARKNESS	Rallying followers, they conjure dark forces or ancient evils to plunge the world into despair.
DECEPTIVE TRICKSTER	Crafty and sly, they manipulate emotions and perceptions to further their hidden agenda.
VENGEFUL GHOST	A spectral entity, seeking vengeance for past grievances, haunting the living.
BETRAYED COMPANION	A former friend turned antagonist, their sense of betrayal fuels a quest for revenge.
PRIMORDIAL DREAD	An ancient, malefic force awakens, spreading chaos and devastation across the realm.
AMBITIOUS ADVISOR	Cunning and manipulative, they undermine rulers for personal power and control.
FALLEN DEITY	Once divine, now corrupted, they seek dominion over mortals, thirsting for power.

THEMES IN FANTASY FICTION

ETERNAL STRUGGLE	Characters confront the age-old battle between good and evil, embodying the clash of opposing forces.
JOURNEY OF THE HERO	Protagonists embark on transformative quests, overcoming trials to emerge as heroes.
PATH TO MATURITY	Young characters experience growth, discovering their identity and purpose as they mature.
BONDS OF FELLOWSHIP	The power of friendship and companionship is celebrated as characters forge unbreakable bonds.
IDENTITY UNVEILED	Characters grapple with self-discovery, unravelling their true selves amid fantastical realms.
PRICE OF VALOUR	Sacrifice and redemption underscore the cost of heroism, leading characters to find redemption through noble acts.
HARMONY WITH NATURE	The balance between nature and society is explored as characters navigate their impact on the world.

THEMES IN FANTASY FICTION

MATTERS OF THE HEART	Love and romance intertwine with fantasy, adding depth and vulnerability to the characters' journeys.
LIGHT IN DARKNESS	Characters demonstrate resilience and hold onto hope, even in the face of overwhelming challenges.
ANCESTRAL ECHOES	The weight of lineage shapes characters' destinies, echoing the actions of their forebears.
UNITY THROUGH DIVERSITY	Themes of prejudice and acceptance illuminate the importance of embracing differences.
TEMPTATION OF POWER	Characters confront the allure and dangers of power, struggling to resist corruption.
THREADS OF FATE	The balance between destiny and free will is questioned as characters navigate their chosen paths.
HOPE AMID DESOLATION	The theme of hope and despair mirrors the characters' ability to find light in the darkest moments.
QUEST FOR WISDOM	Characters seek knowledge and truths, delving into ancient mysteries and prophecies.

TITLES

A FRAMEWORK FOR FANTASY FICTION TITLES

THE [NOUN] OF [PLACE/CHARACTER/ARTEFACT]

This classic framework combines a significant noun with a location, character, or mythical artefact, creating intrigue and setting the stage for the story's central focus.

Example: "The Sword of Avalon" or "The Chronicles of Elaria."

[CHARACTER NAME]'S [JOURNEY/QUEST/ADVENTURE]

Highlight the protagonist's name followed by an exciting word that represents their journey, quest, or adventure, offering readers a glimpse into the character's heroic path.

Example: "Elena's Quest for the Enchanted Amulet" or "The Adventures of Willard the Brave."

TITLES

A FRAMEWORK FOR FANTASY FICTION TITLES

[THE] [ADJECTIVE] [NOUN] [OF PLACE]

Incorporate the sense of wonder and discovery by introducing an adjective and noun tied to a specific location or realm.

Example: "The Crystal City of Atlantis" or "The Lost Crown of Thorns."

THE [ADJECTIVE] [NOUN]

Use a descriptive adjective to enhance the mystery or atmosphere and pair it with a compelling noun to evoke the essence of the story.

Example: "The Enchanted Forest" or "The Forbidden Scroll."

TITLES

COMMON LENGTHS FOR FANTASY FICTION TITLES

Fantasy fiction titles often range from 3 to 5 words in length.

Longer titles are occasionally used, but concise and impactful titles are generally preferred to capture readers' attention.

COMMON WORDS FEATURED IN FANTASY FICTION TITLES

MAGIC/MAGICAL	SWORD/SORCERER	DRAGON/DRAKE	QUEST/ADVENTURE
CHRONICLES	KINGDOM/REALM	JOURNEY	ENCHANTED
PROPHECY	SHADOW	CROWN	LOST/FORGOTTEN
ANCIENT	CHRONICLES	LEGEND	DESTINY

MOST POPULAR WORDS IN FANTASY FICTION

MAGIC	Supernatural powers or abilities are used to manipulate reality or perform extraordinary feats.
ADVENTURE	An exciting and daring journey or quest filled with challenges and risks.
QUEST	A mission or expedition undertaken by a hero or group to achieve a specific goal.
SWORD	A weapon often associated with heroes and warriors, symbolising courage and strength.
DRAGON	A mythical creature with scaly skin, wings, and the ability to breathe fire, often representing power and danger.
ENCHANTED	Under the influence of magic, bewitched, or possessing magical qualities.
REALM	A kingdom or domain, often associated with magical or fantastical elements.
HERO/HEROINE	The central character who embarks on a journey or quest and displays bravery and noble qualities.

MOST POPULAR WORDS IN FANTASY FICTION

SORCERER/SORCERESS	A skilled magic practitioner, often possessing a vast knowledge of the mystical arts.
PROPHECY	A prediction or foretelling of future events, often crucial to the plot.
KINGDOM	A realm ruled by a monarch, often with magical or mythical elements.
MYTHICAL	Associated with myths or legendary stories, involving gods or magical creatures.
ANCIENT	From a distant past, often involving ancient civilizations or artefacts.
JOURNEY	A passage or progress from one place or state to another, often involving personal growth.
WIZARD/WITCH	A magic practitioner, usually skilled in the arcane arts and possessing magical knowledge.
QUEST	A mission or expedition undertaken by a hero or group to achieve a specific goal.
SPELL	A magical formula or incantation with specific effects or outcomes.

SHOW NOT TELL TECHNIQUES IN FANTASY WRITING

SENSORY ENCHANTMENT

Instead of directly telling the reader, use sensory details to bring the scene to life. Describe the sights, sounds, smells, tastes, and textures that immerse them in your fantasy world.

Telling: The forest was mysterious.

Showing: The forest exhaled an earthy aroma, its mist-shrouded trees concealing secrets as the distant howl of a hidden creature sent shivers down spines.

CHARACTER SUBTEXT

Let characters' actions and reactions unveil their emotions and intentions. Allow readers to decipher their feelings without explicitly stating them.

Telling: He was excited about the adventure.

Showing: His eyes lit up like stars, and an impulsive grin spread across his face as he eagerly examined the treasure map.

DIALOGUE UNVEILED

Craft dialogue that carries underlying meanings or subtext, giving insight into characters' thoughts and conflicts.

Telling: She felt betrayed.

Showing: "You promised this wouldn't happen," her voice trembled, her eyes reflecting a wounded trust.

SYMBOLIC LANGUAGE

Enhance your descriptions with metaphors and symbolism that evoke emotions and deepen readers' connections to the narrative.

Telling: The castle was imposing.

Showing: The castle stood tall, its towering spires a defiant challenge to the heavens, a sentinel of authority and power.

SCIENCE FICTION

FICTION SQUARE

CHARACTER	SETTING	GOAL	CONFLICT	CONSEQUENCE
CYBER ENGINEER	MEGACITY	DEVELOP GROUNDBREAKING TECHNOLOGY	TECHNOLOGY HACKED	DEATH
ASTRONAUT	SPACESHIP	MISSION SUCCESS	BETRAYAL	VIRUS
EXPLORER	PLANET	FIND CURE	GREED	DISEASE
SPACE SALVAGER	LAB	FIND MEDICINE	RUNNING OUT OF TIME	COLLAPSE
RESEARCHER	RESEARCH FACILITY	EXPLORATION	MORAL DILEMMA	CHAOS
SCIENTIST	DYSTOPIAN FUTURE	EVADE ENEMY	POWERS FADING	DEFEAT
SOLDIER	A.I. CITY	FIND SECRET	ROGUE AGENTS	WAR

	RESEARCHER	LAB	DEVELOP GROUNDBREAKING TECHNOLOGY	TECHNOLOGY HACKED	WAR
IDEA 1	A researcher working in a high-tech lab aspires to create groundbreaking technology. However, he finds himself becoming the target of a relentless hacking attempt. As the stakes escalate, the researcher must navigate the threat of his technology falling into the wrong hands, with the potential consequence being the ignition of a world war fueled by the misuse of his revolutionary invention.				
WHY?	Driven by a vision of advancing humanity, the researcher is compelled to create revolutionary technology that could reshape the world for the better.				
WHAT IF...?	His groundbreaking invention attracts the attention of malicious actors aiming to exploit its power for negative purposes, posing an imminent threat to global security.				
AND THEN...?	In a race against time, the researcher must find and stop hackers, secure his invention, and navigate global tensions to prevent a world war sparked by the misuse of his own creation.				

FICTION SQUARE

You should have: A character, setting, goal, conflict and consequence

IDEA 2

WHY?

WHAT IF...?

AND THEN...?

You should have: A character, setting, goal, conflict and consequence

IDEA 3

WHY?

WHAT IF...?

AND THEN...?

WHAT TO DO

WHAT TO DO	HOW
WORLD-BUILD	Develop a timeline of historical events that shaped your world, including technological advancements, conflicts, and key cultural shifts
RESEARCH SCIENTIFIC CONCEPTS	Consult scientific journals or reliable sources to understand the latest theories related to your story's scientific elements.
IDENTIFY CORE THEMES	Brainstorm real-world parallels to your themes, drawing inspiration from contemporary issues to add relevance and depth.
ADD STRENGTHS AND FLAWS TO CHARACTERS	Create a character questionnaire detailing their fears, proudest moments, and most embarrassing memories to flesh out their complexities
ALTERNATE PACE BETWEEN ACTION AND REFLECTION	Use short chapters or sections to switch between intense action scenes and quieter moments of introspection.

WHAT TO DO

WHAT TO DO	HOW
REPRESENT DIFFERENT BACKGROUNDS	Conduct interviews or surveys with individuals from diverse backgrounds to gain insights and create authentic characters.
CREATE MORAL GREY AREAS	Develop a list of challenging ethical questions and brainstorm scenarios that force characters to confront these dilemmas
FORESHADOW PLOT TWISTS WITH CARE	Hide subtle clues in dialogue or descriptions that only become meaningful when the plot twist is revealed.
DEVELOP CHARACTER-DRIVEN EMOTIONS	Write a scene from your character's past that evokes a strong emotion, even if it doesn't make it into the final story. This exercise helps you understand
BE VISIONARY	Collaborate with artists to create visual representations of your futuristic world, sparking your imagination and helping you envision its details.

WHAT TO AVOID DOING

AVOID LENGTHY INFO-DUMPS AND EXCESSIVE EXPOSITION	Reveal world-building details through character interactions and experiences, allowing readers to discover your world naturally as the story unfolds.
STEER CLEAR OF OVERUSED TROPES AND CLICHÉD PLOTLINES	Challenge yourself to put a unique twist on a familiar trope, subverting reader expectations and breathing new life into the narrative.
AVOID ONE-DIMENSIONAL CHARACTERS DEFINED SOLELY BY PLOT ROLES	Write a scene that explores a character's past or personal thoughts, even if it doesn't make it into the final draft. This exercise deepens your understanding of their motivations.
DON'T SACRIFICE PLAUSIBILITY	Create a "science bible" detailing the rules and limitations of your fictional science and technology, and refer to it while writing to ensure consistency.
AVOID SUDDEN AND IMPROBABLE SOLUTIONS	When faced with a plot challenge, brainstorm at least three plausible solutions that align with the established rules of your world, choosing the one that best fits your narrative.
DON'T IGNORE THEMES AND MESSAGES	Incorporate real-world news or events as inspiration for your story's themes, grounding your narrative in current societal discussions.
DON'T STEREOTYPE CHARACTERS OR CULTURES	Conduct research or consult with individuals from the cultures you're representing to ensure accurate and respectful depictions.
DON'T RUSH THE ENDING	Review your story's major plotlines and ensure that each one receives a satisfying resolution, addressing lingering questions and character arcs.
DON'T NEGLECT EMOTIONS	Write a scene where a character experiences a powerful emotion and describe the physical sensations and thoughts they go through, intensifying the emotional impact.

COMMON SCIENCE FICTION SETTINGS

SPACE EXPLORATION	Stories set in vast space with spaceships, planets, and aliens. Research real space missions and technologies to add authenticity to your spacefaring world.
DYSTOPIAN EARTH	Future Earth is in decline, highlighting oppression and survival. Analyse current societal trends to create a plausible dystopian scenario.
POST-APOCALYPTIC WORLD	Civilisation's aftermath after catastrophic events. Consider how ecosystems and societies might evolve in a post-apocalyptic world.
CYBERPUNK CITYSCAPES	Futuristic urban areas with advanced tech and AI. Study emerging technologies and predict their societal impact.
TIME TRAVEL	Characters navigate different eras, altering history. Map out a timeline to maintain consistent time travel logic.
EXTRATERRESTRIAL WORLDS	Alien planets with diverse life forms and cultures. Draw inspiration from Earth's extreme environments to design alien landscapes.
PARALLEL UNIVERSES	Alternate realities with different outcomes. Create a "hub" event that diverges to form alternate realities.
ARTIFICIALLY CREATED ENVIRONMENTS	Controlled habitats like space stations. Explore the psychological and practical challenges of isolated living.
VIRTUAL REALITY WORLDS	Characters immersed in digital realms. Consider the moral implications of living in a virtual world.
UTOPIAN SOCIETIES	Idealised societies, questioning perfection. Address flaws and conflicts within the seemingly perfect society.

SCIENCE FICTION TIME PERIODS/ERAS

THE FUTURE	Speculate on advanced technology, space exploration, and societal changes. Research current scientific trends to make future predictions more plausible.
ALTERNATE FUTURES	Explore different paths from the present due to pivotal events. Choose a significant historical event to alter and trace its consequences.
POST-APOCALYPTIC	Depict survival in a world changed by global catastrophes. Study real-world environmental concerns to inform your post-apocalyptic setting.
TIME TRAVEL	Visit historical periods, offering unique perspectives on the past. Maintain consistent rules for time travel to avoid confusion.
PARALLEL UNIVERSES	Uncover alternate realities with differing historical outcomes. Establish a key event that led to branching realities.
STEAMPUNK/ VICTORIAN ERA	Blend Victorian aesthetics with futuristic technology. Research Victorian culture and technology for accurate world-building.
SPACE EXPLORATION IN THE PRESENT	Focus on current-day space exploration and encounters. Learn about current space missions and possibilities for realism.
RETROSPECTIVE FUTURE	Imagine past eras' visions of the future. Explore historical science fiction literature to capture past imaginings.

KEY CHARACTER ROLES IN SCIENCE FICTION

THE PROTAGONIST (HERO/HEROINE)	Drives the story, and faces challenges. Give them clear motivations and personal stakes.
THE ANTAGONIST (VILLAIN)	Opposes the protagonist, and creates conflict. Develop their backstory and reasons for opposing the protagonist.
THE MENTOR/GUIDE	Offers guidance and wisdom. Establish a unique teaching method or valuable knowledge they provide.
THE SIDEKICK/COMPANION	Provides support and companionship. Give them strengths that complement the protagonist's weaknesses
THE REBEL/OUTLAW	Challenges norms, fights for change. Create a backstory that explains their reasons for rebelling.
THE SCIENTIST/INVENTOR	Drives technological advancement. Integrate their inventions into plot progression.
THE ARTIFICIAL INTELLIGENCE (AI)	Explores AI's impact on humanity. Develop their self-awareness journey throughout the story.
THE ALIEN BEING	Adds cultural complexity and diversity. Design distinct alien customs and behaviours.
THE EXPLORER/ADVENTURER	Sparks discovery, uncovers secrets. Use their curiosity to reveal hidden aspects of the setting.
THE RELUCTANT HERO	Overcomes inner conflict, steps up. Gradually reveal their transformation through key moments.

CHARACTER NAMES

MALE CHARACTERS		FEMALE CHARACTERS	
KAI	ORION	LUNA	VEGA
ZANDER	ASHER	ARIA	LYRA
JAXON	PHOENIX	EMBER	AURORA
RYDER	THANE	SERAPHINA	NOVA
AXEL	NOVA	SORA	CELESTE

These names evoke a sense of adventure and mystery, making them popular choices for characters in science fiction stories.

As a writer, feel free to mix and match or create your own unique names that align with the themes and setting of your science fiction world. The key is to create names that resonate with readers and suit the imaginative and futuristic atmosphere of your narrative.

MOST COMMON OCCUPATIONS

SPACE EXPLORER/PILOT	Characters who explore distant planets, galaxies, or outer space, piloting advanced spacecraft, are common in science fiction. They may be astronauts, spacefarers, or intergalactic adventurers.
SCIENTIST/ RESEARCHER	Scientists and researchers play significant roles in science fiction, studying advanced technologies, extraterrestrial life, or futuristic scientific concepts.
SOLDIER/MILITARY OFFICER	Military personnel are often featured in science fiction, especially in stories involving space battles, alien invasions, or conflicts between planets or civilisations.
ENGINEER/ TECHNICIAN	Engineers and technicians design and maintain advanced technologies, spacecraft, or robots in science fiction narratives.
MEDIC/DOCTOR	Medical professionals in science fiction may deal with futuristic medical advancements, treat alien species, or face unique medical challenges in space or otherworldly settings.
SMUGGLER/ MERCENARY	Characters who engage in shady or morally ambiguous activities like smuggling or mercenary work are popular in science fiction stories with themes of space piracy or lawlessness.
MERCHANT/TRADER	Merchants and traders facilitate commerce in the fantasy world, dealing with rare magical items, artefacts, or exotic goods.
HACKER/ CODEBREAKER	Tech-savvy characters skilled in hacking or deciphering advanced computer systems often play pivotal roles in science fiction plots.
AI PROGRAMMER/ ROBOTICS SPECIALIST	Occupations related to artificial intelligence and robotics are prevalent in science fiction, often involving characters who interact with sentient machines.

CHALLENGES AND CONFLICTS

ALIEN ENCOUNTERS	Create tensions through cultural clashes. Develop unique alien societies and customs for authenticity.
TECHNOLOGICAL MALFUNCTIONS	Raise stakes by tying malfunctions to critical moments. Foreshadow malfunctions subtly to increase suspense
SURVIVAL IN HARSH ENVIRONMENTS	Emphasise resourcefulness and adaptation. Introduce innovative tools or solutions for survival.
ETHICAL DILEMMAS	Explore characters' internal struggles and choices. Present dilemmas that directly challenge their values.
SPACE TRAVEL HAZARDS	Intensify suspense with unexpected hazards. Research real space dangers for accurate portrayals.
OPPRESSIVE GOVERNMENTS/ CORPORATIONS	Amplify conflict with personal stakes. Tie characters' backgrounds to the conflict's origin.
INVASION OR ALIEN THREATS	Convey urgency through escalating threats. Gradually reveal the true extent of the alien threat.
INTERSTELLAR CONFLICT	Develop complex motivations for each faction. Showcase internal divisions within factions.
TIME PARADOXES	Maintain clarity through clear cause-and-effect. Establish rules for time travel in your universe.
RESISTANCE AGAINST OPPRESSION	Highlight characters' emotional journeys. Showcase their growth from fear to courage.

HIGH STAKES IN SCIENCE FICTION

LIFE AND DEATH	Characters often face life-threatening situations, where the consequence is the loss of their own lives or the lives of those they care about.
EXTINCTION OR DESTRUCTION	The stakes may involve the potential extinction of an entire species, the destruction of a planet or civilisation, or the annihilation of a crucial resource.
THE FATE OF WORLDS	Characters may hold the fate of an entire world or galaxy in their hands, with the choices they make impacting the future of vast populations.
TECHNOLOGICAL ADVANCEMENTS	The consequences of advanced technology falling into the wrong hands can be catastrophic, leading to misuse or dangerous experimentation.
SOCIETAL COLLAPSE	Characters may face the risk of societal collapse or widespread chaos due to conflicts, technological disasters, or alien invasions.
ETHICAL DILEMMAS AND MORAL CONSEQUENCES	The choices characters make can have profound ethical and moral consequences, affecting not only themselves but also the world around them.
LOSS OF IDENTITY	Characters may face the risk of losing their identities, memories, or consciousness due to mind-altering technology, memory manipulation, or AI control.
BETRAYAL AND LOYALTY	The consequences of betrayal can be severe, fracturing alliances and leading to dire circumstances for characters and their goals.
INTERSTELLAR DIPLOMACY	The stakes may involve maintaining peace between different alien civilisations or preventing interstellar conflicts from escalating.
THE BALANCE OF POWER	Characters might strive to preserve the balance of power in the universe, preventing the dominance of one faction or individual over others.

HEROIC GOALS IN SCIENCE FICTION

SAVING THE WORLD/GALAXY	Infuse urgency by revealing escalating threats. Introduce unexpected complications to the salvation plan.
EXPLORATION AND DISCOVERY	Enhance intrigue with gradual revelations. Develop clues that lead characters deeper into mysteries.
SURVIVAL	Create tension through resource scarcity and challenges. Have characters adapt and innovate to stay alive.
ADVANCING TECHNOLOGY/ KNOWLEDGE	Foster stakes by highlighting potential consequences. Explore ethical debates surrounding the technology.
ESCAPE AND FREEDOM	Amplify emotional resonance by showcasing personal struggles. Develop characters' connections to the world they seek to escape.
RESOLVING TIME TRAVEL PARADOXES	Deepen complexity by introducing unintended consequences. Establish clear rules for time travel's cause and effect.
SEEKING REVENGE OR JUSTICE	Develop empathy by delving into the characters' motivations. Challenge characters' notions of revenge and justice.
UNCOVERING SECRETS	Maintain suspense by unravelling secrets gradually. Use foreshadowing to hint at hidden truths.
REDEMPTION OR PERSONAL GROWTH	Illuminate transformation through character arcs. Create internal conflicts that hinder their growth.
UNDERSTANDING ALIEN LIFE	Deepen empathy by exploring cultural barriers. Showcase characters' efforts to bridge communication gaps.

NOTORIOUS VILLAINS IN SCIENCE FICTION

THE EVIL OVERLORD/DARK LORD	Elevate menace by revealing layers of their ruthless ambition. Develop a tragic backstory that fuels their lust for power.
CORRUPT AI/ROBOT	Intensify tension by exploring the AI's motives and twisted logic. Showcase the AI's skewed interpretation of human values.
ALIEN INVADERS	Enhance conflict by delving into their species' motivations and history. Present internal divisions within the alien invaders.
ROGUE AI SYSTEM	Generate suspense by unravelling the AI's malfunction and intentions. Gradually expose the AI's descent into chaos.
BOUNTY HUNTER/MERCENARY	Humanise them with conflicting loyalties and moral dilemmas. Force them to question their loyalty or motive.
MAD SCIENTIST	Add complexity by portraying their twisted ethical justifications. Reveal personal traumas that led to their descent.
TRAITOR/DOUBLE AGENT	Create uncertainty by masking their true intentions. Plant subtle clues hinting at their double-cross.
ALIEN PARASITE/INFECTION	Amplify horror by exploring the parasite's biology and origin. Show its impact on infected individuals' minds.
CORPORATE OR GOVERNMENT VILLAIN	Expose their manipulation tactics and hidden agendas. Reveal whistleblowers within their ranks.
THE FALLEN HERO	Evoke empathy by unravelling their tragic fall from grace. Mirror their journey with the protagonist's growth.

THEMES IN SCIENCE FICTION

EXPLORATION AND DISCOVERY	Foster a sense of wonder by emphasising the transformative journey of discovery. Use vivid sensory details to immerse readers in new, uncharted worlds.
TECHNOLOGY AND ITS IMPACT	Engage readers by focusing on the moral dilemmas and societal shifts caused by groundbreaking technology. Explore personal stories that highlight the human side of technological advancements.
FUTURE SOCIETIES AND GOVERNMENTS	Build intrigue by depicting the intricate dynamics of alternative societies and their power structures. Introduce subtle cultural practices that reflect society's values
ALIEN ENCOUNTERS AND EXTRATERRESTRIAL LIFE	Spark curiosity by examining the complexities of inter-species interactions. Create a diverse range of alien cultures, each with distinct norms and beliefs.
TIME TRAVEL AND TEMPORAL PARADOXES	Challenge readers' perceptions by constructing intricate timelines and exploring the butterfly effect. Foreshadow the consequences of time-altering decisions.
SURVIVAL AND POST-APOCALYPTIC WORLDS	Evoke empathy by focusing on the characters' emotional struggles and adaptability in dire circumstances. Show characters finding unexpected sources of hope and resilience.
ARTIFICIAL INTELLIGENCE AND HUMANITY	Prompt reflection by blurring the lines between human and AI emotions and experiences. Create poignant moments that emphasise shared emotions between AI and human characters.
CLIMATE CHANGE AND ENVIRONMENTAL ISSUES	Elicit urgency by depicting the tangible effects of environmental neglect on both nature and society. Highlight characters' personal connections to the changing world
IDENTITY AND EXISTENCE	Challenge perceptions by blurring reality in ways that make characters question their own existence. Employ symbolism to reflect the characters' journeys of self-discovery.

TITLES

A FRAMEWORK FOR SCIENCE FICTION TITLES

KEY ELEMENT OR THEME + EVOCATIVE PHRASE

Start with a key element or theme from your story and combine it with an evocative phrase that sparks curiosity.

Example: "Galactic Chronicles: The Starforged Legacy"

THE NAME OF THE WORLD OR GALAXY + ADVENTUROUS NOUN

Use the name of the world or galaxy in which your story is set and pair it with an adventurous or mysterious noun.

Example: "Andromeda's Odyssey" or "Nebula Quest"

TITLES

A FRAMEWORK FOR SCIENCE FICTION TITLES

ACTION VERB + SCI-FI ELEMENT

Use an action verb paired with a sci-fi element to create a dynamic and attention-grabbing title.

Example: "Stellar Resurgence" or "Cybernetic Rebellion"

THE UNEXPLORED + DESTINATION OR OBJECTIVE

Highlight the unexplored or unknown aspect of your story and combine it with a destination or objective.

Example: "The Uncharted Frontier: Expedition to Orion" or "Into the Nebula: Secrets of the Hyperdrive"

TITLES

COMMON LENGTHS FOR SCIENCE FICTION TITLES

As for the length of sci-fi titles, they can range from a few words to several words, but most commonly, they consist of 2 to 5 words.

Shorter titles can be punchy and memorable, while longer ones may offer more context and intrigue.

The key is to ensure that the title captures the essence of your story, sparks curiosity, and reflects the themes and elements of your science fiction narrative. As a new writer, feel free to experiment with different title structures and styles to find the one that best represents your story and resonates with your readers.

COMMON WORDS FEATURED IN SCIENCE FICTION TITLES

SPACE	ALIEN	TECHNOLOGY	FUTURE
GALAXY	ROBOT	TIME	INVASION
SPACESHIP	EXTRATERRESTRIAL	CYBERNETICS	ARTIFICIAL INTELLIGENCE
TELEPORTATION	INTERSTELLAR	MUTATION	ALTERNATE
PARALLEL	NANOTECHNOLOGY	WARP	TELEPATHY
DYSTOPIAN	VIRTUAL	GENETICS	COSMOS

SHOW NOT TELL TECHNIQUES IN SCIENCE FICTION WRITING

USE TECHNOLOGICAL SENSORY DETAILS

Instead of directly stating how a futuristic setting feels, use sensory details that reflect advanced technology and unique environments. Describe the hum of machines, the glow of holographic displays, the scent of ionised air, and the touch of futuristic materials to immerse the reader in the sci-fi realm.

Telling: The space station was impressive

Showing: The colossal space station loomed before them, its sleek surfaces adorned with pulsating lights, and the low thrum of hyperdrive engines reverberated through the metal floor.

TECHNOLOGICAL ACTIONS AND REACTIONS

Reveal characters' interactions with advanced technology and their emotional responses to futuristic events. Let readers deduce characters' feelings and motivations through their use of technology and their reactions to sci-fi phenomena.

Telling: She was astonished by the holographic display

Showing: Her eyes widened in awe as she reached out, fingers brushing the holographic projection, marvelling at the virtual marvel before her.

FUTURISTIC DIALOGUE WITH SUBTEXT

Craft dialogue that incorporates futuristic jargon, technological slang, and underlying meanings. Characters can indirectly convey their thoughts and emotions through their futuristic language and interactions.

Telling: They were suspicious of each other.

Showing: Their eyes met, each one assessing the other's cybernetic enhancements, and a tense silence settled between them, like a data transfer between rival AI cores.

POWER WORDS IN SCIENCE FICTION

FUTURISTIC	Advanced, innovative, modern, visionary, cutting-edge
EXTRATERRESTRIAL	Alien, otherworldly, cosmic, non-human, celestial
INTERSTELLAR	Spacefaring, celestial, cosmic, intergalactic, star-travelling
GALACTIC	Cosmic, celestial, interstellar, spacefaring, extraterrestrial
ALIEN	Extraterrestrial, foreign, non-human, unearthly, unfamiliar
SPACE	Celestial, cosmic, astral, interstellar, galactic
CYBERNETIC	Robotic, mechanical, artificial, bionic, electronic
ARTIFICIAL INTELLIGENCE	AI, smart, intelligent, sentient, robotic
TIME TRAVEL	Temporal, chronological, time-bending, time-bending, time-warping
APOCALYPTIC	Cataclysmic, world-ending, catastrophic, doomsday, post-apocalyptic
DYSTOPIAN	Oppressive, totalitarian, grim, nightmarish, bleak
ALTERNATE REALITY	Parallel, different, alternative, otherworldly, separate
VIRTUAL	Simulated, computer-generated, digital, virtual reality, simulated
NANOTECHNOLOGY	Nano, microscopic, molecular, tiny, micro-scale

POWER WORDS IN SCIENCE FICTION

TELEPORTATION	Instantaneous, instantaneous, transportation, beaming
ROBOTIC	Mechanical, automated, artificial, android, machine-like
COSMIC	Celestial, astronomical, intergalactic, space, universal
INNOVATIVE	Inventive, creative, groundbreaking, revolutionary, pioneering
ADVANCED	Sophisticated, high-tech, cutting-edge, progressive, state-of-the-art
PARALLEL UNIVERSE	Alternate, parallel, alternate reality, separate, divergent
HOLOGRAPHIC	Three-dimensional, projected, hologram, virtual, simulated
INTERGALACTIC	Galactic, spacefaring, cosmic, celestial, extraterrestrial
EXOPLANET	Alien, celestial, distant, non-native, extrasolar
UTOPIAN	Ideal, perfect, idyllic, harmonious, peaceful
BIOENGINEERING	Biotechnological, genetically engineered, modified, genetic
STARSHIP	Spacecraft, star-traveling, interstellar, galactic, cosmic
CLONING	Replication, genetic duplication, reproduction, cloning
CYBERSPACE	Virtual, digital, computerised, online,

POWER WORDS IN SCIENCE FICTION

INVASION	Incursion, attack, assault, intrusion
TRANSCENDENT	Elevated, spiritual, divine, beyond, surpassing
ASTRONOMICAL	Cosmic, celestial, immense, vast, colossal
SPACECRAFT	Starship, spaceship, celestial vessel, interstellar craft, space vehicle
FUTURISM	Forward-looking, visionary, progressive, modern, innovative
GENETIC	Hereditary, inherited, biological, genomic
AUGMENTED REALITY	AR, enhanced, computer-generated, overlaid, mixed reality
ROBOTICS	Automated, mechanised, AI-driven, technological
WARP DRIVE	Hyperspace, space warp, FTL, faster-than-light, warp speed
QUANTUM	Subatomic, atomic, quantum physics, quantum mechanics
ASTROBIOLOGY	Extraterrestrial life, space life, celestial biology, astrobiological
NEUROMANCER	Futuristic, cybernetic, AI-driven, technologically enhanced, virtual
TELEPATHY	Mind-reading, psychic, mental communication, telepathic
EXTRAPOLATE	Project, deduce, infer, calculate, estimate

POWER WORDS IN SCIENCE FICTION

TECHNOLOGICAL	High-tech, advanced, digital, computerised, innovative
GALAXY	Galactic, cosmic, celestial, interstellar, astral
STEAMPUNK	Retro-futuristic, Victorian, steam-powered, neo-Victorian, vintage
SUPERNOVA	Explosive, catastrophic, stellar explosion, cosmic, celestial
ANDROID	Robotic, mechanical, artificial, humanoid, automaton
CYBORG	Part-human, part-machine, robotic, bionic, mechanical
DRONES	Unmanned, automated, robotic, remote-controlled, UAV
SINGULARITY	Technological, AI-driven, post-human, advanced, artificial

Now mix and match these words to create plot twists/ and or endings:

We picked the following words in BLUE:

A GROUNDBREAKING DRONE can now CALCULATE every HUMAN'S weakness by their body heat, and gets left in the wrong hands...

Use these power words to add lots of vivid imagery to your writing

ROMANCE

FICTION SQUARE

CHARACTER	SETTING	GOAL	CONFLICT	CONSEQUENCE
WRITER	SMALL TOWN	TO HEAL	TIME RUNNING OUT	LOST CHANCE
BAKER	CITY	LOVE AGAIN	LACK OF IDEAS	HEARTBREAK
MUSICIAN	OFFICE	SECOND-CHANCE	GRIEF	REPUTATION
ARTIST	RURAL	HELP OTHERS	COMPLICATED HISTORY	UNEXPRESSED FEELINGS
BUSINESS PERSON	COUNTRY ESTATE	DISCOVER THEMSELVES	FEELING VULNERABLE	NO HAPPINESS
WIDOWED PERSON	COASTAL AREA	TO BREAK UP	DISTRACTED	FEELING LOST
SPOUSE	BAR	TO REIGNITE	LONG-DISTANCE	LONLINESS

	WRITER	SMALL TOWN	HELP OTHERS	FEELING VULNERABLE	LONLINESS

IDEA 1 — In a small town, a writer, who pens about helping others find love while still healing from their own heartbreak. As they meet someone special, the struggle with their vulnerability and opening up becomes a barrier that could lead the writer to the brink of loneliness, testing their ability to embrace a new chapter in their own love story.

WHY? — Driven by a deep desire to heal from their own heartbreak, the writer immerses themselves in helping others find love.

WHAT IF...? — However, as they meet someone special, the writer's struggle with vulnerability intensifies, hindering their chance at a new and genuine connection.

AND THEN...? — Faced with the looming threat of loneliness, the writer must confront their fear, take a leap of faith, and navigate the complexities of opening up to embrace a potential new love story.

FICTION SQUARE

You should have: A character, setting, goal, conflict and consequence

IDEA 2					
WHY?					
WHAT IF...?					
AND THEN...?					

You should have: A character, setting, goal, conflict and consequence

IDEA 3					
WHY?					
WHAT IF...?					
AND THEN...?					

WHAT TO DO

CRAFT AN ENGAGING ROMANCE STORY

ENGAGING AND RELATABLE CHARACTERS

CHARACTER PROFILES	Create detailed backgrounds, personalities, strengths, and flaws
EMOTIONAL CORE	Give characters relatable vulnerabilities and emotional struggles.
DIALOGUE AND INTERACTIONS	Craft authentic speech and meaningful relationships.

CHEMISTRY AND EMOTIONAL DEPTH

ESTABLISH COMMON BONDS	Share experiences, interests, or values for a genuine connection.
CONFLICT AND TENSION	Introduce challenges that test and strengthen the relationship.
VULNERABILITY AND EMOTIONAL MOMENTS	Allow characters to open up and deepen their bond.

WHAT TO DO

CRAFT AN ENGAGING ROMANCE STORY

CONFLICT AND OBSTACLES

VARIED CHALLENGES	Create internal and external conflicts for growth.
CHARACTER-SPECIFIC CONFLICTS	Tailor challenges to individual traits and histories.
RESOLUTION AND GROWTH	Overcome conflicts believably, with lessons learned.

CLEAR MOTIVATIONS

INDIVIDUAL GOALS	Define meaningful aspirations for each character.
SHARED VALUES	Identify common interests that draw characters together.
EVOLVING MOTIVATIONS	Show how their relationship impacts their goals.

WHAT TO DO

CRAFT AN ENGAGING ROMANCE STORY

SENSORY DETAILS

VIVID SETTING DESCRIPTIONS	Use descriptive language to engage senses.
SENSORY EXPERIENCES	Describe sensations during romantic moments.
METAPHORS AND SIMILES	Use figurative language for emotional impact.

EMOTIONAL IMPACT

PORTRAY VULNERABILITY	Allow characters to express fears and insecurities.
CRAFT INTENSE EPISODES	Mix heartwarming and poignant scenes.
EMOTIONAL LANGUAGE	Show emotions through actions and thoughts.

WHAT TO DO

CRAFT AN ENGAGING ROMANCE STORY

REALISTIC DEVELOPMENT

GRADUAL EVOLUTION	Show characters' feelings for each other developing over time.
INTERNAL AND EXTERNAL INFLUENCES	Explore growth from personal and shared experiences.
CONFLICT AND COMMUNICATION	Overcome challenges through authentic communication.

SATISFYING RESOLUTION

CLOSURE FOR CHARACTER ARCS	Resolve personal conflicts and goals.
RESOLVE CENTRAL CONFLICT	Address the main obstacle to the romance.
EMOTIONAL CATHARSIS	Provide a meaningful moment of realisation or connection.

WHAT TO DO

CRAFT AN ENGAGING ROMANCE STORY

AUTHENTIC DIALOGUE

DISTINCT CHARACTER VOICES	Show characters' feelings for each other developing over time.
RELEVANCE AND INTENT	Explore growth from personal and shared experiences.
CONFLICT	Show conflict in tough situations through dialogue

FRESH AND ORIGINAL APPROACH

SUBVERT TROPES	Put a unique twist on common themes.
EXPLORE UNIQUE SETTINGS	Use unconventional locations or time periods.
UNCONVENTIONAL CHARACTERS	Create diverse and unexpected character traits.

WHAT TO AVOID DOING

DON'T RELY ON CLICHÉS AND TROPES	Avoid overusing: Common clichés and tropes make the story predictable
	Bring freshness: Add innovation to keep readers engaged and surprised.
DON'T RUSH THE ROMANCE	Avoid insta-love: Sudden emotional connections lack depth.
	Build naturally: Develop the romance over time for believability.
DON'T NEGLECT CHARACTER DEVELOPMENT	Avoid sole focus: Well-rounded characters enrich the romance.
	Add compelling depth: Individual growth enhances relatability.
DON'T IGNORE CONSENT AND BOUNDARIES	Emphasise respect: Intimate scenes should prioritise consent and boundaries.
	Avoid harmful portrayals: Steer clear of non-consensual behaviour.
DON'T SACRIFICE PLOT FOR ROMANCE	Balance themes: A strong plot complements the central romance.
	Integrate seamlessly: Weave romantic elements into the storyline.

WHAT TO AVOID DOING

DON'T OVERLOAD ON DIALOGUE TAGS	Avoid excess: Dialogue tags can disrupt natural conversation flow. Use context: Attribute dialogue through action for immersion.
DON'T DISREGARD RESEARCH	Ensure accuracy: Thoroughly research professions, cultures, or experiences. Avoid misrepresentation: Authenticity maintains credibility.
DON'T SHY AWAY FROM CONFLICT	Embrace challenges: Conflict is vital for engaging romance. Facilitate growth: Meaningful obstacles foster character development.
DON'T NEGLECT EDITING AND PROOFREADING	Avoid errors: Typos detract from the reader's experience. Edit carefully: Review and seek feedback for improvement.
DON'T LIMIT DIVERSITY AND REPRESENTATION	Be inclusive: Embrace diversity in backgrounds and orientations. Expand appeal: Inclusive storytelling resonates with a broader audience.

COMMON ROMANCE SETTINGS

SMALL TOWN OR RURAL SETTING	Small towns and rural areas are popular settings for romance fiction. These settings often provide a cosy and intimate atmosphere where characters can form strong connections.
BIG CITY OR URBAN SETTING	On the other hand, big cities or urban environments offer a vibrant backdrop for romance stories. The fast-paced lifestyle can create exciting encounters and opportunities for the characters to meet and interact.
HISTORICAL SETTINGS	Romance stories set in the past can be highly captivating. Writers can explore different time periods, such as Regency, Victorian, or Medieval eras, adding a layer of charm and intrigue to the romance.
CONTEMPORARY SETTINGS	Contemporary settings are widely popular in romance fiction, allowing writers to explore modern relationships, challenges, and cultural references.
BEACH OR RESORT SETTING	Beach or resort settings provide a romantic and picturesque backdrop for love stories. The beauty of the natural surroundings enhances the atmosphere of romance.
WORKPLACE OR OFFICE SETTING	Workplace romances are a common trope in romance fiction. They allow characters to connect professionally and personally, often leading to tension and forbidden love.
SECOND-CHANCE SETTING	Second-chance romances often take place in familiar locations where characters reunite after a period of separation, giving them an opportunity to rekindle their relationship.
TRAVEL OR ADVENTURE SETTINGS	Travel or adventure settings can take characters on thrilling journeys, offering opportunities for personal growth and unexpected romance.

ROMANCE TIME PERIODS/ERAS

CONTEMPORARY/MODERN TIMES	Use current technology and societal issues to add realism and relatability.
REGENCY ERA (1811-1820)	Embrace the elegance of the period by focusing on intricate social dynamics and etiquette.
VICTORIAN ERA (1837-1901)	Capture the essence of Victorian ideals and societal shifts by incorporating themes of change and hidden desires.
MEDIEVAL TIMES	Create authentic medieval settings by researching castles, clothing, and chivalry to enhance the atmosphere.
WILD WEST/PIONEER ERA	Infuse resilience and determination in your characters as they navigate challenges, mirroring the spirit of the Wild West
ROARING TWENTIES	Explore the liberating and experimental spirit of the era through characters who challenge conventions.
WORLD WAR I OR II ERA	Delve into the emotional impact of war on relationships, highlighting personal growth and resilience.
GEORGIAN ERA (1714-1830)	Spotlight the complexities of class distinctions and societal norms, adding depth.
WORLD WAR II POST-WAR RECONSTRUCTION	Showcase the themes of healing and rebuilding as characters find hope and love amidst the aftermath of war.
FUTURE/FUTURISTIC SETTINGS	Develop imaginative worlds and relationships that push the boundaries of convention, while maintaining emotional resonance.

KEY CHARACTER ROLES IN ROMANCE

THE PROTAGONIST (HERO/HEROINE)	Give your protagonist relatable flaws and strengths to create a compelling and dynamic central character.
THE LOVE INTEREST	Develop the love interest's unique qualities and motivations to make their connection with the protagonist more engaging and authentic.
THE BEST FRIEND/CONFIDANTE	Use the best friend's insights to reveal the protagonist's internal conflicts, adding depth to their emotional journey.
THE ANTAGONIST (RIVAL/OBSTACLE)	Make the antagonist's motivations clear, whether they're a romantic rival or an external obstacle, to enhance the story's conflict.
THE MENTOR/GUIDE	Showcase the mentor's personal growth through their guidance, demonstrating the impact of their wisdom on the protagonist.
THE SIDEKICK	Infuse the sidekick's interactions with humour or unique perspectives to enrich the story's tone and dynamic.
THE FAMILY/FRIENDS	Create well-developed relationships between the protagonist and their family/friends, adding layers of complexity to the romance.
THE VILLAIN (NOT ALWAYS PRESENT)	Craft a multi-dimensional villain, if present, by exploring their motivations and backstory, making them more than just an obstacle.
THE UNREQUITED LOVE	Convey the unrequited love's growth and self-discovery as they navigate their feelings and find their own happiness.
THE BROKEN HEARTED	Depict the broken-hearted character's gradual healing and emotional transformation, showing their journey to opening up to love again.

CHARACTER NAMES

MALE CHARACTERS	FEMALE CHARACTERS	UNISEX CHARACTERS
ALEXANDER (ALEX)	OLIVIA	TAYLOR
LIAM	SOPHIA	JORDAN
NICHOLAS (NICK)	AVA	RILEY
BENJAMIN (BEN)	GRACE	AVERY
SEBASTIAN (SEB)	EMILY	ALEX
ETHAN	EMMA	MORGAN
WILLIAM (WILL)	ISABELLA (BELLA)	CAMERON
JAMES (JAMIE)	MIA	CASEY
GABRIEL (GABE)	CHARLOTTE (CHARLIE)	QUINN
RYAN	AMELIA (MIA)	JAMIE

Again, these are just a few examples, and there are countless other names you can use to create unique and memorable characters in your romance fiction. Consider the personalities, backgrounds, and time periods of your characters when selecting names to ensure they fit seamlessly into your story.

Ultimately, choosing names that resonate with you and suit the overall tone of your romance will contribute to crafting well-rounded and relatable characters.

MOST COMMON OCCUPATIONS

BUSINESS EXECUTIVE/CEO	Explore the CEO's vulnerability beneath their success, allowing their personal struggles to contribute to the romance's emotional depth.
ARTIST/WRITER	Infuse the creative process into the narrative, showcasing the character's artistic journey and the impact of their work on the romance.
DOCTOR/NURSE/ MEDICAL PROFESSIONAL	Use medical challenges to highlight the character's empathy and determination, shaping their growth throughout the romance.
LAWYER/ ATTORNEY	Develop moral dilemmas that challenge the lawyer's sense of justice, leading to personal growth and relationship dynamics.
ENTREPRENEUR/ SMALL BUSINESS OWNER	Create conflicts between work and romance, emphasising the character's dedication to their business and their evolving priorities.
TEACHER/ PROFESSOR	Incorporate themes of mentorship and learning, showcasing how the character's role as an educator influences the romance.
POLICE OFFICER/DETECTIVE	Explore the character's internal conflict between duty and personal life, adding depth to their relationship struggles.
FIREFIGHTER/ PARAMEDIC	Highlight moments of bravery and sacrifice, demonstrating the character's commitment to others and their romantic partner.
CHEF/RESTAURANT OWNER	Utilise sensory descriptions during cooking scenes to enhance the sensuality and emotional connection in the romance.
ACTOR/ACTRESS	Delve into the character's journey of self-discovery and identity, portraying the challenges of fame and authentic relationships.

CHALLENGES AND CONFLICTS

MISCOMMUNICATION OR LACK OF COMMUNICATION	Use internal monologues to reveal characters' thoughts, creating tension as readers see their misunderstandings while hoping for eventual clarity.
PAST TRAUMA OR HEARTBREAK	Gradually unveil characters' pasts, allowing their vulnerabilities to emerge over time and fostering a deeper emotional connection.
SOCIAL OR CLASS DIFFERENCES	Develop characters' growth by having them challenge societal norms, highlighting the power of love to transcend social boundaries.
FORCED PROXIMITY OR RELUCTANT PARTNERSHIPS	Show evolving dynamics through shared experiences, gradually building trust and chemistry within the forced partnership.
EXTERNAL OPPOSITION OR ANTAGONISTS	Humanise antagonists with nuanced motivations, giving them a chance for redemption or change to create a more complex conflict.
SECRETS AND HIDDEN IDENTITIES	Use dramatic reveals to fuel character development, leading to moments of vulnerability and strengthening the emotional bond.
COMMITMENT PHOBIA OR FEAR OF INTIMACY	Depict characters' internal struggles, allowing readers to empathise with their emotional journey towards overcoming their fears.
TIME CONSTRAINTS OR LONG-DISTANCE RELATIONSHIPS	Utilise technology creatively to maintain communication, showcasing efforts to bridge the gap and deepen emotional connection.
CAREER AMBITIONS OR PERSONAL GOALS	Create scenarios where characters' paths intersect, forcing them to reevaluate their priorities and reconcile their ambitions.
EXTERNAL CIRCUMSTANCES OR LIFE EVENTS	Use unexpected events to test the strength of the romance, allowing characters to prove their commitment and resilience.

HIGH STAKES IN ROMANCE

EMOTIONAL VULNERABILITY	Show characters' internal struggles through introspection, allowing readers to empathise with their fear of opening up.
FRIENDSHIP AND RELATIONSHIP DYNAMICS	Highlight characters' conflicts and dilemmas, illustrating the challenges they face in maintaining both romance and friendships.
SELF-DISCOVERY AND GROWTH	Depict characters' evolving self-awareness through their actions and decisions, emphasising personal growth as a result of the romance.
CAREER OR PERSONAL SACRIFICE	Create moments of tough choices, where characters must weigh their priorities and values to add depth to their emotional journey.
REPUTATION OR SOCIAL STANDING	Develop societal pressures and internal conflicts, emphasising characters' choices between love and external expectations.
FAMILY APPROVAL OR DISAPPROVAL	Showcase characters' inner turmoil and dilemmas as they navigate familial relationships, adding layers to their emotional stakes.
PROFESSIONAL REPERCUSSIONS	Introduce workplace challenges that test characters' commitment, highlighting the tension between personal desires and professional responsibilities.
REGRET AND WHAT-IFS	Use inner monologues or flashbacks to convey the characters' internal struggles, emphasising the weight of potential regrets.
PHYSICAL SAFETY OR WELL-BEING	Create suspenseful situations where characters' safety is at risk, heightening the urgency of their choices and actions.
UNREQUITED LOVE OR LOSS OF FRIENDSHIP	Illustrate characters' emotional turmoil through their interactions, revealing the internal battle between desire and potential loss.

When integrating consequences and stakes, ensure they are tightly connected to the characters' motivations and development. By making the stakes resonate on a personal level, you can deepen the emotional impact of the romance, keeping readers invested in the characters' choices and outcomes.

HEROIC GOALS IN ROMANCE

FIND TRUE LOVE	The primary goal in many romance stories is for the characters to find true love and a deep emotional connection with each other.
OVERCOME PAST HEARTBREAK	Characters may aim to heal from past heartbreak or traumatic experiences and open their hearts to love again.
SELF-DISCOVERY AND PERSONAL GROWTH	Characters often strive for self-discovery and personal growth, which can be accelerated or influenced by their romantic relationship.
PURSUE PROFESSIONAL ASPIRATIONS	Characters may have career-related goals or dreams that they want to achieve while navigating their romantic journey.
ACHIEVE INDEPENDENCE	Some characters aim to achieve independence and self-sufficiency before fully committing to a romantic relationship.
RECONCILE WITH FAMILY OR FRIENDS	Characters may have goals of reconciling with estranged family members or friends, with their romantic partner's support.
PROTECT LOVED ONES	Characters may prioritise protecting their loved ones, even if it means sacrificing their own happiness.
PROVE THEMSELVES	Some characters may seek to prove their worth, talent, or capabilities to others, including their romantic interest.
RESOLVE INTERNAL CONFLICTS	Characters may have internal conflicts, such as fear of commitment, that they want to overcome to fully embrace the romance.
DEFEAT ANTAGONISTS OR OVERCOME OBSTACLES	In romantic suspense or action-orientated romances, characters may have the goal of defeating antagonists or overcoming external obstacles that threaten their relationship.

NOTORIOUS VILLAINS IN ROMANCE

THE RIVAL LOVE INTEREST	Build tension through interactions and competitions, highlighting the rival's appeal while showcasing the depth of the protagonists' connection.
THE DISAPPROVING FAMILY MEMBER OR FRIEND	Develop the disapproving character's motivations and backstory, revealing their reasons for opposing the relationship and adding complexity to their role.
THE MANIPULATIVE OR DECEPTIVE CHARACTER	Employ subtle hints and foreshadowing to create intrigue, allowing readers to piece together the manipulative character's true intentions.
THE SOCIETAL OR CULTURAL OPPOSITION	Use inner conflicts to show characters grappling with societal expectations, illustrating the internal struggle caused by the cultural antagonist.
THE BUSINESS RIVAL OR COMPETITOR	Introduce professional challenges that force characters to navigate between their career aspirations and romantic desires.
. THE EX-SPOUSE OR PARTNER	Showcase the ex-partner's emotional journey, revealing vulnerabilities that contribute to their actions and adding depth to their character.
THE MISUNDERSTOOD CHARACTER	Gradually unveil the misunderstood character's motivations, allowing readers to empathise and potentially sympathise with their perspective.
THE EXTERNAL THREAT OR DANGER	Create suspenseful scenes that emphasise the danger posed by the external threat, intensifying the protagonists' bond as they face challenges together.
THE INTERNAL STRUGGLE OR FLAW	Depict moments of vulnerability that expose the internal struggle, leading to character growth and eventual resolution.
THE TIME OR CIRCUMSTANCE	Infuse urgency into the romance as characters confront the constraints of time or circumstance, emphasising their determination to overcome obstacles.

When crafting a villain role, ensure that their actions and motivations align with the overall theme and development of the romance. By incorporating multidimensional antagonists, you can create a more layered and engaging narrative that adds complexity and depth to the protagonists' journey toward love.

THEMES IN ROMANCE FICTION

SECOND CHANCES	Use flashbacks and shared memories to highlight the depth of the characters' past relationships, enhancing the emotional impact of their second chance.
OPPOSITES ATTRACT	Create engaging dialogues that showcase the characters' differences while also revealing their underlying similarities and mutual understanding.
FORBIDDEN LOVE	Develop internal conflicts that reflect the characters' struggle between societal expectations and their genuine feelings, heightening the tension.
FRIENDS-TO-LOVERS	Utilise inner monologues to convey the characters' evolving feelings, capturing the nuances of their emotional transition.
LOVE TRIANGLES	Deepen the connections between all three characters, ensuring each love interest has distinct qualities that resonate with the protagonist.
SELF-DISCOVERY AND PERSONAL GROWTH	Show character development through their actions and choices, allowing the romance to catalyse their growth.
FAKE RELATIONSHIPS	Incorporate humourous and heartfelt moments that blur the line between pretence and reality, creating a dynamic emotional arc.
HEALING AND REDEMPTION	Use introspective scenes to explore the characters' emotional wounds and their gradual journey toward healing.
SMALL TOWN ROMANCE	Infuse the town's unique charm and quirky characters into the narrative, making the setting an integral part of the story.
ARRANGED OR FORCED MARRIAGES	Develop the characters' shifting attitudes toward the arranged marriage, allowing their feelings to evolve naturally.

Remember that themes in romance fiction provide a framework to explore the dynamics of love and relationships. As a writer, your creativity shines when you intertwine these themes with well-developed characters and engaging plots, allowing readers to immerse themselves in the emotional journey of your story.

TITLES

A FRAMEWORK FOR ROMANCE FICTION TITLES

DESCRIPTIVE ELEMENT

A key word or phrase that describes the central theme, emotion, or setting of the romance.

Example: "Whispers of Desire"

EMOTIONAL TRIGGER

Words that evoke strong emotions associated with love, desire, or heartbreak.

Example: "Emma's Enchanting Embrace"

TITLES

A FRAMEWORK FOR ROMANCE FICTION TITLES

CHARACTER ELEMENT

Names of the main characters or terms of endearment related to the protagonists.

Example: "Emily's New Dream"

SETTING OR TIME PERIOD

If the romance is set in a specific time period or location, it may be included in the title.

Example: "Midnight in Paris"

TITLES

COMMON LENGTHS FOR ROMANCE FICTION TITLES

Romance fiction book titles typically consist of 3 to 5 words, although there can be variations.

Romance fiction book titles often evoke emotions, capturing the essence of the love story.

They may hint at the central theme, setting, or the type of romance portrayed in the book.

Many titles use poetic or descriptive language to create an alluring and romantic feel.

COMMON WORDS FEATURED IN ROMANCE FICTION TITLES

LOVE	HEART	KISS	PASSION
SECRET	DESIRE	FOREVER	DREAM
FIRE	TEMPTATION	HEARTBREAK	SWEET
SEDUCTION	FATE	ENCHANTMENT	PROMISE
MIDNIGHT	BRIDE	SURRENDER	FORBIDDEN

MOST POPULAR WORDS IN ROMANCE FICTION

LOVE	The deep affection and strong emotional bond between characters that drives the central theme of the romance story.
ROMANCE	The genre focuses on love, relationships, and emotional connections between characters, often with a strong emphasis on passion and desire.
HEART	Symbolises the emotional core of the characters' feelings, representing love and vulnerability.
PASSION	Intense and overwhelming emotions, especially related to physical and romantic desire.
DESIRE	The strong feeling of wanting or longing for someone, often associated with romantic and sensual attraction.
KISS	An intimate physical gesture that can signify love, passion, and affection between characters.
EMBRACE	A tender and loving gesture of hugging or holding closely, representing emotional closeness.
RELATIONSHIP	The connection and interaction between characters, often portraying their romantic journey.
ATTRACTION	The magnetic pull and interest characters feel toward each other, sparking the development of a romantic bond.
CHEMISTRY	The undeniable connection and spark between characters that enhances their romantic interactions.

MOST POPULAR WORDS IN ROMANCE FICTION

INTIMACY	The emotional and physical closeness characters share, often portrayed through romantic or sensual moments.
AFFECTION	Warm feelings of fondness and tenderness displayed between characters.
TENDERNESS	Acts of gentleness and care that demonstrate the depth of characters' emotions.
DEVOTION	Characters' strong commitment and loyalty to each other, even in the face of challenges.
CONNECTION	The emotional link that binds characters together and forms the foundation of their romance.
ADORATION	Characters' deep admiration and love for each other, often expressed through gestures and words.
FLIRTATION	Playful and teasing interactions that suggest romantic interest and create a sense of anticipation.
SWEETHEART	A term of endearment used to express affection and love between characters.
SOULMATE	The idea of a perfect match, someone with whom characters feel a profound and spiritual connection.
HEARTFELT	Genuine and sincere emotions expressed by characters, reflecting the depth of their love and romance.

SYMBOLS FOUND IN ROMANCE FICTION

ROSE	A universal symbol of love and romance, often given as a gesture of affection.
HEART	Represents love and emotional connections between characters.
RING	Symbolises commitment and often used in proposals or as a token of love.
LOVE LETTER	A handwritten letter expressing deep emotions and affection.
CANDLE	Creates a romantic ambiance and signifies intimacy and warmth.
CHOCOLATE	A sweet treat associated with romance and expressing love.
CHAMPAGNE	A celebratory drink often enjoyed during romantic moments.
LOCKET	A piece of jewellery that holds sentimental value, often containing a picture of a loved one.
PENDANT	Symbolises a connection between characters or love and devotion.
KISS	A tender and intimate gesture of affection between characters.
SUNSET	A romantic setting often used to enhance emotional moments.
MOON	Symbolises love and romance, often associated with a sense of magic and mystery.
BEACH	A popular setting for romantic walks and heartwarming moments.
STARRY SKY	Creates an enchanting backdrop for romantic scenes and declarations of love.

POWER WORDS IN ROMANCE FICTION

PASSIONATE	Fiery, intense, fervent, ardent, zealous
LOVE	Affectionate, adoring, caring, tender, devoted
DESIRE	Yearning, craving, longing, lustful, eager, unexpected
SEDUCTION	Alluring, enticing, captivating, tempting, beguiling
HEARTFELT	Sincere, genuine, earnest, heartfelt, profound
INTENSE	Powerful, fervid, strong, deep, emotional
AFFECTION	Loving, tender, warm, fond, gentle
EMBRACE	Enveloping, loving, warm, tight, intimate
ATTRACTION	Magnetic, appealing, captivating, charming, enticing
ADORATION	Reverent, worshipful, idolising, loving, devoted
CONNECTION	Bond, link, tie, relationship, attachment
CHEMISTRY	Magnetic, electric, powerful, strong, alluring
ENCHANTMENT	Charming, magical, captivating, enchanting, bewitching
ROMANTIC	Amorous, affectionate, loving, passionate, tender

POWER WORDS IN ROMANCE FICTION

SENSUAL	Sensuous, passionate, alluring, erotic, seductive
TENDER	Gentle, soft, loving, affectionate, caring
YEARNING	Longing, craving, eager, pining, desiring
DEVOTION	Dedicated, loyal, committed, faithful, steadfast
LONGING	Aching, yearning, craving, wistful
ENRAPTURED	Captivated, enchanted, entranced, mesmerised, spellbound
AMOUROUS	Loving, affectionate, romantic, passionate, tender
EUPHORIA	Ecstasy, bliss, elation, joy, happiness
CUDDLE	Embrace, snuggle, nestle, hug, cuddly
INFATUATION	Smitten, besotted, lovesick, infatuated, captivated
BLISS	Joyful, ecstatic, euphoric, content, blissful
WHISPER	Softly spoken, murmur, hushed, intimate, secret
BELOVED	Cherished, loved, dear, adored, treasured
PASSIONATE	Intense, fervent, ardent, zealous, enthusiastic

POWER WORDS IN ROMANCE FICTION

CHERISH	Treasure, value, appreciate, hold dear, love
BUTTERFLIES	Nervous excitement, flutter, anticipation, thrill, tingling
HEARTS	Loving, affectionate, tender, caring, heartfelt
KISS	Romantic, tender, passionate, loving, sweet
HUG	Warm, comforting, loving, tender, affectionate
ROMANCE	Love, passion, affection, courtship, relationship
SWOON	Faint, be overwhelmed, enchanted, entranced, infatuated
ENAMOURED	Smitten, captivated, charmed, in love, infatuated
ENDEARMENT	Loving, affectionate, sweet, tender, fond
INTIMACY	Closeness, connection, togetherness, affection, love
WARMTH	Affection, love, tenderness, comfort, intimacy
LUST	Desire, passion, craving, longing, sensuality
CARING	Nurturing, loving, kind, thoughtful, considerate
CHARMING	Enchanting, charismatic, captivating, alluring, lovely

POWER WORDS IN ROMANCE FICTION

TENDERNESS	Gentle, loving, affectionate, caring, soft
FASCINATION	Enchantment, captivation, allure, mesmerising, entrancement
GLOWING	Radiant, shining, bright, beaming, luminescent, spark
SENTIMENT	Emotional, heartfelt, touching, moving, expressive
SERENDIPITY	Fortunate, chance, unexpected, providence, luck
PASSIONATELY	Intensely, fervently, wholeheartedly, deeply, ardently
EMOTIONAL	Heartfelt, intense, passionate, sentimental, moving, fiery

Now mix and match these words to create plot twists/ and or endings:

We picked the following words in BLUE:

An UNEXPECTED SPARK develops between two work friends, who were FIERY enemies and puts their individual work projects in jeopardy.

What happens now?

Use these power words to add lots of vivid imagery to your writing

SHOW NOT TELL TECHNIQUES IN ROMANCE WRITING

CHARACTER IN LOVE

Telling: She couldn't deny the fluttering feeling in her chest whenever she received a message from him.

Showing: Her heart raced as she saw his name on her phone, and a shy smile tugged at the corner of her lips.

ROMANTIC MOMENT

Telling: In that instant, amidst the library's hushed ambience, they felt an undeniable connection that left them both breathless.

Showing: Their fingers brushed lightly as they reached for the same book, and their eyes locked in a shared moment of warmth.

HEARTBREAK

Telling: The ache in her chest intensified every time she thought of him, a constant reminder of the love she had lost.

Showing: She traced her fingertip over the empty coffee cup, her gaze distant and haunted as memories of their laughter echoed in her mind.

TENSION BETWEEN CHARACTERS

Telling: Their arguments had become more frequent lately, an underlying tension that neither of them could ignore.

Showing: He leaned in, his voice low and tinged with frustration as their eyes clashed in a battle of wills.

CRIME

FICTION SQUARE

CHARACTER	SETTING	GOAL	CONFLICT	CONSEQUENCE
DETECTIVE	URBAN	SEEKING REDEMPTION	INTERNAL STRUGGLE	INNOCENT LIVES LOST
PRIVATE INVESTIGATOR	RURAL	UNCOVER THE TRUTH	BETRAYAL WITHIN THE TEAM	FRAMED FOR A CRIME
REFORMED CRIMINAL	COAST	PROTECT LOVED ONES	RACE AGAINST TIME	ETERNAL GUILT
FORENSIC EXPERT	PRISON	CLEAR THEIR NAME	INTERFERENCE FROM AUTHORITIES	RISE OF A NEW CRIMINAL POWER
JOURNALIST	WAREHOUSE	STOP A SERIAL KILLER	PERSONAL VENDETTA	PERSONAL TRAGEDY
JUDGE	ISLAND	PREVENT A CATASTROPHE	UNPREDICTABLE ALLIANCES	CHAOS
EX-COP	CORPORATE	DISMANTLE AN ORGANISATION	SOMEBODY WASN'T WHO THEY SAID THEY WERE	GLOBAL CATASTROPHE

	WRITER	SMALL TOWN	HELP OTHERS	FEELING VULNERABLE	LONLINESS
IDEA 1	A determined detective stationed along the coast must race against time to clear their name as they uncover a web of corruption, all while facing the looming threat of a personal tragedy that will strike if the truth remains elusive.				
WHY?	A once-trusted partner frames the Detective [Character Name] for a high-profile crime, leading to their expulsion from the force and tarnished reputation.				
WHAT IF...?	In a desperate bid to clear their name, the detective discovers a city-wide conspiracy.				
AND THEN...?	With the clock ticking, the detective must unearth the truth before a personal tragedy strikes, unraveling a sinister plot that goes deeper than they ever imagined.				

FICTION SQUARE

You should have: A character, setting, goal, conflict and consequence

IDEA 2

WHY?

WHAT IF...?

AND THEN...?

You should have: A character, setting, goal, conflict and consequence

IDEA 3

WHY?

WHAT IF...?

AND THEN...?

WHAT TO DO

STRONG HOOK	Detective Williams is called to the crime scene, where a single red rose lay on the victim's lifeless body.
COMPLEX CRIME	A burglary reveals a hidden safe with missing contents, turning it into a murder investigation.
ENGAGING DETECTIVE	Detective Jane Watson, haunted by an unsolved case, uses her forensic expertise to uncover the truth.
CLUES AND RED HERRINGS	A mysterious phone call leads the detective astray, diverting attention from the real culprit.
BUILD SUSPENSE	Cryptic messages left by the killer escalate tension as the detective inches closer to solving the case.
MOTIVES AND BACKSTORIES	A suspect's financial troubles and history with the victim make them a compelling figure in the investigation.
TWISTS AND SURPRISES	The victim's closest friend is revealed to be the mastermind behind the crime, challenging assumptions.
EFFECTIVE DIALOGUE	"I saw him that night at the bar," she said, her voice trembling. "He was acting strangely."
CONVEY SETTING	The eerie aura of a dilapidated mansion on the hill serves as the backdrop for the final confrontation.
SATISFYING RESOLUTION	Detective Watson confronts the killer after a thrilling chase, exposing their identity and motive.

WHAT TO AVOID DOING

AVOID OVERCOMPLICATING THE PLOT	Outline the main plot points before writing to maintain a clear and focused storyline.
AVOID UNNECESSARY VIOLENCE OR GORE	Use violence sparingly and ensure it serves the story's progression or character development.
AVOID LEAVING PLOT HOLES	Review your story for unanswered questions before finalising, and consider seeking feedback from others.
AVOID MAKING THE DETECTIVE PERFECT	Give your detective relatable flaws to make them more human and engaging.
AVOID RELYING ON COINCIDENCES	Integrate clues and logical deductions to drive the plot forward, minimising reliance on chance.
AVOID STEREOTYPING CHARACTERS	Develop unique traits and backgrounds for your characters to avoid clichés and add depth.
AVOID PREDICTABLE ENDINGS	Experiment with unexpected twists and conclusions to keep readers intrigued.
AVOID NEGLECTING RESEARCH	Research legal and procedural details to add authenticity and credibility to your story.
AVOID RUSHING THE CLIMAX	Build tension gradually through rising stakes and well-paced reveals leading to the climax.
AVOID NEGLECTING SETTING AND ATMOSPHERE	Use descriptive language to create a sensory-rich setting that enhances the mood and tone.

COMMON CRIME SETTINGS

URBAN CITY	The bustling streets and diverse neighbourhoods of a city provide a dynamic backdrop for crime fiction. The urban setting often involves detective agencies, police precincts, and a mix of social classes.
SMALL TOWN	The close-knit and seemingly peaceful atmosphere of a small town can hide dark secrets and conflicts, making it a compelling setting for crime fiction.
COUNTRYSIDE OR RURAL AREA	Remote and isolated settings offer a sense of danger and mystery, as crimes may go unnoticed or be harder to solve.
POLICE STATION	The heart of law enforcement, police stations are common settings for interrogations, crime-solving discussions, and interactions between detectives and officers.
CRIME SCENE	Whether it's a crime scene in a home, an alleyway, or a deserted area, it is a pivotal setting where clues are discovered and investigations begin.
FORENSIC LAB	A space where scientific experts analyse evidence, such as DNA, fingerprints, and ballistics, to aid in solving crimes.
PRISON	A setting where interactions with suspects, witnesses, or criminals can take place, and where protagonists may find key information or confront adversaries.
COURTROOM	A location for legal proceedings, where tension rises during trials and suspects are brought to justice.
UNDERGROUND WORLD	Criminal hideouts, black markets, and secretive organisations can add intrigue and danger to crime fiction.
FOREIGN COUNTRIES	Crime fiction set in foreign lands adds cultural complexity and challenges for the protagonists.

CRIME TIME PERIODS/ERAS

CONTEMPORARY TIMES	Crime fiction set in the present day, involving modern technology, current societal issues, and contemporary police procedures.
GOLDEN AGE (1920S-1940S)	Inspired by the works of authors like Agatha Christie, crime fiction in the Golden Age features classic whodunits, locked-room mysteries, and amateur sleuths.
NOIR ERA (1940S-1950S)	Set in post-World War II America, noir crime fiction focuses on gritty urban settings, morally ambiguous characters, and themes of corruption and betrayal.
VICTORIAN ERA (1837-1901)	Crime fiction set in the Victorian era often includes Sherlock Holmes-type detectives and elaborate, mysterious crimes in historical London.
PROHIBITION ERA (1920S-1930S)	Crime fiction during the Prohibition era involves bootlegging, gangsters, and speakeasies, providing a backdrop for organised crime stories.
POST-WAR ERA (1950S-1960S)	Stories set in the post-war era can explore the impact of wartime experiences on characters and crimes that emerged during this period.
WILD WEST ERA (LATE 1800S)	Crime fiction set in the Wild West includes sheriffs, outlaws, and robberies in frontier towns.

CRIME TIME PERIODS/ERAS

MODERN HISTORICAL (1960S-1990S)	Crime fiction set in recent history allows for the exploration of historical events, such as political scandals or serial killer cases.
FUTURISTIC OR DYSTOPIAN	Crime fiction set in a futuristic or dystopian world offers opportunities for exploring advanced technology, societal breakdowns, and unconventional crimes.
MEDIEVAL OR RENAISSANCE ERA	Crime fiction set in medieval or Renaissance times involves unique challenges and investigative techniques in historical settings.
PRE-MODERN TIMES (ANCIENT EGYPT, ROME, ETC.)	Stories set in ancient civilisations can feature historical detectives solving crimes using ancient methods and traditions.
EDWARDIAN ERA (1901-1910)	Crime fiction during the Edwardian era may focus on societal changes and class divides, similar to the Victorian era.
SWINGING SIXTIES (1960S)	Crime fiction set in the 1960s captures the atmosphere of cultural revolutions and societal changes.
ROARING TWENTIES (1920S)	Stories set in the Roaring Twenties can explore the Jazz Age, prohibition, and organised crime.

KEY CHARACTER ROLES IN CRIME

DETECTIVE/INVESTIGATOR	Give your detective a unique backstory or personal motivation that drives their dedication to solving the case.
SIDEKICK/PARTNER	Create a dynamic between the detective and sidekick that adds depth to both characters, showcasing complementary skills and contrasting personalities.
VICTIM	Develop the victim's character before the crime occurs, allowing readers to empathise and connect with them.
WITNESS	Use the witness to reveal clues gradually, creating suspense and keeping readers engaged in the investigation.
SUSPECT	Develop distinct motives and backgrounds for each suspect, making the detective's decision-making process more complex.
CRIMINAL/PERPETRATOR	Build intrigue around the identity of the perpetrator, dropping subtle hints without giving away their role too early.
POLICE CHIEF/AUTHORITY FIGURE	Use the authority figure to introduce conflicts, obstacles, or additional pressure on the detective's investigation.
JOURNALIST/REPORTER	Utilise the journalist to provide external perspectives on the case and create ethical dilemmas for the detective.
INFORMANT	Develop a layered relationship between the detective and informant, including mutual benefits and potential risks.
RED HERRING	Introduce the red herring as a seemingly crucial character, only to reveal their true purpose later in the story.
ALIBI WITNESS	Play with the reliability of the alibi witness, adding uncertainty and complicating the detective's assessment.

CHARACTER NAMES

MALE CHARACTERS

JAMES	CHRISTOPHER
JOHN	MARK
ROBERT	JOSEPH
WILLIAM	BRIAN
MICHAEL	MATTHEW
DAVID	RICHARD
JACK	THOMAS
DANIEL	RONNIE

FEMALE CHARACTERS

MARY	EMILY
JENNIFER	NICOLE
SUSAN	AMANDA
LINDA	SAMANTHA
KAREN	ELIZABETH
PATRICIA	MICHELLE
SARAH	RACHEL
JESSICA	JOANNE

These names are frequently used in crime fiction due to their familiarity and widespread popularity in English-speaking regions. However, as a new writer, you are not limited to these names. Feel free to explore other names that suit your characters and their backgrounds, adding diversity and uniqueness to your crime fiction story.

MOST COMMON OCCUPATIONS

LAW ENFORCEMENT AND INVESTIGATION

POLICE DETECTIVE	PRIVATE INVESTIGATOR	FBI AGENT
FORENSIC SCIENTIST	CRIME SCENE INVESTIGATOR (CSI)	HOMICIDE DETECTIVE
UNDERCOVER AGENT	INTELLIGENCE ANALYST	INTERPOL OFFICER

LEGAL PROFESSIONS

DEFENCE ATTORNEY	PROSECUTOR	DISTRICT ATTORNEY
JUDGE	PARALEGAL	BARRISTER

JOURNALISM AND MEDIA

INVESTIGATIVE JOURNALIST	CRIME REPORTER	PHOTOJOURNALIST
NEWS ANCHOR	TV PRODUCER	EDITOR

CRIMINAL PROFILING AND PSYCHOLOGY

CRIMINAL PROFILER	FORENSIC PSYCHOLOGIST	PHOTOJOURNALIST
PSYCHIATRIST	CRIMINAL BEHAVIOUR ANALYST	COUNSELLOR

MOST COMMON OCCUPATIONS

MEDICAL AND FORENSIC

MEDICAL EXAMINER	CORONER	PATHOLOGIST
FORENSIC PATHOLOGIST	TOXICOLOGIST	CONSULTANT

CRIMINAL ELEMENTS

MOB BOSS	GANG LEADER	HITMAN/ASSASSIN
SMUGGLER	HACKER	THIEF/BURGLAR

GOVERNMENT AND SECURITY

CIA AGENT	SECRET SERVICE AGENT	HOMELAND SECURITY OFFICER
DIPLOMATIC SECURITY AGENT	WHITEHOUSE STAFF	GUARD

OTHER PROFESSIONS

SECURITY GUARD	CORRUPT POLITICIAN	BUSINESS TYCOON
BOUNTY HUNTER	BLACKMAIL SPECIALIST	COMPUTER PROGRAMMER

CHALLENGES AND CONFLICTS

MURDER OR HOMICIDE	The central crime that sets the story in motion and serves as the main obstacle to be solved.
MISSING PERSON	The disappearance of a character, often involving a race against time to find them before it's too late.
KIDNAPPING	The abduction of a person, leading to negotiations, ransom demands, or a rescue mission.
HEIST OR ROBBERY	A planned theft that involves complex schemes and challenges for both criminals and law enforcement.
ORGANISED CRIME	The presence of powerful and dangerous criminal organisations that hinder investigations and pose significant threats.
CORRUPTION	Characters within the law enforcement or legal system who are corrupt and obstruct the pursuit of justice.
FALSE ACCUSATION	The protagonist or a suspect being falsely accused of the crime, leading to their efforts to clear their name.
RACE AGAINST TIME	A limited timeframe to solve the crime before dire consequences occur, like another murder or a looming disaster.
WITNESS INTIMIDATION	Witnesses who are too scared to testify or provide crucial information due to intimidation or fear.

CHALLENGES AND CONFLICTS

JURISDICTIONAL CONFLICTS	Conflicts between different law enforcement agencies or legal jurisdictions that hinder cooperation.
RED TAPE AND BUREAUCRACY	Obstacles caused by bureaucratic procedures that slow down or complicate the investigation.
PERSONAL CONFLICTS	Internal conflicts within the protagonist's personal life, such as strained relationships or personal demons.
FALSE LEADS AND DEAD ENDS	Misleading clues or evidence that divert the investigation off track and delay the discovery of the truth.
LIMITED RESOURCES	The protagonist facing limited manpower, funds, or equipment, making the investigation more challenging.
UNCOOPERATIVE WITNESSES/SUSPECTS	Witnesses or suspects who are uncooperative or deliberately misleading investigators.
MEDIA AND PUBLIC PRESSURE	Pressure from the media or public demands for quick results, adding stress to the investigation.
LACK OF EVIDENCE	The absence of crucial evidence that hinders the case's progress and requires innovative methods to gather information.
UNSOLVABLE MYSTERY	An initially unsolvable crime that forces the protagonist to think outside the box to find a breakthrough.

HIGH STAKES IN CRIME FICTION

CAPTURE OR FREEDOM	The stakes involve the difference between the criminal being caught and facing justice or escaping and remaining free to commit more crimes.
LIFE OR DEATH	The consequences can be a matter of life or death for characters involved, such as victims, suspects, or law enforcement.
JUSTICE SERVED OR ESCAPING JUSTICE	The stakes revolve around whether the truth will be revealed and justice served, or if the guilty party will evade punishment.
SAFETY OF LOVED ONES	Characters may be motivated by the need to protect their loved ones from harm, making the stakes deeply personal.
CAREER AND REPUTATION	The consequences can impact the protagonist's career and reputation, especially if they are in law enforcement or a position of authority.
PUBLIC SAFETY	The stakes involve the safety of the public, as the crime may have the potential to harm others.
REDEMPTION OR DAMNATION	The protagonist may be seeking redemption for past mistakes or facing the risk of being damned by failing to solve the case.
MORAL DILEMMAS	Characters may face ethical dilemmas, where their decisions have significant consequences for themselves and others.
SURVIVAL	In some cases, the stakes are simply about surviving the dangers and threats posed by criminals or the pursuit of justice.
PSYCHOLOGICAL IMPACT	The consequences may include the psychological toll of the investigation on characters, such as trauma, guilt, or obsession.

These consequences and stakes add depth and urgency to crime fiction stories, keeping readers engaged and invested in the outcome of the investigation. As a new writer, using these elements effectively can elevate your narrative and create a compelling reading experience.

HEROIC GOALS IN CRIME FICTION

SOLVE THE CRIME	The central goal of the protagonist, typically a detective or investigator, is to solve the crime and bring the perpetrator to justice.
CATCH THE KILLER	Similar to solving the crime, the protagonist's primary objective is to apprehend the murderer responsible for the crime.
CLEAR ONE'S NAME	A character may be falsely accused of the crime and their goal is to prove their innocence and clear their name.
PROTECT LOVED ONES	The protagonist may be driven by the desire to protect their family or friends from harm, especially if they become targets of the criminal.
REVENGE	A character seeks revenge against the perpetrator for a personal vendetta, especially if the crime affected them or their loved ones.
STOP A SERIAL KILLER	The protagonist's goal is to stop a serial killer who has been committing a series of murders
RECOVER STOLEN PROPERTY	The objective is to recover stolen items or valuable objects taken during a robbery or heist
EXPOSE CORRUPTION	The protagonist aims to expose corruption within law enforcement or other institutions that hinders the investigation.
STOP A TERRORIST PLOT	The protagonist works to prevent a large-scale terrorist attack from taking place.
PREVENT FURTHER CRIMES	The goal is to prevent the criminal from committing more crimes or causing additional harm.

NOTORIOUS VILLAINS IN CRIME FICTION

THE MASTERMIND	The mastermind is the brains behind the crime, orchestrating intricate plans and manipulating others to achieve their goals. They are often cunning, calculating, and several steps ahead of the protagonists.
THE SERIAL KILLER	This villain is driven by a compulsion to commit multiple murders, often following a specific pattern or signature. They may have a twisted motivation, such as seeking notoriety or fulfilling a dark desire.
THE CORRUPT AUTHORITY	This villain operates within the system, abusing their position of power for personal gain. They may be a corrupt cop, politician, or high-ranking official, obstructing the investigation to protect their interests.
THE RUTHLESS MOB BOSS	The mob boss is a powerful and dangerous figure leading an organised crime syndicate. They control illegal activities and are willing to resort to extreme violence to maintain their dominance.
THE FEMME FATALE	A seductive and manipulative female villain who uses her charm to deceive and betray others. She often plays various characters against each other to achieve her objectives
THE HENCHMAN/WOMAN	The loyal and often brutal accomplice of the main villain, carrying out their orders and doing the dirty work. They can be a formidable physical threat to the protagonist.
THE PSYCHOPATH	This villain lacks empathy or remorse, making them exceptionally dangerous and unpredictable. They may commit violent crimes without any rational motive.

NOTORIOUS VILLAINS IN CRIME FICTION

THE BLACKMAILER	The villain who uses incriminating information to manipulate and control others, often for financial gain or to achieve a specific objective.
THE REVENGE-SEEKER	This villain is motivated by a desire for revenge against a specific individual or group, often due to a perceived past injustice.
THE INSIDER BETRAYER	A character who betrays their colleagues, friends, or family by secretly aiding the criminals or leaking vital information.
THE PROFESSIONAL THIEF	A skilled and elusive thief who specialises in high-stakes heists and daring robberies.
THE IDEOLOGICAL EXTREMIST	A villain who commits crimes driven by strong ideological beliefs or political motivations, seeking to promote their cause through violence.
THE SABOTEUR	This villain's goal is to disrupt operations, cause chaos, or obstruct the investigation, making it difficult for the protagonists to solve the crime.
THE MANIPULATIVE PUPPETEER	A villain who manipulates events and people from behind the scenes, pulling strings to achieve their dark objectives without directly getting their hands dirty.

These villain roles bring depth and complexity to crime fiction stories, providing formidable challenges for the protagonists to overcome. As a writer, developing well-rounded and compelling villains can elevate your narrative and keep readers captivated.

THEMES IN CRIME FICTION

JUSTICE AND REDEMPTION	Exploring the concept of justice, the quest for redemption, and the idea of atoning for past sins.
GOOD VS. EVIL	Portraying the battle between protagonists who seek justice and villains who commit crimes.
MORAL AMBIGUITY	Examining ethical dilemmas where characters must make difficult choices with no clear right or wrong answers.
CORRUPTION AND BETRAYAL	Uncovering corruption within institutions, and the theme of betrayal by those once trusted.
POWER AND CONTROL	Investigating the misuse of power and control that can lead to crime and abuse.
OBSESSION AND COMPULSION	Delving into the minds of characters with obsessions, compulsions, or fixations that drive their criminal actions.
IDENTITY AND DISGUISE	Exploring the theme of mistaken identity, secret identities, and characters wearing masks to conceal their true selves.
REVENGE	Focusing on the desire for vengeance and its consequences on individuals and society.
CONSEQUENCES OF CRIME	Portraying the ripple effects of crime on victims, perpetrators, and society as a whole.

THEMES IN CRIME FICTION

BETRAYAL AND LOYALTY	Examining the themes of loyalty and betrayal among friends, family, and colleagues.
THE ANATOMY OF CRIME	Unravelling the intricacies of how crimes are planned, executed, and investigated.
FRAMED OR WRONGLY ACCUSED	Following characters who are framed for crimes they didn't commit and their fight to clear their names.
INJUSTICE AND INEQUALITY	Addressing social issues related to discrimination, socioeconomic disparities, and how they impact crime and its investigation.
FACING THE PAST	Characters confronting their past mistakes, crimes, or traumas that come back to haunt them.
GREED AND AMBITION	Exploring the consequences of characters driven by greed, ambition, or an insatiable desire for power.
FEAR AND PARANOIA	Delving into the psychological effects of crime on individuals and communities, leading to fear and paranoia.
BETRAYAL OF TRUST	Exploring the devastating effects of trust betrayed in personal and professional relationships.
THE SEARCH FOR TRUTH	Following characters as they unravel the truth behind a crime, often in the face of deception and misinformation.

These themes offer rich storytelling opportunities for crime fiction writers, allowing them to delve into the complexities of human behaviour and society while crafting captivating and thought-provoking narratives.

TITLES

A FRAMEWORK FOR CRIME FICTION TITLES

ATTENTION-GRABBING WORDS

Crime fiction titles often include powerful and descriptive words that pique readers' curiosity and create an immediate sense of intrigue.

Example: "killer," "murder," "danger," "deadly," "puzzle," "conspiracy," and "investigation" are commonly used.

SHORT AND IMPACTFUL

Many crime fiction titles are short and to the point, usually consisting of one to three words. This brevity allows for quick recognition and memorability.

Example: "Need You Dead"

TITLES

A FRAMEWORK FOR CRIME FICTION TITLES

EMOTION AND SUSPENSE

Titles may evoke emotions or convey a sense of suspense, fear, or urgency. These emotions can draw readers into the story before they even read the blurb.

Example: "Her Last Breath"

SETTING OR LOCATION

Titles may incorporate the setting or location of the crime, adding a layer of atmosphere and intrigue.

Example: "Silent Bay Murders"

TITLES

COMMON LENGTHS FOR CRIME FICTION TITLES

Crime fiction titles commonly range from one to five words, with two to three words being the most prevalent. The goal is to create a title that is memorable, impactful, and easily recognisable, drawing readers' attention to the story's themes and genre.

As a new writer, crafting an attention-grabbing title that captures the essence of your crime fiction story can entice readers and enhance the overall appeal of your work.

Consider the elements of suspense, mystery, and intrigue when brainstorming your title to create a compelling representation of your narrative.

COMMON WORDS FEATURED IN CRIME FICTION TITLES

MURDER	KILLER	DEATH	DANGER
DEADLY	BETRAYAL	CONSPIRACY	SECRET
INVESTIGATION	MYSTERY	DETECTIVE	SUSPICION
WITNESS	INTRIGUE	THRILLER	HUNT

MOST POPULAR WORDS IN CRIME FICTION

MURDER	MYSTERY	DETECTIVE	FORENSIC
INVESTIGATION	CRIME	THRILLER	CRIMINAL
SUSPENSE	DANGER	DANGEROUS	TREACHERY
CONSPIRACY	SECRET	BETRAYAL	WHODUNIT
INTRIGUE	POLICE	CRIMINAL	MANHUNT
REVENGE	SUSPICIOUS	KILLER	WANTED
KILLING	MOTIVE	UNDERCOVER	CHASE
CORRUPTION	CLUE	SUSPECT	REVEAL
WITNESS	EVIDENCE	INVESTIGATE	DECEPTION
PURSUIT	FUGITIVE	BLACKMAIL	ALIBI
HEIST	ROBBERY	MAFIA	SOLVE
GANGSTER	RIVALRY	VENGEANCE	CRIME SCENE

SYMBOLS FOUND IN CRIME FICTION

MAGNIFYING GLASS	A symbol of investigation and close examination of evidence.
CRIME SCENE TAPE	Yellow tape used to cordon off crime scenes, signifying restricted access.
HANDCUFFS	Representing the apprehension and restraint of suspects or criminals.
EVIDENCE BAG	Used to preserve and transport items collected from the crime scene.
FINGERPRINT	A unique mark left by a person's fingertip, crucial for identification and evidence.
POLICE BADGE	Symbolises the authority and role of law enforcement in the story.
GUN	Often a significant object in crime fiction, linked to acts of violence and danger.
KNIFE	A weapon commonly found in crime stories, often associated with murder.
MASK	Used by criminals to conceal their identity during illegal activities.
BRIEFCASE	May contain stolen goods or act as a symbol of secretive dealings.
LOCK PICK	Represents illicit activities, such as breaking into locked spaces.
FLASHLIGHT	Used to investigate dark and hidden areas during crime scenes.
FORENSIC KIT	Contains tools used by investigators to gather and analyse evidence.
BULLET SHELL	Found at crime scenes and serves as evidence in shooting incidents.

SYMBOLS FOUND IN CRIME FICTION

LOOT/ VALUABLES	Stolen items that drive the plot in heist or burglary narratives.
HIDDEN SAFE	A secretive container for valuable possessions or evidence.
SURVEILLANCE CAMERA	Symbolises constant observation and potential evidence.
BLUEPRINTS/ FLOOR PLANS	Used by thieves and investigators to navigate locations.
GLOVES	Worn by criminals to avoid leaving fingerprints or DNA at the crime scene.
TAPE RECORDER	Used to document witness statements or capture important conversations.
SAFE COMBINATION	A crucial piece of information for cracking a safe in the story.
WANTED POSTER	Represents the search for a criminal or a person of interest.
BALACLAVA	A type of ski mask used to conceal a person's identity during crimes.
FLASH DRIVE	Contains digital evidence or important information in modern crime stories.
PISTOL/RIFLE	Firearms used by characters, such as detectives or criminals, in action scenes.

These objects and symbols help create a vivid and engaging crime fiction narrative, building suspense and intrigue as readers follow the investigation and uncover the truth behind the criminal activities.

POWER WORDS IN CRIME FICTION

INTRIGUE	Mysterious, captivating, alluring, secretive, puzzling
MYSTERY	Enigmatic, puzzling, baffling, perplexing, enigmatic
THRILLER	Gripping, intense, heart-pounding, suspenseful, thrilling
SUSPENSE	Tense, gripping, nail-biting, suspenseful, thrilling
DETECTIVE	Investigative, sleuthing, inquisitive, probing, observant
INVESTIGATION	Investigative, thorough, meticulous, thorough, systematic
CRIME	Criminal, unlawful, illicit, illegal, illicit
MURDER	Homicidal, deadly, lethal, killing, fatal
GANGSTER	Criminal, mobster, thug, racketeer, gangland
HEIST	Robbery, theft, burglary, robbery, caper
MAFIA	Organised crime, underworld, mob, criminal organisation
UNDERWORLD	Criminal, illicit, clandestine, subterranean, hidden
UNDERCOVER	Covert, secret, hidden, clandestine, stealthy
ESPIONAGE	Spy, secret, covert, clandestine, undercover

POWER WORDS IN CRIME FICTION

CONSPIRACY	Secretive, clandestine, covert, secretive
CRIMINAL	Unlawful, illicit, illegal, felonious, lawless
DANGER	Perilous, risky, hazardous, unsafe, precarious
PUZZLE	Enigmatic, mysterious, puzzling, perplexing, cryptic
UNRAVEL	Reveal, solve, decipher, uncover, untangle
DECEPTION	Deceptive, deceitful, misleading, dishonest, tricky
CLUE	Evident, hint, indication, trace, sign
SLEUTH	Investigative, inquisitive, perceptive, observant, astute
EVIDENCE	Incriminating, corroborating, proof, testimony, indication
FORENSIC	Investigative, scientific, analytical, detective, evidentiary
CORRUPTION	Unethical, dishonest, fraudulent, immoral, tainted
RIVALRY	Competitive, antagonistic, opposing, hostile, combative
BETRAYAL	Deceptive, treacherous, disloyal, unfaithful, deceitful
ROBBERY	Theft, larceny, burglary, heist, plunder

POWER WORDS IN CRIME FICTION

FUGITIVE	Runaway, escapee, absconder, on the run, escaped
NOIR	Dark, shadowy, grim, bleak, gloomy
BLACKMAIL	Extortion, threatening, coercion, manipulation, blackmailing
WITNESS	Observant, knowledgeable, eyewitness, informant, informant
INFILTRATE	Infiltration, stealthy, covert, undercover, clandestine
CRIME SCENE	Investigative, forensic, evidence, forensic, police
INTERROGATE	Question, probe, inquire, interview, cross-examine
VIGILANTE	Avenger, justice seeker, self-appointed enforcer, avenging
CAPER	Heist, caper, robbery, theft, burglary
WHODUNIT	Mystery, detective, enigma, puzzling, suspenseful
RANSOM	Demand, extortion, payment, price, release
INFORMANT	Informative, knowledgeable, reliable, informant, witness
ALIBI	Excuse, justification, defence, explanation, pretext
INCRIMINATE	Accuse, implicate, blame, frame, charge

POWER WORDS IN CRIME FICTION

MASTERMIND	Brilliant, ingenious, cunning, clever, masterful
CONCEAL	Hide, cover, mask, disguise, obscure
DOUBLE-CROSS	Betrayal, treachery, deception, disloyalty, duplicity
PURSUIT	Chase, hunt, tracking, follow
TREASON	Betrayal, disloyalty, treachery, sedition, rebellion
REVENGE	Retribution, vengeance, retaliation, payback, reprisal
MANHUNT	Search, pursuit, chase, hunt, investigation

Now mix and match these words to create plot twists/ and or endings:

We picked the following words in BLUE:

A ROBBERY takes place, but the WITNESS to it is WANTED in connection to a MURDER that the MAIN CHARACTER thought was solved. This blows that case, and this, wide open.

What happens now?

Use these power words to add lots of vivid imagery to your writing

SHOW NOT TELL TECHNIQUES IN CRIME WRITING

INSTEAD OF TELLING FEAR

Telling: She was afraid of the dark alley and quickened her pace.

Showing: Her heart pounded in her chest as she hurried through the dimly lit alley, glancing over her shoulder at every shadow that seemed to creep closer.

INSTEAD OF TELLING SUSPICION

Telling: He suspected the witness was lying.

Showing: His eyes narrowed, and he leaned in closer, studying the witness's body language for any signs of deception.

INSTEAD OF TELLING SURPRISE

Telling: She was surprised by the sudden appearance of the masked figure.

Showing: Gasping, she stumbled back as the masked figure materialised from the shadows, causing her heart to race in shock.

INSTEAD OF TELLING ANGER

Telling: He was angry at the betrayal.

Showing: His face turned red, his fists clenched, and he struggled to keep his voice steady as he confronted the traitor.

INSTEAD OF TELLING EXCITEMENT

Telling: She was excited to solve the case.

Showing: A wide smile spread across her face, and her eyes sparkled with anticipation as she pieced together the final clue.

SHOW NOT TELL TECHNIQUES IN CRIME WRITING

INSTEAD OF TELLING PANIC

Telling: He panicked when he realised he was trapped.

Showing: His breath quickened, and he frantically searched for an escape route, his heart pounding in his ears.

INSTEAD OF TELLING REGRET

Telling: He regretted his past actions.

Showing: His shoulders slumped, and he avoided eye contact, haunted by memories of the decisions he wished he could undo.

INSTEAD OF TELLING INTUITION

Telling: She had a hunch about the suspect.

Showing: The silence was palpable as everyone in the room avoided eye contact, their bodies stiff with apprehension.

INSTEAD OF TELLING TENSION

Telling: There was tension in the room.

Showing: His face turned red, his fists clenched, and he struggled to keep his voice steady as he confronted the traitor.

INSTEAD OF TELLING RELIEF

Telling: He felt relieved when he saw his partner was safe.

Showing: A sigh of relief escaped his lips, and a weight lifted from his shoulders as he saw his partner emerge from the danger unharmed.

PSYCHOLOGICAL

FICTION SQUARE

CHARACTER	SETTING	GOAL	CONFLICT	CONSEQUENCE
TRAUMA SURVIVOR	HOUSE	HEAL OTHERS	FAMILY	TRAPPED
THERAPIST	HOSPITAL	TO RECOVER MEMORIES	OWN MEMORIES	DEATH
DETECTIVE	PRISON	TO SOLVE MYSTERY	LACK OF BELIEF FROM OTHERS	LOSS OF IDENTITY
NURSE	TOWN	UNCOVER TRUTH	LACK OF BOUNDARIES	DETERIORATION
PATIENT	CITY	TO GET BETTER	INTERNAL STRUGGLES	SUCCUMBS
SPOUSE	COMMUNITY	CONFRONT PAST	MANIPULATION	SILENCED
HOUSE GUEST	VILLAGE	TO FACE FEAR	THREATS	CYCLE OF DESTRUCTION

	PATIENT	COMMUNITY	UNCOVER TRUTH	OWN MEMORIES	TRAPPED
IDEA 1	Recently released from a psychiatric hospital, a patient, fearing recommitment, strives to uncover sinister truths during about her community, fearing they are messing with her memories. Balancing the pursuit of truth, she faces going back into hospital, and being trapped forever. Caught in a haunting struggle for freedom, will she uncover the truth?				
WHY?	Recently released from a psychiatric hospital, a patient, fearing recommitment, strives to uncover sinister truths about her community, suspecting manipulation of her memories.				
WHAT IF…?	Balancing the pursuit of truth, she unearths evidence of a widespread conspiracy.				
AND THEN…?	As the threat of going back into the hospital looms, and the possibility of being trapped forever intensifies, she must decide whether to confront the chilling truth or risk succumbing to a fabricated reality, caught in a haunting struggle for freedom with an uncertain outcome.				

342

FICTION SQUARE

You should have: A character, setting, goal, conflict and consequence

IDEA 2

WHY?

WHAT IF...?

AND THEN...?

You should have: A character, setting, goal, conflict and consequence

IDEA 3

WHY?

WHAT IF...?

AND THEN...?

WHAT TO DO

EXPLORE INNER CONFLICTS	Use introspective moments and internal dialogue to delve deep into the protagonist's thoughts and emotions, revealing their inner struggles gradually.
UTILISE UNRELIABLE PERSPECTIVES	Drop subtle hints that suggest the unreliability of the narrator, gradually building doubt and intrigue in the reader's mind.
EMPLOY PSYCHOLOGICAL SYMBOLISM	Choose symbols that resonate with the story's themes and characters, and weave them consistently throughout the narrative for added depth.
PLAY WITH PERCEPTION AND REALITY	Incorporate sensory details and vivid descriptions to blur the lines between reality and imagination, making the reader question the character.
BUILD TENSION THROUGH MIND GAMES	Develop intricate power dynamics and subtle manipulations between characters, allowing tension to escalate naturally.
CREATE MORAL DILEMMAS	Present dilemmas that challenge the character's core values, and explore their internal struggle as they grapple with making difficult choices.
EMPLOY REVERSE CHRONOLOGY	Begin with an enigmatic climax and work backward, revealing key moments that shed light on the character's psychological journey.

WHAT TO DO

USE PSYCHOLOGICAL THRILLS	Foreshadow psychological twists through subtle clues and foils, setting the stage for a shocking revelation that reshapes the narrative.
CRAFT UNSETTLING ATMOSPHERES	Describe sensory details that evoke discomfort and unease, creating an environment that reflects the characters' psychological turmoil.
DEVELOP COMPLEX RELATIONSHIPS	Explore characters' motivations and vulnerabilities, and use dialogue to showcase power shifts and emotional dynamics.
CREATE LAYERS OF DECEPTION	Gradually expose characters' hidden motives and agendas, leaving breadcrumbs of doubt and suspicion for the reader to follow.
USE INTERNAL MONOLOGUES	Intersperse internal monologues with external action, providing insights into the character's psyche while maintaining pacing.
INCORPORATE PSYCHOLOGICAL DISORDERS	Approach the portrayal of disorders with sensitivity and accuracy, using research to portray the experiences authentically.
EXPLORE DREAMS AND NIGHTMARES	Integrate dreams and nightmares seamlessly into the narrative, using vivid descriptions and symbolism to unravel subconscious conflicts.
CRAFT MIND-BENDING ENDINGS	Conclude with an ending that raises thought-provoking questions, leaving room for interpretation and encouraging readers to reflect.

WHAT TO AVOID DOING

AVOID STEREOTYPES	Don't use clichés about mental health issues. Instead, research and portray conditions accurately and sensitively.
LIMIT SHOCKING CONTENT	Don't include excessive violence for shock value. Focus on tension and emotional turmoil instead.
STAY GROUNDED	Avoid introducing supernatural elements that don't fit the story's tone or theme.
DEVELOP CHARACTERS	Don't make characters one-dimensional. Create depth with diverse motivations and weaknesses.
BE UNPREDICTABLE	Avoid predictable plots and twists. Challenge readers' expectations with unexpected turns.
RESEARCH ACCURATELY	Don't spread misinformation about mental health. Research thoroughly to portray it realistically.
SHOW REALISTIC CHANGE	Avoid sudden and unrealistic character transformations. Portray gradual healing that makes sense.
EXPLORE COMPLEX MOTIVES	Don't simplify characters' motivations. Delve into multiple factors driving their actions.
USE SUBTLE EXPOSITION	Avoid explaining emotions directly. Show feelings through actions, reactions, and inner struggles.
BALANCE TWISTS AND DEPTH	Don't rely only on twists. Keep psychological exploration and character development at the story's core.

By avoiding these mistakes, your psychological fiction short stories will offer nuanced, engaging, and relatable experiences for your readers.

COMMON PSYCHOLOGICAL SETTINGS

PSYCHIATRIC HOSPITALS OR ASYLUMS	Set the story in a mental health facility to delve into the characters' inner struggles. Create an eerie atmosphere and explore trauma and the complexities of the mind.
ISOLATED HOUSES OR CABINS	Choose secluded places to heighten tension. Use the setting to intensify feelings of vulnerability and paranoia, enhancing psychological turmoil.
ABANDONED OR HAUNTED PLACES	Opt for mysterious, spooky locations. Characters can confront past traumas or supernatural elements that mirror their inner conflicts.
URBAN JUNGLES	Place the story in a bustling city to evoke alienation. Show characters lost in the urban chaos, struggling with their identity and purpose.
SMALL TOWNS WITH DARK SECRETS	Select close-knit communities with hidden mysteries. The town's secrets can reflect the characters' psychological struggles.
REMOTE ISLANDS OR BEACH RESORTS	Use these settings to isolate characters. Explore their inner fears and desires away from everyday distractions.
MINDSCAPES OR DREAMS	Create surreal dream-like environments to symbolise characters' subconscious thoughts. This allows for creative psychological exploration.
THERAPY SESSIONS OR SUPPORT GROUPS	Utilise safe spaces like therapy sessions for emotional exploration. Characters can delve into past traumas and their journey towards healing.
SCHOOLS OR UNIVERSITIES	Set the story in educational institutions to explore young minds. Touch on academic pressures, social dynamics, and personal growth.
GOTHIC MANSIONS OR CASTLES	Psychological fiction set in foreign lands adds cultural complexity and challenges for the protagonists.

PSYCHOLOGICAL FICTION TIME PERIODS/ERAS

MODERN-DAY	Present settings unravel current mental battles, societal issues, and relationships.
VICTORIAN ERA	Unveils repressed emotions, societal constraints, impacting minds and desires.
WORLD WARS	Delves into wartime trauma, PTSD, conflict-induced mental strains.
ROARING TWENTIES	Probes hedonism, societal shifts, and their psychological aftermath.
GREAT DEPRESSION	Depicts poverty's toll, resilience, and hope amid struggles.
POST-WAR	Examines post-conflict psychological coping and rebuilding.
1960S-70S	Explores counterculture, norm-challenging minds seeking freedom.
CONTEMPORARY HISTORY	Delves into near-past eras, blending nostalgia with psychological depth.

KEY CHARACTER ROLES IN PSYCHOLOGICAL FICTION

PROTAGONIST	Story's core, facing inner turmoil and emotional conflicts, shaping plot and growth.
UNRELIABLE NARRATOR	Doubtful perspective adds suspense, questioning event truths.
ANTIHERO	Morally complex lead, challenges good vs. evil norms.
PSYCHOLOGICAL EXPERT	Unravels minds, guides emotional journeys.
MANIPULATOR	Masters mind games, fuels tension and conflict.
VICTIM	Trauma-stricken, adds emotional depth, susceptible to manipulation.
OBSESSIVE	Driven by irrational fixations, charts gripping paths.
LONER/OUTCAST	Explores isolation's impact on identity and belonging.
MENTOR/GUIDE	Supports, aids psychological struggles, offers insight.
SPLIT PERSONALITY	Multiple identities, central psyche exploration.
TROUBLED CHILD	Childhood trauma influences development and coping.
ENIGMATIC STRANGER	Mysterious motives add intrigue.

CHARACTER NAMES

MALE CHARACTERS		FEMALE CHARACTERS	
DAVID	JAMES	SARAH	JESSICA
MICHAEL	JOHN	EMILY	EMMA
ROBERT	JOSEPH	OLIVIA	GRACE
THOMAS	DANIEL	ELIZABETH	SOPHIA
WILLIAM	MATTHEW	NATALIE	ISABELLA

Remember that while these names are commonly used, they are by no means restrictive. Feel free to explore various names and consider the significance they hold for your characters' psychological journeys.

The names you choose can add depth and resonance to your story, helping readers connect with the characters on a deeper level.

MOST COMMON OCCUPATIONS

THERAPIST/COUNSELLOR	Guides emotional journeys, fosters growth.
DETECTIVE/INVESTIGATOR	Unveils psychological motives behind crimes.
WRITER/AUTHOR	Wrestles with inner demons, creativity challenges.
DOCTOR/MEDICAL PRO	Explores mental and physical health link.
ARTIST/MUSICIAN/PHOTOGRAPHER	Channels emotions, blurs reality.
TEACHER/EDUCATOR	Supports troubled students, faces own battles.
LAWYER/ATTORNEY	Tackles ethical dilemmas, own struggles.
JOURNALIST/REPORTER	Uncovers hidden psychological truths.
POLICE OFFICER	Confronts trauma, ethical choices.
SOCIAL WORKER	Advocates, tackles social issues, self-reflection.
CORPORATE EXECUTIVE	Balances ambition, workplace dynamics' toll.
CAREGIVER/NURSE	Supports mental health, ethical decisions.

CHALLENGES AND CONFLICTS

INTERNAL STRUGGLE	Turmoil from emotions, memories, dilemmas.
IDENTITY CRISIS	Self-definition doubts, purpose loss.
MENTAL HEALTH CHALLENGES	Battling depression, anxiety, trauma.
TRUST VS. BETRAYAL	Emotionally charged deceptions.
UNRESOLVED TRAUMA	Past pain obstructing growth.
OBSESSION/COMPULSION	Destructive fixation battles.
GUILT AND REGRET	Past actions haunt, self-forgiveness struggle.
MANIPULATION AND GASLIGHTING	Confusing psychological games.
REALITY VS. PERCEPTION	Questioning sanity, reality's grip.
FEAR OF ABANDONMENT	Overcoming rejection fears.
POWER STRUGGLES/CONTROL	Inner and relational dominance clashes.
ADDICTION AND DEPENDENCY	Breaking destructive cycles.
FAMILY SECRETS/DYSFUNCTION	Hidden truths, emotional trauma.
SURVIVOR'S GUILT	Coping with surviving trauma.
ISOLATION/LONELINESS	Emotional barriers, relationship strains.

HIGH STAKES IN PSYCHOLOGICAL FICTION

EMOTIONAL STRAIN	Characters battle anxiety, guilt, despair.
PSYCHOLOGICAL FRACTURE	Risk of breakdown, inner turmoil's grip.
SANITY AT RISK	Confronting trauma tests mental stability.
SELF-DESTRUCTION	Inner turmoil drives dangerous choices.
BROKEN BONDS	Emotional conflicts fracture vital relationships.
IDENTITY LOSS	Risk of self-identity dissolution.
MORAL QUANDARIES	Tough choices torment conscience.
ISOLATION/LONELINESS	Emotional walls breed seclusion.
SECRETS EXPOSED	Unveiling hidden truths fuels shame.
BETRAYAL'S IMPACT	Trust shatters, emotions unravel.
REVENGE CYCLE	Retaliation spirals, repercussions loom
THREAT TO OTHERS	Inner battles endanger those around.
CONTROL ERODES	Chaos ensues from faltering restraint.
UNHEALTHY COPING	Consequences of maladaptive strategies.

Crafting these stakes propels characters' emotional depth, enhancing psychological narratives' impact and reader engagement.

HEROIC GOALS IN PSYCHOLOGICAL FICTION

SELF-DISCOVERY	Unravel emotions, unveil identity.
HEALING FROM TRAUMA	Confront past wounds, find peace.
CONQUERING DEMONS	Battle inner obstacles, grow.
ACCEPTANCE/ BELONGING	Crave inclusion, find self-worth.
SEEKING REDEMPTION	Atone for errors, seek forgiveness.
BREAKING MANIPULATION	Gain autonomy, defy control.
UNVEILING SECRETS	Discover truths, unravel mysteries.
EMOTIONAL RESILIENCE	Face challenges, grow stronger.
CONFRONTING FEARS	Overcome insecurities, empower.
ESCAPING ISOLATION	Forge connections, end loneliness.
DEFEATING ANTAGONIST	Triumph over inner/outer foe.
UNDERSTANDING BONDS	Decode complex relationships.
EXPRESSING SELF	Share emotions, break silence.
MENTAL BALANCE	Find calm, clarity amid thoughts.

NOTORIOUS VILLAINS IN PSYCHOLOGICAL FICTION

MANIPULATOR	Controls through psychological tricks.
GASLIGHTER	Distorts reality, causing turmoil.
SHADOW SELF	Manifests protagonist's darker side.
OBSESSIVE STALKER	Fear-inducing, invasive fixation.
ENIGMATIC MASTERMIND	Orchestrates complex schemes.
PSYCHOPATHIC ANTAGONIST	Lacks empathy, distorts emotions.
TORMENTED SOUL	Projects trauma, inflicts pain.
SPLIT PERSONALITY	Multiple identities, unique challenges.
DOPPELGÄNGER	Identity crisis, uncanny resemblance.
RESENTFUL AVENGER	Seeks revenge, fuelled by past issues.
CULT LEADER	Charismatic manipulator, cult dynamics.
INTERNAL SABOTEUR	Undermines growth, sows doubt
MEMORY MANIPULATOR	Alters memories, induces distress
EMOTIONAL BLACKMAILER	Guilt-driven control tactics.
UNSEEN PRESENCE	Shadows psyche, unseen turmoil.

THEMES IN PSYCHOLOGICAL FICTION

IDENTITY/SELF-DISCOVERY	Unravelling who characters truly are.
MENTAL HEALTH/WELL-BEING	Coping, trauma's impact explored.
REALITY VS. ILLUSION	Challenging perception, truth blurred.
ISOLATION/LONELINESS	Yearning for connection, emotional solitude.
MEMORY/PERCEPTION	Unreliable memories shape understanding.
GUILT/REDEMPTION	Past actions, seeking forgiveness.
MANIPULATION/DECEPTION	Gaslighting, mind games unfold.
FEAR/PHOBIAS	Inner fears drive decisions.
POWER/CONTROL	Dynamics explored, wielding influence.
OBSESSION/COMPULSION	Fixations guide characters.

THEMES IN PSYCHOLOGICAL FICTION

TRAUMA/HEALING	Coping, recovery's journey.
DUALITY OF NATURE	Inner contradictions faced.
EMOTIONAL RESILIENCE	Adversity, coping strength.
UNRELIABLE NARRATORS	Hidden motives, skewed stories.
EXISTENTIAL QUESTIONS	Life's meaning, purpose pondered.
COPING MECHANISMS	Strategies for emotional turmoil.
IDENTITY CRISIS	Roles, self-exploration questioned.
TRUST/BETRAYAL	Distrust's toll, betrayal's impact.
DESIRE FOR CONTROL	Grasping life's reins, lacking command.
CONFRONTING DEMONS	Striving for self-improvement.

TITLES

A FRAMEWORK FOR PSYCHOLOGICAL FICTION TITLES

THE [EMOTION/THEME] OF [CHARACTER OR EVENT]

Psychological fiction titles often evoke strong emotions or feelings related to the themes explored in the story. They aim to capture the psychological depth of the narrative.

Example: "The Fragility of Sanity: A Psychological Thriller"

[DESCRIPTIVE ADJECTIVE] MINDS AND [EMOTION/THEME]

Titles can include phrases or expressions that reflect the characters' internal thoughts, emotions, or psychological states.

Example: "Twisted Minds and Dark Secrets: A Psychological Mystery"

[SYMBOL/METAPHOR] OF [EMOTION/THEME]

Psychological fiction titles may use symbolism and metaphors to represent the characters' psychological struggles and the overall mood of the story.

Example: "The Mirror of Despair: A Psychological Exploration"

TITLES

A FRAMEWORK FOR PSYCHOLOGICAL FICTION TITLES

THE [PSYCHOLOGICAL STRUGGLE/CONFLICT] WITHIN

Titles that carry multiple interpretations or have dual meanings can create an air of mystery, drawing readers into the complexities of the narrative.

Example: "The Battle Within: An Emotional Psychological Drama"

COMMON LENGTHS FOR PSYCHOLOGICAL FICTION TITLES

Psychological fiction book titles typically range from 3 to 8 words, with an average of 4 to 6 words.

COMMON WORDS FEATURED IN PSYCHOLOGICAL FICTION TITLES

MIND	SOUL	SHADOWS	SECRETS
MADNESS	ECHOES	UNRAVELLING	LIES
REFLECTIONS	SHATTERED	DEPTHS	DISGUISE
DARK	FRAGILE	ILLUSION	HUNT

TITLES

CREATING INTRIGUING PSYCHOLOGICAL FICTION TITLES

EXPLORE THE THEME	Identify the central theme or emotion that drives your story and try to encapsulate it in a few powerful words.
EMPHASISE MYSTERY	Use words or phrases that hint at the psychological mystery or conflicts readers will encounter in the story.
CREATE CONTRAST	Combine contradictory or contrasting words to emphasise the complexities of the characters' minds and emotions.
USE SYMBOLISM	Incorporate symbolic or metaphorical elements from the story to add depth and intrigue to the title
ASK QUESTIONS	Pose intriguing questions in the title that pique readers' curiosity and compel them to delve into the psychological journey.
FOCUS ON EMOTIONS	Choose words that evoke strong emotions or feelings related to the psychological experiences within the narrative.
SEEK DUAL MEANINGS	Opt for titles that carry multiple interpretations, allowing readers to discover deeper layers of meaning as they read.

Remember, an intriguing title is like a glimpse into the mind of the story. It should capture the essence of the psychological journey and entice readers to dive into the complexities of your characters' minds and emotions.

MOST POPULAR WORDS IN PSYCHOLOGICAL FICTION

MIND	PSYCHE	MYSTERY	PERCEPTION
IDENTITY	REALITY	SUBCONSCIOUS	TWISTED
OBSESSION	UNRAVEL	MANIPULATE	DECEPTION
PARANOIA	UNRAVELLING	SURREAL	DYSFUNCTIONAL
TRAUMA	DELUSION	HALLUCINATION	MIND GAMES
UNRELIABLE	FRAGMENTED	UNCONSCIOUS	INSANITY
INTRIGUE	DISTORT	CONFRONT	UNSETTLING
MENTAL	PSYCHOANALYSIS	EMOTIONALLY	PHOBIA
DISTORTED	HAUNTED	AMNESIA	REPRESSED
ISOLATION	NIGHTMARE	COMPULSION	DARK
REVELATION	UNPREDICTABLE	INTROSPECTION	TORTURED
GUILT	EMOTION	PSYCHOTIC	FRAGMENTATION

SYMBOLS FOUND IN PSYCHOLOGICAL FICTION

MIRROR	Represents self-reflection, identity, and the exploration of one's inner psyche.
MASK	Symbolises hidden identities, secrets, and the complexities of human behaviour.
LABYRINTH/MAZE	Represents the intricate and confusing nature of the human mind.
LOCKED ROOM	A confined space that becomes a symbol of entrapment and psychological isolation.
DIARY/JOURNAL	Contains the inner thoughts and emotions of a character, revealing their psyche.
CLOCK	Represents the passage of time and the ticking tension in psychological narratives.
STAIRCASE	Symbolises the descent into darkness or the exploration of different levels of consciousness.
DOLL	Often used to portray a sense of uncanny or eerie presence.
BROKEN GLASS	Symbolises shattered perceptions, fractured realities, and psychological trauma.
COBWEB	Represents entanglement, hidden dangers, and the intricacies of the mind.
CHESSBOARD	Symbolises strategic thinking, manipulation, and psychological mind games.
EMPTY SWING	Suggests a sense of abandonment and loss, evoking emotions of suspense.
BROKEN CLOCK	Represents distorted perceptions of time and a fractured psyche.

SYMBOLS FOUND IN PSYCHOLOGICAL FICTION

PUZZLE	Represents the unravelling of a complex mystery or psychological enigma
CRUMPLED PAPER	Symbolises inner turmoil, repressed emotions, or discarded thoughts.
REFLECTION ON WATER	A visual metaphor for distorted realities and altered perceptions.
HANDWRITING SAMPLE	Used for analysing characters' personality traits and psychological state.
SHADOW	Symbolises hidden desires, fears, or subconscious thoughts.
LOCKED BOX	A mysterious container representing hidden secrets or memories.
WATCH/ TIMEPIECE	Creates a sense of urgency and adds to the psychological tension.
CANDLE	Represents the flickering nature of the mind and the fragile state of emotions.
DARK TUNNEL	Symbolises a journey into the unknown and facing psychological fears.
BLEEDING INK	Represents the merging of reality and imagination in a character's mind.
SPINNING TOP	Symbolises a character's struggle with reality and illusion.
ABANDONED BUILDING	A setting that reflects a character's psychological state or history.

These objects and symbols contribute to the psychological depth and suspense in thriller fiction, allowing writers to explore the complexities of the human mind and keep readers on the edge of their seats.

POWER WORDS IN PSYCHOLOGICAL FICTION

MIND-BENDING	Puzzling, perplexing, confusing, intricate, complex
PSYCHOLOGICAL	Mental, emotional, cognitive, psychiatric
MYSTERIOUS	Enigmatic, puzzling, baffling, cryptic
PERCEPTIVE	Insightful, observant, intuitive, discerning, keen
REALITY-ALTERING	Surreal, hallucinatory, dreamlike, disorienting, otherworldly
SUBCONSCIOUS	Unconscious, hidden, submerged, underlying, latent
TWISTED	Distorted, contorted, warped, convoluted
OBSESSIVE	Compulsive, fixated, preoccupied, consuming, fanatical
UNRAVELLING	untangling, disentangling, unwinding
MANIPULATIVE	Deceptive, scheming, cunning, crafty, calculating
DECEPTIVE	Misleading, deceitful, dishonest, duplicitous, false
PARANOID	Suspicious, mistrustful, fearful, apprehensive, anxious
UNRELIABLE	Untrustworthy, undependable, inconsistent, uncertain
FRAGMENTED	Broken, fractured, disjointed, shattered

POWER WORDS IN PSYCHOLOGICAL FICTION

SURREAL	Dreamlike, bizarre, fantastical, unreal, strange
DYSFUNCTIONAL	Malfunctioning, abnormal, defective, impaired
TRAUMATIC	Distressing, distressing, painful, upsetting, agonising
DELUSIONAL	Illusory, misguided, false, hallucinatory, deluded
HALLUCINATORY	Illusory, unreal, dreamlike, surreal, hallucinogenic
UNSETTLING	Disturbing, troubling, disconcerting
MENTAL	Emotional, psychological, cognitive, intellectual
PSYCHOANALYTIC	Analytical, psychological, Freudian, introspective
EMOTIONALLY	sentimentally, passionately, affectively
PHOBIC	Fearful, afraid, anxious, scared
DISTORTED	Twisted, misshapen, deformed, contorted
HAUNTED	Tormented, plagued, troubled, possessed
AMNESIAC	Forgetful, memory-impaired
REPRESSED	Suppressed, inhibited, restrained, held back
ISOLATED	Secluded, solitary, lonely, remote

POWER WORDS IN PSYCHOLOGICAL FICTION

NIGHTMARISH	Terrifying, horrifying, dreadful, frightening
COMPULSIVE	Obsessive, impulsive, driven, compelled, irresistible
DARK	Gloomy, shadowy, dim, sombre
REVELATORY	Revealing, disclosing, illuminating, enlightening
UNPREDICTABLE	Unforeseen, uncertain, capricious, erratic
INTROSPECTIVE	Reflective, contemplative, thoughtful, self-examining, soul-searching
TORTURED	Tormented, anguished, suffering, agonised
GUILT-RIDDEN	Ashamed, remorseful, regretful, culpable, guilty
EMOTIONAL	Affective, feeling, heartfelt, passionate
PSYCHOTIC	Insane, mad, mentally ill, deranged
FRAGMENTED	Broken, shattered, disconnected, disorganised
SELF-DISCOVERY	Self-awareness, self-realisation, self-exploration, self-understanding
COMPELLING	Captivating, engaging, powerful, gripping, persuasive

Now mix and match these words to create plot twists/ and or endings:

MIND GAMES DISTORT a character's version of their past which leads to a TROUBLING outcome of a past allegation.

What happens now?

SHOW NOT TELL TECHNIQUES IN PSYCHOLOGICAL WRITING

INSTEAD OF TELLING ANXIETY

Telling: She was feeling anxious and scared about the upcoming therapy session.

Showing: As she entered the therapist's office, her heart pounded, her palms turned clammy, and she couldn't help but fidget with her necklace. Her mind raced with worries about what might be uncovered during the session.

INSTEAD OF TELLING ANGER

Telling: He was very angry with his friend's betrayal.

Showing: His face flushed red, and his fists clenched tightly at his sides. He shot his friend a piercing stare, his jaw tense with suppressed rage.

INSTEAD OF TELLING SADNESS

Telling: She was devastated by the loss of her job.

Showing: Tears streamed down her face, and her shoulders shook with silent sobs. She stared blankly at the termination letter in her hands, unable to process the sudden end of her career.

INSTEAD OF TELLING GUILT

Telling: He felt guilty for his actions.

Showing: He couldn't look her in the eye, his gaze avoiding hers as shame clouded his expression. He sighed heavily and took a step back as if trying to distance himself from his own actions.

SHOW NOT TELL TECHNIQUES IN PSYCHOLOGICAL WRITING

HOW TO DO IT

USE SENSORY DETAILS	Engage the reader's senses by describing what characters see, hear, feel, smell, and taste. This adds depth to emotions and experiences.
DIALOGUE AND BODY LANGUAGE	Allow characters' interactions and nonverbal cues to reveal their emotions and intentions, creating more realistic and immersive scenes.
INTERNAL MONOLOGUE	Show characters' thoughts and inner conflicts through internal monologues or introspective narration, allowing readers to understand their emotional turmoil.

BENEFITS OF SHOW NOT TELL IN PSYCHOLOGICAL FICTION

EMOTIONAL IMPACT	Showing emotions and experiences immerses readers in the characters' feelings, creating a deeper emotional connection with the story.
CHARACTER DEVELOPMENT	Demonstrating characters' thoughts and actions rather than telling them helps develop well-rounded, three-dimensional characters.
IMMERSIVE READING EXPERIENCE	Show, not tell, creates a more engaging and immersive reading experience, allowing readers to experience the story alongside the characters.
READER EMPATHY	By showing characters' struggles and vulnerabilities, readers can empathise with them and become emotionally invested in their journey.
AVOIDING INFORMATION DUMP	Showing instead of telling allows the story's information to unfold naturally, avoiding information dumps that can disrupt the flow of the narrative.
PROMOTING INTERPRETATION	Showing allows readers to interpret characters' emotions and motives, encouraging critical thinking and engagement with the story.

HORROR

369

FICTION SQUARE

CHARACTER	SETTING	GOAL	CONFLICT	CONSEQUENCE
INVESTIGATOR	MANSION	UNCOVER TRUTH	RESISTANCE	DEATH
RESEARCHER	OLD PRISON	RESEARCH	ISOLATION	TORTURE
PRIEST	WOODS	GET EVIDENCE	LACK OF EVIDENCE	ENDLESS NIGHTMARES
MEDIUM/PSYCHIC	BASEMENT	TO SOLVE MYSTERY	LACK OF BELIEF	MADNESS
EXPLORER	ABANDONED ASYLUM	MAINTAIN ORDER	DARK FORCE	PRISON
DETECTIVE	SMALL TOWN	KEEP THINGS HIDDEN	BETRAYAL	TRAGEDY
CURSED PERSON	COASTAL TOWN	SAVE PEOPLE	LACK OF TIME	GENERATIONAL CURSE

IDEA 1	INVESTIGATOR	BASEMENT	TO SOLVE MYSTERY	DARK FORCE	GENERATIONAL CURSE
	\multicolumn{5}{l}{An investigator delves into a peculiar basement to solve a mystery but confronts a dark force that threatens to unleash a generational curse, casting a sinister shadow over both the family and himself.}				

WHY?	Driven by a series of unexplained events, the investigator is compelled to research the eerie basement, believed to hold the key to a family's malevolent legacy.
WHAT IF...?	Upon entering, the investigator unwittingly awakens a malevolent force, triggering a chain of horrifying events that unravel the very fabric of reality.
AND THEN...?	Faced with the looming threat of a generational curse, the investigator must unravel the basement's secrets before it consumes not only the family but his own.

FICTION SQUARE

You should have: A character, setting, goal, conflict and consequence

IDEA 2					
WHY?					
WHAT IF...?					
AND THEN...?					

You should have: A character, setting, goal, conflict and consequence

IDEA 3					
WHY?					
WHAT IF...?					
AND THEN...?					

WHAT TO DO

SET A CREEPY ATMOSPHERE	Eerie descriptions conjure dread. Example: "The moonlit mansion stood, windows boarded like vacant eyes, the wind's haunting whispers through cracked walls."
DEVELOP COMPELLING CHARACTERS	Relatable, empathetic figures engage readers. Example: "Sara, a sceptic journalist, explores the haunted house, determined to debunk myths."
BUILD GRADUAL TENSION	Suspense escalation keeps readers on edge. Example: "Sara's steps echoed, faint footsteps behind, growing louder with each stride."
HARNESS IMAGINATION'S POWER	Suggest terror, withhold full revelation. Example: "Unseen presence brushed Sara's shoulder, spine shivers."
UNLEASH UNEXPECTED TWISTS	Surprises amplify scares. Example: "Alone illusion shatters, cold grip pulls her into darkness."
APPEAL TO BASIC FEARS	Darkness, isolation, unknown exploit common fears. Example: "Sara's flashlight flickers, heartbeat echoes in the dark."
CREATE OMINOUS FOREBODING	Foreshadowing heightens anticipation. Example: "Faded sign warns 'Enter at your own risk' before mansion's threshold."
USE VIVID DESCRIPTIVE LANGUAGE	Evocative language immerses in horror. Example: "Icy air, misty breath, unseen presence's chilling breath."
LEAVE QUESTIONS UNANSWERED	Unresolved mysteries ignite the imagination. Example: "Haunted escape, lingering doubt: malevolent spirit's return?"
CRAFT A MEMORABLE ENDING	Chilling finale, twist etches in memory. Example: "Sara leaves, mansion reflects her, trapped, haunting forever."

WHAT TO AVOID DOING

AVOID EXCESSIVE EXPLANATIONS	Let imagination foster fear; don't over-explain horrors.
AWKWARD GORE AND SUSPENSE	Limit shock value; emphasise psychological tension.
PREDICTABLE TROPES	Transform clichés, add fresh twists for impact.
POOR EMOTIONAL CONNECTION	Don't make characters one-dimensional. Create depth with diverse motivations and weaknesses.
POORLY PACED SUSPENSE	Pace suspense; hasty plot weakens horror's grip.
TOO QUICK REVELATIONS	Conceal horrors; revelations keep suspense alive.
WEAK ATMOSPHERIC SETTING	Setting matters; immerse readers in a chilling ambience.
NO UNPREDICTABILITY	Surprise with twists, evade predictable patterns.
UNBALANCED STORYTELLING ESSENCE	Blend horror and narrative; harmonious structure.
WEAK FEAR TACTICS	Don't rely solely on jumps; weave psychological elements.

By avoiding the above, your horror tale can captivate, terrify, and resonate powerfully with readers.

COMMON HORROR FICTION SETTINGS

DESOLATE HAUNTED HOUSE	"A desolate house stood at the street's end, windows boarded, its door groaning eerily. Shadows danced on cracked walls; whispers, distant yet chilling, painted a haunting aura."
FORGOTTEN ASYLUM	"Against twilight's canvas, the asylum loomed, its broken eyes watching. Vines gripped like spectral hands; tormented cries echoed, a symphony of forgotten souls."
FOREST	"In the dense woods, silence reigned, branches weaving eerie tapestries. Unseen creatures rustled; distant howls wrote a tale of isolation and impending dread."
CARNIVAL	"Under the moon's pale gaze, a carnival frozen in time faded and forlorn. Phantom laughter lingered as if children played in the spectral night."
ISLAND	"Emerging from mist, an island guarded by cliffs. A lone lighthouse beckoned, revealing hidden truths in its eerie light."
HOSPITAL	"A hospital, corridors empty, rooms dim. Antiseptic's scent mingled with decay. Creaking doors, ghostly whispers, inviting the living into a haunted embrace."
ANCIENT RESTING GROUND	"Burial ground, aged and sombre, tombstones telling tales. A sorrowful breeze, spirits restless, as forgotten whispers rode the wind."
SINISTER HEART OF TOWN	"A town, deceptively quaint, masks secrets sinister. Smiles hid unease, streets silent at night, darkness waiting, an unwelcome embrace."
CRYPTIC UNDERGROUND MAZE	"Labyrinth below, darkness suffocates. Torches flicker, cryptic symbols adorn walls, and water drips like footsteps of spectral wanderers."
BEYOND, UNEARTHLY REALM	"Crossing realms, reality twists, colours shift. Shapes unknown lurk; a realm beyond, a tapestry woven in the fabric of fear."

HORROR FICTION TIME PERIODS/ERAS

GOTHIC SHADOWS OF THE VICTORIAN AGE	"Within the gas-lit labyrinth of Victorian London, fog shrouds cobblestone alleys. Unseen forces stir beneath the repressed emotions of a society captivated by death's allure."
WHISPERS OF THE EDWARDIAN TWILIGHT	"Amid opulent estates, an unsettling air blankets the Edwardian era. Echoes of times past haunt polished facades, concealing the tremors of a changing world."
SPEAKEASIES AND SUPERNATURAL SECRETS	"In the roaring twenties, jazz's rhythmic heartbeats mingle with the whisper of hidden horrors. Speakeasies conceal more than just contraband, as a gilded era conceals its darker truths."
WAR-TORN NIGHTMARES OF THE 1940S	"Within war's chaotic embrace, shadows awaken darker fears. Amidst bomb-shattered landscapes, a malevolent force thrives, feeding on the horrors of a world at war."
MODERN ECHOES OF DARKNESS	"In today's realm, technology's web both connects and isolates. Reality blurs and human darkness takes on new forms, reminding us that the unknown still holds terror."
UNEARTHLY AFTERMATH IN THE POST-APOCALYPSE	"In the wake of apocalyptic cataclysms, survivors confront a new world order. Humanity's struggle intertwines with the monstrous unknown, born from the ruins."
FOLKLORE'S HAUNTING EMBRACE	"In medieval enclaves, myths dance with reality. Villages, shrouded in ancient secrets, echo with the chilling footsteps of supernatural beings."

KEY CHARACTER ROLES IN HORROR FICTION

THE PROTAGONIST	The central character through whose eyes the story unfolds. Often faces terrifying situations and is the primary focus of the reader's empathy. **Example:** Sarah, a young woman who moves into a haunted house, becomes the protagonist as she unravels its dark secrets.
THE FINAL GIRL (OR BOY)	Typically the last surviving character in a horror story faces off against the antagonist. Exhibits resilience, intelligence, and determination to survive the horror. **Example:** Alex, the lone survivor of a group terrorised by a serial killer, emerges as the final girl.
THE SCEPTIC	Initially doubts or dismisses the existence of supernatural or malevolent forces. Provides contrast to other characters who may believe in the horror. **Example:** Dr Michael, a rational scientist, refuses to believe in the cursed artefact's supernatural powers until it's too late.
THE INVESTIGATOR	Takes on the role of uncovering the mystery behind the horror, often delving into the history and origins of malevolence. Acts as a driving force in unravelling the plot and revealing the truth. **Example:** Detective Jane, determined to solve a series of mysterious disappearances in a small town, becomes the investigator.

KEY CHARACTER ROLES IN HORROR FICTION

THE RELUCTANT HERO	Initially unwilling or unprepared to confront the horror, but circumstances force them into action. Often undergoes significant character development, growing into a courageous figure. **Example:** John, a regular person who must face a demonic entity, reluctantly becomes the hero to protect his family.
THE ANTAGONIST (OPTIONAL FOR DUAL PERSPECTIVES)	In some horror stories, the antagonist's perspective is explored alongside the protagonist's. Provides insight into the malevolent force's motives, psyche, and actions. **Example:** The tragic backstory of a ghostly apparition haunting the old mansion is revealed.
THE HAUNTED	A character who is directly affected or possessed by the horror becomes a victim or a threat to others. Often undergoes internal struggles as the malevolent influence takes hold. **Example:** Emily, haunted by a malevolent spirit, battles to regain control over her mind and body.
THE MENTOR (OPTIONAL)	A guiding figure who possesses knowledge or experience with the horror, aiding the protagonist. Offers advice, guidance, or warnings to navigate the terrifying situation. **Example:** Elderly Mr Johnson, who survived an encounter with the supernatural, becomes the mentor to the young protagonist.

CHARACTER NAMES

MALE CHARACTERS		FEMALE CHARACTERS	
JAMES	JOHN	SOPHIA	AVA
DAVID	MICHAEL	CHARLOTTE	LILY
WILLIAM	ROBERT	ABIGAIL	VICTORIA
JACK	THOMAS	HANNAH	ELIZABETH
RICHARD	DANIEL	NATALIE	GRACE
ANDREW	CHRISTOPHER	OLIVIA	EMMA
MATTHEW	BENJAMIN	JENNIFER	SARAH

These names are popular in horror fiction as they are familiar to readers, making it easier for them to connect with the characters.

However, writers are encouraged to use a mix of common and unique names to create a diverse and memorable cast of characters in their horror stories.

MOST COMMON OCCUPATIONS

INVESTIGATOR/DETECTIVE	Often the protagonist, they delve into the mysteries behind the horror, trying to solve crimes or paranormal occurrences.
JOURNALIST/REPORTER	Curiosity-driven, they seek to uncover the truth behind supernatural events or urban legends.
PSYCHIATRIST/PSYCHOLOGIST	Their expertise in the human mind helps them understand and confront psychological horror or possession.
PARANORMAL INVESTIGATOR	Specialises in exploring haunted locations and dealing with supernatural phenomena.
MEDIUM/SPIRITUALIST	Able to communicate with the spirit world, they aid in exorcisms or unravelling ghostly mysteries.
POLICE OFFICER	Often faced with solving crimes involving monsters or supernatural elements.
MEDICAL PROFESSIONAL/DOCTOR	Confronts medical or supernatural horrors, dealing with cursed diseases or unexplained phenomena.
CLERGY/EXORCIST	Tasked with battling malevolent entities and performing exorcisms.
ARCHAEOLOGIST/ANTHROPOLOGIST	Delves into ancient curses or unearthed malevolent artefacts.
TEACHER/PROFESSOR	Guides and protects young characters as they face supernatural threats in schools or academies.

MOST COMMON OCCUPATIONS

LIBRARIAN/RESEARCHER	Holds crucial knowledge or forbidden texts that can reveal the horror's origins.
WRITER/AUTHOR	May be a horror novelist, basing their work on real-life encounters with the supernatural.
HAUNTED HOUSE CARETAKER	Takes on the challenging job of maintaining and investigating a haunted property.
GHOST HUNTER	A modern-day explorer seeking evidence of spirits and hauntings.
WITCH/WARLOCK	Often portrayed as either antagonists or allies, their knowledge of the occult plays a significant role.
MONSTER HUNTER	Fearless individuals who dedicate their lives to protecting others from supernatural creatures.
SURVIVALIST	Thrust into horror scenarios, their resourcefulness and survival skills are put to the test.
FIREFIGHTER/RESCUE WORKER	Faces horrors beyond ordinary emergencies, such as supernatural disasters.
SECURITY GUARD/NIGHT WATCHMAN	Guards against malevolent forces or haunted locations during the night.
CURATOR/COLLECTOR	Guards and studies cursed or haunted artefacts in private collections or museums.

CHALLENGES AND CONFLICTS

MALEVOLENT ENTITY/PSYCHOLOGICAL HORROR	The main obstacle is a malevolent spirit, ghost, demon, or supernatural force that terrorises the characters. Psychological horror presents internal conflicts, where characters grapple with their sanity and fears.
CURSED OBJECTS/ARTEFACTS	Characters face the challenge of dealing with cursed or haunted objects that bring misfortune or supernatural occurrences.
SURVIVAL	The primary conflict revolves around characters trying to survive a deadly threat, such as a serial killer, monster, or supernatural entity.
ISOLATION	Characters are cut off from help or society, facing their fears alone in remote locations, haunted houses, or isolated landscapes.
INVESTIGATION AND DISCOVERY	The obstacle is unravelling the mystery behind the horror, often leading to dangerous revelations.
LOSS AND GRIEF	Characters must cope with loss, death, or the haunting memory of a loved one, which can also become a source of conflict.
BETRAYAL AND DECEPTION	Characters might not know whom to trust, leading to betrayal or deception that worsens their situation.

CHALLENGES AND CONFLICTS

DARK PAST OR FAMILY SECRETS	Characters confront their own dark past or uncover family secrets linked to the horror, making them vulnerable to the malevolent force.
SUPERNATURAL RULES AND CURSES	Characters face complex rules or ancient curses that dictate their fate and drive the conflict.
TIME CONSTRAINTS/ COUNTDOWN	Characters must act quickly to resolve the horror, adding urgency to their conflict and decisions.
DOUBT AND SCEPTICISM	Characters might struggle to accept the existence of the horror, leading to doubt and scepticism that hinder their ability to combat it.
HUMAN NATURE AND MORALITY	The horror brings out the worst in the characters, testing their morality and survival instincts.
INESCAPABLE LOCATION/TRAP	Characters find themselves in a location from which they cannot escape, such as a haunted house or cursed land.
POSSESSION AND CONTROL	Characters may become possessed or controlled by a malevolent force, leading to internal conflicts and struggles for control.
FATE AND PREDESTINATION	Characters might face a sense of inevitability or inescapable fate, making their conflict even more ominous.

HIGH STAKES IN HORROR FICTION

DEATH OR HARM	Characters risk their lives or physical well-being from malevolent forces.
POSSESSION OR CORRUPTION	Characters risk losing identity and humanity to control.
INSANITY AND MADNESS	Characters risk mental breakdown from horrors witnessed.
LOSS OF LOVED ONES	Characters risk losing dear ones to the malevolence.
CURSES AND DAMNATION	Characters risk eternal suffering or afterlife consequences.
ETERNAL CONFINEMENT	Characters risk forever trapped souls.
REALITY ALTERATION	Characters risk world distortion by malevolence.
APOCALYPTIC OUTCOME	Characters risk catastrophe if horror prevails.
EXPOSURE AND VULNERABILITY	Characters risk manipulation or attacks.
UNVEILING DARK SECRETS	Characters risk sanity and global impact.
SACRIFICE AND BETRAYAL	Characters face moral dilemmas and self-sacrifice.
LOSS OF INNOCENCE	Characters confront inner darkness.
HAUNTED LEGACY	Characters risk generational torment.
INESCAPABLE PURSUIT	Characters relentlessly pursued by malevolence.

By infusing these high-stakes consequences, writers forge engaging, emotionally charged narratives, anchoring readers in the characters' battle against terror.

HEROIC GOALS IN HORROR FICTION

SURVIVAL	Characters aim to escape the malevolent force and stay alive.
UNCOVER TRUTH	Characters seek origins and motives behind horror.
PROTECT LOVED ONES	Characters keep friends and family safe.
STOP EVIL	Characters end malevolence or break curses.
REDEMPTION	Characters seek closure for past mistakes.
ESCAPE LOCATION	Characters flee haunted places.
OVERCOME FEARS	Characters conquer personal demons.
PREVENT APOCALYPSE	Characters save the world from catastrophe.
LIFT CURSES	Characters remove malevolence's effects.
SURVIVE COUNTDOWN	Characters solve mysteries under time pressure.
RESCUE OTHERS	Characters save trapped victims.
REGAIN CONTROL	Characters reclaim power over horror.
EXORCISE ENTITY	Characters remove malevolent beings.
FIND SAFE HAVEN	Characters seek refuge from the horror.
BREAK THE CYCLE	Characters end recurring curses.

NOTORIOUS VILLAINS IN HORROR FICTION

MALEVOLENT ENTITY	Supernatural being haunting and terrorising characters.
SERIAL KILLER	Human antagonist inflicting pain and fear.
MONSTER/CREATURE	Terrifying, supernatural creature
CURSED OBJECT/ARTEFACT	Object possessed by malevolence.
POSSESSED INDIVIDUALS	Humans controlled by evil spirits.
CULT/CULT LEADER	Group worshiping dark forces.
VENGEFUL SPIRIT	Ghost seeking revenge.
SUPERNATURAL DEITIES	Malevolent, powerful entities.
PSYCHOLOGICAL VILLAIN	Mind-manipulating antagonist.
UNSEEN THREAT	Mysterious, lurking presence.
REVENGE-DRIVEN CHARACTER	Dark, vengeance-seeking figure.

THEMES IN HORROR FICTION

FEAR OF THE UNKNOWN	Unseen forces and mysteries evoke terror.
SURVIVAL INSTINCTS	Characters fight to stay alive.
CONFRONTING DEMONS	Inner struggles and past traumas explored.
LOSS OF CONTROL	Terrifying consequences of losing control.
ISOLATION AND CLAUSTROPHOBIA	Tension in confined settings.
POWER OF BELIEF	Superstition shapes characters' fates.
MORAL AMBIGUITY	Ethical dilemmas blur right and wrong.
HAUNTED PAST	Past haunts characters and places.
CORRUPTION OF INNOCENCE	Malevolence targets the vulnerable.
INESCAPABLE FATE	Themes of destiny and doom.
DARK SIDE OF TECHNOLOGY	Consequences of scientific exploration.
SUPERNATURAL VS. RATIONAL	Blurring reality with the paranormal.
REDEMPTION AND ATONEMENT	Seeking forgiveness amidst horror.
LOSS OF INNOCENCE	Youth's purity shattered by darkness.
UNRELIABLE NARRATOR	Narrators' sanity and perceptions doubted.

TITLES

COMMON LENGTHS FOR HORROR FICTION TITLES

Horror fiction titles can vary in length, but they are typically concise and impactful. They often consist of one to five words, capturing the essence of the story in a brief, attention-grabbing phrase.

COMMON WORDS FEATURED IN HORROR FICTION TITLES

DARK	NIGHTMARE	HAUNTING	SHADOWS
BLOOD	TERROR	CHILLS	SCREAMS
GHOSTS	CURSE	DREAD	CREEP
DEAD	VENGEANCE	ABYSS	VAMPIRE

EXAMPLES OF HORROR FICTION TITLES

WHISPERS IN THE SHADOWS	THE HAUNTING OF BLACK MANOR	THE MALEVOLENT ENTITY
CHILLS DOWN THE SPINE	CRIMSON MOONRISE	DREADFUL SECRETS
THE CURSED DOLLHOUSE	NIGHTMARE'S EMBRACE	THE DEVIL'S TRANCE
THE VEIL OF DARKNESS	HOUSE OF ECHOES	FANGS OF THE NIGHT
THE BLOODCURDLING MURDERS	SCREAMS IN THE ATTIC	THE SINISTER REFLECTION

TITLES

CREATING INTRIGUING HORROR FICTION TITLES

EVOKING FEAR AND INTRIGUE	A successful horror title should evoke fear, curiosity, and intrigue in the reader. It should hint at the unsettling elements within the story, enticing the audience to explore further.
FOCUS ON EMOTIONS	Consider the emotions you want to evoke in readers, such as fear, dread, or curiosity.
HIGHLIGHT KEY ELEMENTS	If there's a central supernatural entity, cursed object, or eerie setting, consider incorporating them into the title.
KEEP IT CONCISE	Aim for brevity while conveying the essence of your story.
EVOKE SETTING	Some titles hint at the story's setting, emphasising haunted houses, haunted forests, or ominous landscapes.
THEMES AND ELEMENTS	Titles may highlight specific themes or elements in the story, such as the supernatural, haunted locations, malevolent entities, psychological terror, or impending doom.

Remember, a compelling horror title is like a gateway into your story's world, setting the tone and drawing readers in with its eerie allure.

Experiment with different words, themes, and emotions to find the perfect title that encapsulates the essence of your horror fiction.

MOST POPULAR WORDS IN HORROR FICTION

HAUNTING	CHILLING	TERRIFYING	DARK
SINISTER	SUPERNATURAL	NIGHTMARISH	EERIE
DREADFUL	MYSTERIOUS	GHOSTLY	MALEVOLENT
SUSPENSEFUL	GRUESOME	MACABRE	CREEPY
UNSETTLING	OMINOUS	SINISTER	ENIGMATIC
CURSED	GORY	DISTURBING	MENACING
SPINE-TINGLING	BONE-CHILLING	PSYCHOLOGICAL	APPARITION
PARANORMAL	TENSE	EVIL	TERRIFIC
UNEARTHLY	WICKED	DIABOLICAL	MYSTERIOUS
FORBIDDEN	DESPERATE	VENGEFUL	PERILOUS

SYMBOLS FOUND IN HORROR FICTION

CANDLE	Represents eerie illumination and the thin line between light and darkness
HAUNTED HOUSE	A classic setting that signifies malevolence and the presence of ghosts.
MIRROR	Symbolises reflections of the unknown and the potential for malevolent doppelgängers.
SPIDER/WEB	Represents entrapment, danger, and the presence of malevolent forces.
DOLL	Often used to evoke uncanny and creepy feelings, especially when associated with the supernatural.
COBWEB	Symbolises neglect, decay, and the presence of malevolent spirits.
KNIFE	A weapon commonly found in horror stories, associated with violence and danger.
SCARECROW	Represents a fear of the unknown, often brought to life in supernatural tales.
WOODS/FOREST	A setting that signifies isolation, darkness, and the unknown.
OUIJA BOARD	A tool used to communicate with spirits, symbolising the gateway to the supernatural.
BATS	Associated with vampires and the supernatural, representing fear and darkness.
FULL MOON	Often used to create an eerie atmosphere and foreshadow supernatural events.
RAVEN	A bird often associated with death, darkness, and the supernatural.

SYMBOLS FOUND IN HORROR FICTION

SKELETON	Symbolises mortality and the fear of death in horror narratives.
CRACKED MIRROR	Represents a broken reality, alternate dimensions, and malevolent spirits.
BLOOD	A common element in horror fiction, symbolising violence, danger, and the supernatural.
GARGOYLE	Represents malevolence and supernatural protection.
CREEPY CRAWLIES	Insects, snakes, or other creatures that evoke fear and disgust.
OLD PHOTOGRAPHS	May reveal ghostly apparitions or haunting memories.
ABANDONED ASYLUM/HOSPITAL	A setting that signifies madness and the unknown.
FOG/MIST	Creates an atmosphere of mystery and uncertainty in horror stories.
BATHTUB	Often used in supernatural or psychological horror scenes.
DAGGER	A weapon used for ritualistic or supernatural purposes.
MOONLIGHT	Creates an eerie and atmospheric setting in horror narratives.

These objects and symbols contribute to the eerie and chilling atmosphere in horror fiction, allowing writers to evoke fear and suspense in their stories.

POWER WORDS IN HORROR FICTION

DREADFUL	Terrifying, horrifying, macabre, gruesome
HAUNTING	Ghostly, eerie
SINISTER	Malevolent, ominous, vengeful
TERRIFYING	Frightening, horrifying, paralysing, ghastly
CHILLING	Bone-chilling, cold, morbid
MENACING	Threatening, dangerous, nightmares
APPARITION	ghostly, spectral
DIABOLICAL	Evil, devilish, demonic
WRAITHLIKE	Wraithlike, ghostly, ethereal
WRETCHED	Miserable, forlorn
CREPUSCULAR	Eerie, twilight
CRYPTIC	Mysterious, enigmatic

Now mix and match these words to create plot twists/ and or endings:

GRUESOME NIGHTMARES start to plague the main character into VENGEFUL acts after visiting an old building.

What happens now?

SHOW NOT TELL TECHNIQUES IN HORROR WRITING

INSTEAD OF TELLING FEAR

Telling: The house was creepy and haunted.

Showing: As she stepped inside, the air turned icy cold, a faint whisper echoed through the dimly lit hallway, walls seemed to watch her every move, and creaking floorboards sounded like distant moans, adding to the unsettling atmosphere.

Telling: He was terrified.

Showing: His heart pounded like a drum, his hands trembled uncontrollably, beads of sweat rolled down his forehead, struggling to catch his breath, fumbling for the light switch to dispel the suffocating darkness.

Telling: The monster was enormous and horrifying.

Showing: The creature's massive form loomed, jagged fangs gleaming, deep growls reverberated, and eyes glowed with otherworldly intensity. Its hulking frame cast a menacing shadow, sending chills down their spines.

Telling: She felt scared.

Showing: Her heart pounded like a trapped animal, breaths came in quick, shallow gasps, palms grew clammy, muscles tensed, ready to flee, every noise magnified, darkness pressed in, making her feel small and vulnerable.

SHOW NOT TELL TECHNIQUES IN HORROR WRITING

HOW TO DO IT

USE SENSORY DETAILS	Engage the reader's senses by describing what characters see, hear, feel, smell, and taste. This adds depth to emotions and experiences.
DIALOGUE AND BODY LANGUAGE	Allow characters' interactions and nonverbal cues to reveal their emotions and intentions, creating more realistic and immersive scenes.
INTERNAL MONOLOGUE	Show characters' thoughts and inner conflicts through internal monologues or introspective narration, allowing readers to understand their emotional turmoil.

BENEFITS OF SHOW NOT TELL IN HORROR FICTION

EMOTIONAL IMPACT	Showing emotions and experiences immerses readers in the characters' feelings, creating a deeper emotional connection with the story.
CHARACTER DEVELOPMENT	Demonstrating characters' thoughts and actions rather than telling them helps develop well-rounded, three-dimensional characters.
IMMERSIVE READING EXPERIENCE	Show, not tell, creates a more engaging and immersive reading experience, allowing readers to experience the story alongside the characters.
READER EMPATHY	By showing characters' struggles and vulnerabilities, readers can empathise with them and become emotionally invested in their journey.
AVOIDING INFORMATION DUMP	Showing instead of telling allows the story's information to unfold naturally, avoiding information dumps that can disrupt the flow of the narrative.
PROMOTING INTERPRETATION	Showing allows readers to interpret characters' emotions and motives, encouraging critical thinking and engagement with the story.

HISTORICAL FICTION

395

FICTION SQUARE

CHARACTER	SETTING	GOAL	CONFLICT	CONSEQUENCE
SOLDIER	PARLIAMENT	SURVIVE AND RETURN HOME	ENEMY	SCARS
NURSE	DOCKS	SAVE WOUNDED COMRADES	TRAUMA	EXECUTION
KNIGHT	CASTLE	RECOGNITION	RESISTANCE	PUBLIC SHAME
RESISTANCE FIGHTER	STREETS	GET HELP	MORAL DILEMMA	EXILE
EXPLORER	PALACE	SECURE INDEPENDENCE	BETRAYAL	DEATH
INVENTOR	CAVE	DEFEAT THE ENEMY	MONEY	LOSS OF REPUTATION
SCIENTIST	MOUNTAINS	PEACE	TIME	DISEASE

IDEA 1	SOLDIER	MOUNTAINS	SAVE WOUNDED COMRADES	BETRAYAL	DEATH
	A weary soldier, desperate to save wounded comrades, escapes to the mountains to try and get help, only to face the harrowing conflict of betrayal from somebody there, where the consequence of discovery is death.				
WHY?	Traumatised by the brutality of war, the soldier seeks solace and safety in the mountains to try and get help for his friends.				
WHAT IF...?	In this isolated sanctuary, a fellow comrade betrays the soldier's trust, jeopardising the fragile hope for survival.				
AND THEN...?	Hunted and cornered, the soldier must navigate the treacherous terrain to evade capture, uncovering a deeper conspiracy that threatens not only their life but of the villages nearby.				

FICTION SQUARE

You should have: A character, setting, goal, conflict and consequence

IDEA 2

WHY?

WHAT IF...?

AND THEN...?

You should have: A character, setting, goal, conflict and consequence

IDEA 3

WHY?

WHAT IF...?

AND THEN...?

WHAT TO DO

THOROUGH RESEARCH	Conduct extensive research on the era, understanding customs, clothing, language, and events for an authentic world.
COMPELLING CHARACTERS	Develop well-rounded characters reflecting beliefs of the time, with distinct personalities and motivations.
IMMERSIVE SETTING	Use sensory details and vivid language to transport readers to the historical atmosphere.
STAY TRUE TO HISTORY	Maintain historical accuracy, blending real events and figures with creative elements.
WEAVE REAL EVENTS	Incorporate actual historical occurrences seamlessly into the narrative.
SOCIAL CONTEXT	Depict social norms, class divisions, and cultural expectations of the era.
AUTHENTIC DIALOGUE	Use period-appropriate language and idioms, avoiding modern expressions.
BALANCE FACT AND FICTION	Merge historical accuracy with compelling storytelling.
PORTRAY CHALLENGES	Highlight political, economic, and personal struggles for depth.
CULTURAL DIVERSITY	Acknowledge varied perspectives and experiences of the time.
STRONG PLOT	Craft engaging plots with conflicts and dilemmas against historical backdrops.
HISTORICAL SYMBOLS	Enrich the narrative with significant artefacts and symbols of the era.

WHAT TO AVOID DOING

HISTORICAL INACCURACY	Ensure accuracy; don't distort or neglect historical facts.
ENSURE LANGUAGE AUTHENTICITY	Avoid modern language in dialogue.
AVOID ANACHRONISTIC VALUES	Don't impose modern values on historical characters.
AVOID OVERWHELMING DETAILS	Avoid excessive historical detail that slows the story.
AVOID PASSIVE CHARACTERS	Characters should have agency, not just observe.
DON'T STEREOTYPE FIGURES	Develop well-rounded characters, not stereotypes.
REALISM OVER ROMANTICISM	Present both positive and negative aspects.
NEVER MISREPRESENT EVENTS	Avoid altering or misrepresenting history.
AVOID MODERN LENS	Don't analyse solely through contemporary views.
AVOID ANACHRONISTIC PLOTS	Ensure the plot aligns believably with the era.
ENSURE PACING BALANCE	Keep pacing engaging, avoiding sluggishness.
AVOID MODERATE JARGON	Don't overwhelm with complex historical terms.

COMMON HISTORICAL FICTION SETTINGS

MEDIEVAL EUROPE	Knights, castles, quests, and royal courts of the Middle Ages.
ANCIENT EGYPT	Pharaohs, pyramids, mysticism in ancient times.
VICTORIAN ENGLAND	19th-century England, industrial revolution, upper class lives.
REGENCY ERA	Early 19th-century elegance, societal norms.
WILD WEST	19th-century American frontier, cowboys, pioneers, outlaws.
WORLD WAR I AND II	Impact of two world wars on society, soldiers, and civilians.
RENAISSANCE ITALY	Renaissance art, politics, Medici family.
ANCIENT GREECE AND ROME	Classical antiquity, philosophers, myths.
FEUDAL JAPAN	Samurai, geishas, unique cultural aspects.
THE ROARING TWENTIES	1920s jazz, flappers, prohibition.
THE GOLD RUSH	19th-century prospectors seeking fortunes worldwide.

KEY CHARACTER ROLES IN HISTORICAL FICTION

COURAGEOUS REBEL	Challenges norms, leads revolutions.
FEARLESS EXPLORER	Discovers new lands, treasures.
RESILIENT SURVIVOR	Overcomes challenges, and shows strength.
INTREPID SPY	Engages in espionage, political intrigue.
INSPIRATIONAL LEADER	Guides through historical events.
EMPOWERED SUFFRAGETTE	Advocates for women's rights.
TALENTED ARTIST	Impacts culture, innovation.
DETERMINED ABOLITIONIST	Fights for freedom, abolition.
CUNNING INTRIGUER	Navigates royal courts, politics.
ROMANTIC ADVENTURER	Love amid historical events.
HONOURABLE WARRIOR	Battles in historical conflicts.
CURIOUS SCHOLAR	Advances knowledge, culture.

CHARACTER NAMES

MALE CHARACTERS		FEMALE CHARACTERS	
WILLIAM	CHARLES	MARY	ELIZABETH
JOHN	GEORGE	ANNE	CATHERINE
JAMES	ROBERT	JANE	MARGARET
HENRY	EDWARD	SARAH	ALICE
THOMAS	RICHARD	ELEANOR	ISABELLA

These names are popular in historical fiction as they are familiar to readers, making it easier for them to connect with the characters.

However, writers are encouraged to use a mix of common and unique names to create a diverse and memorable cast of characters in their period stories.

MOST COMMON OCCUPATIONS

FARMER	Cultivates land, raises livestock.
BLACKSMITH	Crafts metal tools, makes armour.
SEAMSTRESS/TAILOR	Creates clothing, garments.
SOLDIER/WARRIOR	Fights in conflicts, battles.
NOBLE/ROYAL	Aristocracy, royalty characters.
SERVANT/MAID	Maintains households.
ARTISAN	Crafts pottery, textiles.
HEALER/HERBALIST	Provides medicinal aid.
MERCHANT/TRADER	Engages in commerce.
INNKEEPER/TAVERN KEEPER	Offers lodging, entertainment.
SCRIBE	Records information, maintains records.
SAILOR/PIRATE	Navigates ships, sometimes pirates.
ARTIST/PAINTER	Contributes to culture, art.
MINSTREL/BARD	Travels, shares stories, songs.

CHALLENGES AND CONFLICTS

WAR AND CONFLICT	Surviving battles, war-torn areas, emotional trauma.
SOCIAL HIERARCHY	Class barriers, societal norms.
PREJUDICE AND DISCRIMINATION	Racial, gender, religious bias.
POLITICAL INTRIGUE	Conspiracies, power struggles.
ECONOMIC HARDSHIP	Poverty, debt, instability.
CULTURAL CLASH	Misunderstandings, conflicting values.
HEALTH AND DISEASE	Illness, epidemics, pandemics.
QUEST FOR INDEPENDENCE	Seeking freedom, autonomy.
FORBIDDEN LOVE	Taboo romances.
RESISTANCE MOVEMENTS	Fighting oppressive regimes.
RELIGIOUS STRIFE	Conflicting beliefs.
INTRIGUING DISCOVERIES	Artefacts, secrets, rival seekers.
FAMILY FEUDS	Long-standing rivalries.
NATURAL DISASTERS	Coping with earthquakes, floods, etc

HIGH STAKES IN HISTORICAL FICTION

LIFE AND DEATH	Facing mortal danger.
LOSS OF FREEDOM	Struggling against captivity.
BETRAYAL	Dealing with shattered trust.
EXILE OR BANISHMENT	Forcing separation from home.
LOSS OF REPUTATION	Facing societal disgrace.
LOVE AND RELATIONSHIPS	Navigating strained bonds.
FAILURE OF QUEST	Dealing with mission failure.
ECONOMIC RUIN	Battling financial collapse.
ENDANGERING LOVED ONES	Risking harm to family.
HISTORICAL REPERCUSSIONS	Influencing the course of history.
SPIRITUAL CONSEQUENCES	Grappling with moral dilemmas.
ISOLATION AND LONELINESS	Suffering from solitude.
LOSS OF HERITAGE/CULTURE	Struggling to preserve identity.
SURVIVAL OF COMMUNITY	Protecting the community's future.

HEROIC GOALS IN HISTORICAL FICTION

SURVIVAL	Navigating life-threatening challenges.
QUEST FOR FREEDOM	Striving to break societal chains.
SEEKING JUSTICE	Confronting corruption and injustice.
CULTURAL PRESERVATION	Safeguarding heritage against suppression.
ACHIEVING SUCCESS/WEALTH	Aiming for societal recognition.
FINDING LOVE/ROMANCE	Pursuing forbidden affection.
PURSUIT OF KNOWLEDGE/DISCOVERY	Uncovering hidden truths.
LEADING OR INSPIRING OTHERS	Guiding through historical upheavals.
OVERCOMING PREJUDICE AND DISCRIMINATION	Defying biased norms.
RESTORING FAMILY HONOUR	Reclaiming lost dignity.
RESISTING OPPRESSION OR OCCUPATION	Fighting for liberation.
REUNITING WITH LOVED ONES	Seeking reconnection amidst turmoil.
CONTRIBUTING TO HISTORICAL EVENTS	Shaping the course of history.
BUILDING A BETTER FUTURE	Striving for lasting positive change.

NOTORIOUS VILLAINS IN HISTORICAL FICTION

TYRANNICAL RULER	Cruel monarch wielding absolute power.
CORRUPT OFFICIAL	Manipulative authority exploiting for personal gain.
VENGEFUL ENEMY	Avenging foe in conflict and conquest.
CUNNING MANIPULATOR	Deceptive plotter advancing hidden motives.
SADISTIC OPPRESSOR	Tormenting antagonist relishing suffering.
TRAITOROUS INSIDER	Betraying collaborator undermining trust.
RELIGIOUS FANATIC	Zealous believer justifying violence.
GREEDY BUSINESSMAN	Ruthless profiteer exploiting resources.
VENGEFUL FAMILY MEMBER	Grudge-bearing kin seeking revenge.
ENSLAVER OR SLAVE OWNER	Treating humans as property.
DARK SORCERER OR WITCH	Using dark magic for evil ends.
SERIAL KILLER	Cold-blooded murderer sowing terror.
OPPRESSIVE PATRIARCH	Controlling figure enforcing norms.
SINISTER COURTIER	Calculating court schemer seeking power.
SUPERNATURAL ENTITY	Malevolent ghost or demon haunting.

THEMES IN HISTORICAL FICTION

IDENTITY AND BELONGING	Characters wrestle with shifting identities and cultural ties.
LOVE AND SACRIFICE	Profound choices made for loved ones.
CONFLICT AND WAR	Impact of battles on individuals and societies.
SOCIAL INJUSTICE AND OPPRESSION	Struggles against discrimination and injustice.
POWER AND CORRUPTION	Consequences of authority gone awry.
COURAGE AND RESILIENCE	Defiance in adversity's face.
CHANGE AND TRANSFORMATION	Personal growth amidst historical context.
TRADITION VERSUS PROGRESS	Balancing old ways with new ideas.
REBELLION AND REVOLUTION	Overthrowing oppressive systems for change.
FAMILIAL BONDS	Importance of family connections.
INNOCENCE AND LOSS	Emotional toll of historical events.
CULTURAL EXCHANGE AND ENCOUNTER	Meeting of diverse worlds.
FAITH AND BELIEF	Spiritual depths shaping characters' paths.
DISCOVERY AND ADVENTURE	Journeys into the unknown.
RESPECT FOR NATURE AND THE ENVIRONMENT	Humanity's relationship with the natural world.

TITLES

COMMON LENGTHS FOR HISTORICAL FICTION TITLES

Historical fiction titles typically range from 2 to 5 words, although there are exceptions. Concise titles can be memorable and impactful, while longer titles can convey more depth and specificity.

COMMON WORDS FEATURED IN HISTORICAL FICTION TITLES

LEGACY	SECRETS	JOURNEY	ECHOES
SHADOWS	LOST/LOST IN	DREAMS/DREAMING	CHRONICLES
TIME/TIMELESS	PROMISE/PROMISES	FORGOTTEN	WINDS
BLOOD	SWORD/SWORDS	EMPIRE	KINGDOM

TITLES

CREATING A COMPELLING HISTORICAL FICTION TITLE STEP-BY-STEP

IDENTIFY THE SETTING OR TIME PERIOD	Think about the historical era or location where your story takes place. Identify key elements that define that time and place. **Example:** Victorian England
DETERMINE THE EMOTION OR THEME	Consider the central emotions or themes that run through your story. Is it a tale of love, betrayal, adventure, or redemption? Choose a word that captures the essence of these emotions or themes. **Example:** Love and Sacrifice
USE SENSORY IMAGERY	Include a descriptive word that evokes sensory images related to the historical era. This helps transport readers to the past and sets the tone for your story. **Example:** Misty Moors
ADD MYSTERY OR INTRIGUE	Consider using a word that sparks curiosity or suggests a hidden layer to your story. A touch of mystery in the title can intrigue potential readers. **Example:** Secrets
COMBINE THE ELEMENTS	Combine the elements from Steps 1 to 5 to create a concise and captivating title that encapsulates the spirit of your historical fiction story. **Example:** "Secrets of the Misty Moors: A Love and Sacrifice Tale set in Victorian England."

Following this framework, you can craft a title that not only reflects the historical context of your story but also entices readers with its emotional resonance and a hint of mystery. Remember that your title is a crucial part of the reader's first impression, so make it engaging and memorable!

MOST POPULAR WORDS IN HISTORICAL FICTION

EPIC	ANCIENT	ADVENTURE	MYSTERY
LOVE	INTRIGUE	BETRAYAL	POWER
CONFLICT	WAR	SECRETS	JOURNEY
PASSION	COURAGE	DESTINY	REVENGE
ROYALTY	FORBIDDEN	REVOLUTION	TREACHERY
DISCOVERY	INJUSTICE	BETRAYAL	SURVIVAL
CONSPIRACY	INTRIGUE	DESIRE	HERO
ESCAPE	TIME	LEGACY	QUEST
SACRIFICE	VENGEANCE	DRAMA	RIVALRY
FATE	DECEPTION	ENCHANTMENT	TRAGEDY
VICTORY	TREASURE	EMPIRE	HERITAGE
MYSTERY	ROMANCE	CONQUEST	DESTINY

SYMBOLS FOUND IN HISTORICAL FICTION

QUILL PEN	Represents writing and communication in historical settings.
SWORD	A symbol of warfare and power, often associated with knights and warriors.
HORSE AND CARRIAGE	Represents transportation in historical eras before automobiles.
POCKET WATCH	Symbolises timekeeping and the passage of time in historical settings.
CROWN	Represents royalty and monarchy, often associated with kings and queens.
PARCHMENT SCROLL	Symbolises historical documents and ancient writings.
COMPASS	Represents exploration and navigation during historical voyages.
SAILING SHIP	Symbolises maritime exploration and trade in historical periods.
DAGGER	A weapon commonly used in historical settings, often associated with intrigue and betrayal.
ARMOUR	Represents medieval warfare and the protection of knights.
CANNON	Symbolises historical warfare and battles.
CHALICE	Represents religious or ceremonial significance in historical contexts.
FLINTLOCK PISTOL	A historical firearm used in the past for personal defence.

SYMBOLS FOUND IN HISTORICAL FICTION

TAPESTRY	Represents intricate and historical artwork, often depicting significant events.
POCKET WATCH	Symbolises timekeeping in historical periods before wristwatches.
QUILL AND INKWELL	Used for writing and composing letters in historical times.
TELESCOPE	Represents scientific exploration and observation in historical eras.
MANUSCRIPT	Symbolises historical writings and literature.
CANDLESTICK	Represents historical lighting before electric lighting.
VICTORIAN DRESS	A symbol of fashion and attire in historical settings.
ANCIENT RUINS	Represents historical civilisations and past glory.
SCEPTRE	Symbolises royalty and authority in historical monarchies.
MUSKET	A historical firearm used in warfare before more modern rifles.
CHARIOT	Represents transportation in ancient historical settings.
SCROLL	Symbolises historical records, writings, and ancient texts.

These objects and symbols help create an authentic historical atmosphere in fiction, immersing readers in the past and providing context for the story's events.

POWER WORDS IN HISTORICAL FICTION

ANCIENT	Time-worn, age-old, archaic
EPIC	Grand, heroic, monumental, legendary
TIMELESS	Enduring, perpetual, ageless
FORGOTTEN	Lost, neglected, abandoned, obscure
GILDED	Ornate, embellished, opulent, luxurious
LOST	Misplaced, vanished, hidden, elusive, secrets
UNTOLD	Unrevealed, concealed, undisclosed, mysterious, forbidden
MAJESTIC	Regal, stately, imposing, magnificent
ENIGMATIC	Cryptic, mysterious, puzzling
INTRIGUING	Captivating, fascinating, engaging, alluring
ENCHANTING	Charming, bewitching, captivating, entrancing
FABLED	Legendary, mythical, renowned, celebrated
PRESTIGIOUS	Stunning, awe-inspiring, breathtaking, magnificent
CONQUERING	Victorious, triumphant, successful

Now mix and match these words to create plot twists/ and or endings:

The main character discovers SECRETS about FORBIDDEN love and has to make a choice...

What happens now?

SHOW NOT TELL TECHNIQUES IN HISTORICAL WRITING

INSTEAD OF TELLING FEAR

Telling: John was scared when he entered the ancient, eerie castle.

Showing: As John stepped into the castle's dimly lit hallway, his heart raced, and a shiver crawled up his spine. The flickering candlelight cast eerie shadows on the stone walls, making him feel like he was being watched.

INSTEAD OF TELLING EXHAUSTION

Telling: The soldiers were exhausted after the long battle.

Showing: His heart pounded like a drum, his hands trembled uncontrollably, beads of sweat rolled down his forehead, struggling to catch his breath, fumbling for the light switch to dispel the suffocating darkness.

INSTEAD OF TELLING HUSTLE AND BUSTLE

Telling: The marketplace was crowded and lively.

Showing: In the bustling marketplace, vendors called out their wares, and the aroma of spices and fresh bread filled the air. Shoppers weaved through the throng, haggling over prices and exchanging gossip.

INSTEAD OF TELLING ANGER

Telling: She was angry at the unfair treatment.

Showing: Her fists clenched, and her face flushed with indignation as she witnessed the injustice. With a voice quivering with anger, she confronted those responsible, demanding change.

SHOW NOT TELL TECHNIQUES IN HISTORICAL WRITING

HOW TO DO IT

USE SENSORY DETAILS	Engage the reader's senses by describing what characters see, hear, feel, smell, and taste. This adds depth to emotions and experiences.
DIALOGUE AND BODY LANGUAGE	Allow characters' interactions and nonverbal cues to reveal their emotions and intentions, creating more realistic and immersive scenes.
INTERNAL MONOLOGUE	Show characters' thoughts and inner conflicts through internal monologues or introspective narration, allowing readers to understand their emotional turmoil.

BENEFITS OF SHOW NOT TELL IN HISTORICAL FICTION

EMOTIONAL IMPACT	Showing emotions and experiences immerses readers in the characters' feelings, creating a deeper emotional connection with the story.
CHARACTER DEVELOPMENT	Demonstrating characters' thoughts and actions rather than telling them helps develop well-rounded, three-dimensional characters.
IMMERSIVE READING EXPERIENCE	Show, not tell, creates a more engaging and immersive reading experience, allowing readers to experience the story alongside the characters.
READER EMPATHY	By showing characters' struggles and vulnerabilities, readers can empathise with them and become emotionally invested in their journey.
AVOIDING INFORMATION DUMP	Showing instead of telling allows the story's information to unfold naturally, avoiding information dumps that can disrupt the flow of the narrative.
PROMOTING INTERPRETATION	Showing allows readers to interpret characters' emotions and motives, encouraging critical thinking and engagement with the story.

YOUNG ADULT

417

FICTION SQUARE

CHARACTER	SETTING	GOAL	CONFLICT	CONSEQUENCE
HACKER	SPACE	TO EXPOSE CORRUPTION	PARENTS	INJURY
MUSICIAN	CITY	WIN COMPETITION	MONEY	CORRUPTION
SPORTS PLAYER	SCHOOL/UNI	SOLVE MYSTERY	THREATS	REMAIN STUCK
STUDENT	SMALL TOWN	ADVENTURE	BETRAYAL	MYSTERY GOES UNSOLVED
TEEN WITH SUPERPOWERS	MAGICAL REALM	FACE FEAR	DANGER	PERSECUTION
ACTIVIST	CAVE	TO CHALLENGE SOCIETY	LACK OF POWERS	RIDICULE
EXPLORER	FOREST	DREAM JOB	LACK OF KNOWLEDGE	SHAME

	MUSICIAN	SMALL TOWN	WIN COMPETITION	PARENTS	RIDICULE
IDEA 1	A young musician, yearning to escape his small town, desperately seeks to win a crucial competition. However, his passion clashes with his parents' disapproval, and failure not only means the continuation of a stifling hometown life but also the looming threat of ridicule from those around him.					
WHY?	Fuelled by a deep longing for a life beyond the confines of his small town, the young musician sees the competition as his ticket to a future filled with possibilities					
WHAT IF...?	His parents, driven by their own unfulfilled dreams, vehemently oppose his pursuit of a musical career, fearing the uncertainty it brings.					
AND THEN...?	As the competition intensifies, the musician must navigate not only the musical challenges but also confront his parents' expectations, risking the chance to break free or facing the weight of their disappointment if he falls short.					

418

FICTION SQUARE

You should have: A character, setting, goal, conflict and consequence

IDEA 2

WHY?

WHAT IF...?

AND THEN...?

You should have: A character, setting, goal, conflict and consequence

IDEA 3

WHY?

WHAT IF...?

AND THEN...?

WHAT TO DO

RELATABLE CHARACTERS	Create diverse characters that resonate with young readers, reflecting various backgrounds and perspectives.
AUTHENTIC VOICE	Use a genuine voice that captures the emotions and complexities of adolescence without being didactic.
COMING-OF-AGE THEMES	Explore self-discovery, identity, friendship, and personal growth in an empathetic manner.
ENGAGING PACE	Maintain a compelling pace and build tension to keep readers invested.
REALISTIC DIALOGUE	Craft natural dialogue that mirrors how young people communicate.
CONTEMPORARY ISSUES	Address relevant topics like mental health, social media, and technology thoughtfully.
DESCRIPTIVE WRITING	Use vivid descriptions to show emotions, scenes, and settings.
INVENTIVE PLOTS	Create diverse and imaginative plots to keep readers engaged.
CHARACTER AGENCY	Empower protagonists to make choices and overcome challenges.
KNOW YOUR AUDIENCE	Understand readers' interests and concerns.
AVOID DIDACTICISM	Let readers draw their own conclusions from characters' experiences.
EMOTIONAL CONNECTION	Evoke reader empathy by exploring characters' feelings.
EMBRACE DIVERSITY WITH POSITIVE MESSAGES	Balance dark themes with hopeful messages. Promote acceptance and inclusivity.

WHAT TO AVOID DOING

DISRESPECT READERS' INTELLIGENCE	Avoid talking down or assuming readers won't grasp complex themes.
AVOID STEREOTYPES	Create authentic, multi-dimensional characters, breaking away from clichéd portrayals.
HARMFUL ROMANTICISATION	Address tough topics but avoid glorifying harmful behaviour like abuse or toxicity.
SLANG AND JARGON	Use contemporary language, but don't overuse slang that may become outdated.
MIND AGE-APPROPRIATENESS	Balance mature themes; limit excessive profanity and explicit content.
UNNATURAL CHARACTER GROWTH	Allow characters to evolve organically; avoid rushed development.
UNBALANCED ROMANCE	If present, ensure romance complements the plot without overshadowing it.
AVOID PREACHING	Address important themes without forcing a specific message.
IRRELEVANT THEMES TO AUDIENCE	Connect with the YA demographic's interests and concerns.

COMMON YOUNG ADULT FICTION SETTINGS

HIGH SCHOOL/SECONDARY SCHOOL	Focus on friendships, relationships, and academics.
FANTASY WORLDS	Magical quests, creatures, and battles.
DYSTOPIAN SOCIETIES	Young rebels in oppressive futures.
URBAN SETTINGS	Complex relationships in cities.
SMALL TOWNS	Coming-of-age tales in close-knit communities.
BOARDING SCHOOLS	Camaraderie, rivalry, and discovery.
POST-APOCALYPTIC LANDSCAPES	Survival in devastated worlds.
HISTORICAL ERAS	Insights into past challenges and cultures.
CONTEMPORARY REALISM	Everyday life, family, and societal issues.
VIRTUAL OR GAMING WORLDS	Digital adventures and virtual realms.
SUMMER CAMPS	Personal growth and friendships
MAGICAL SCHOOLS/INSTITUTES	Fantasy mixed with school.
RURAL COUNTRYSIDE	Self-discovery in serene landscapes.
FUTURISTIC CITIES	Tech-driven future challenges.

YOUNG ADULT FICTION TIME PERIODS/ERAS

CONTEMPORARY TIMES	Current issues, tech, modern challenges.
VICTORIAN ERA	Historical drama, societal norms
WORLD WARS	Bravery, impact of conflict.
ROARING TWENTIES	Jazz, social changes.
1960S AND 1970S	Activism, cultural shifts.
MEDIEVAL TIMES	Knights, quests, fantasy.
ANCIENT CIVILISATIONS	Cultures, mythologies.
REGENCY ERA	Manners, romance.
STEAMPUNK ERA	Fantasy, steam tech.
POST-APOCALYPTIC FUTURES	After catastrophes.
WILD WEST	Adventure, survival.
RENAISSANCE	Art, culture, history.
WWII HOME FRONT	Unseen experiences.
FUTURE AND DYSTOPIA	Techno-changes, consequences.

KEY CHARACTER ROLES IN YOUNG ADULT FICTION

PROTAGONIST	Central character facing challenges and self-discovery.
RELUCTANT HERO/HEROINE	Resists, then confronts challenges.
OUTCAST	Struggles to fit in, relatable to readers.
CHOSEN ONE	Special destiny, fights evil.
REBEL	Challenges norms, seeks change.
LOVE INTEREST	Adds romance, emotional depth.
SIDEKICK/BEST FRIEND	Supports and accompanies.
MENTOR	Guides and imparts wisdom.
ANTAGONIST	Opposes and creates conflict.
SURVIVOR	Navigates trauma and challenges.
COMING-OF-AGE PROTAGONIST	Learns in transformative journey.
MISFIT	Embraces uniqueness for self-worth.
SCAPEGOAT	Takes blame, redeems.
IDENTITY-STRUGGLING PROTAGONIST	Explores belonging and self-acceptance.

CHARACTER NAMES

MALE CHARACTERS		FEMALE CHARACTERS	
JASON	NICK	ABBY/ABIGAIL	ANNA
RYAN	TOM/THOMAS	LAUREN	HANNAH
SAM	MATT/MATTHEW	LILY	SOPHIE
JAKE	BEN	GRACE	EMILY
CHRIS	ALEX	MEGAN	OLIVIA

Remember that while these names are commonly used in YA fiction, there is no hard and fast rule when it comes to naming characters.

As a writer, you have the creative freedom to choose names that suit your characters and their personalities.

MOST COMMON OCCUPATIONS

STUDENT	Common school or college life focus.
ARTIST	Creatives exploring self-expression.
ATHLETE/SPORTS	Sports involvement and competition.
WAITER/WAITRESS	Part-time restaurant work.
BABYSITTER	Childcare experiences and challenges.
RETAIL SALESPERSON	Retail dynamics and interactions.
JOURNALIST/REPORTER	Mysteries and uncovering truths.
INTERN	Learning through professional experience.
TUTOR	Teaching and personal growth.
CAMP COUNSELLOR	Summer adventures and friendships.
BARISTA	Coffee shop stories and romance.
VOLUNTEER/ACTIVIST	Advocacy and community impact.
BOOKSTORE/LIBRARY ASSISTANT	Love for literature and connections.
WAITER/WAITRESS	Part-time restaurant work.
NANNY	Childcare and meaningful relationships.

CHALLENGES AND CONFLICTS

INTERNAL STRUGGLES	Self-doubt, fears, past traumas.
ROMANTIC TENSIONS	Love triangles, emotional turmoil.
FRIENDSHIP DRAMA	Misunderstandings, reconciliation.
FAMILY ISSUES	Divorce, loss, strained relationships.
SOCIETAL EXPECTATIONS	Conformity vs. desires.
ACADEMIC CHALLENGES	Grades, self-discovery.
COMING-OF-AGE THEMES	Responsibility, decisions.
SECRETS AND LIES	Truth, betrayal, misunderstandings.
BULLYING AND PEER PRESSURE	Resilience, self-assertion.
SOCIAL ISSUES AND INJUSTICE	Activism, growth.
SURVIVAL AND ADVENTURE	Thrilling situations, resilience.
QUESTS AND CHALLENGES	Obstacles, adversaries.
OPPOSING BELIEFS	Debates, self-reflection.
BETRAYAL AND LOYALTY	Trust, alliances.
FIGHTING TYRANNY	Revolutions, rebellions.

HIGH STAKES IN YOUNG ADULT FICTION

LIFE-THREATENING DANGER	Characters confront life-or-death situations, risking their lives or others'.
LOSS OF LOVED ONES	Risk of losing friends, family, or love interests due to actions or conflict.
PERSONAL SACRIFICE	Characters make tough choices, sacrificing well-being for the greater good.
DESTRUCTION OF HOME/TOWN	Failure could destroy their community.
BETRAYAL AND BROKEN TRUST	Risk of betrayal, shattered trust.
END OF A RELATIONSHIP	Romance may end due to conflict.
FAILED MISSION OR QUEST	High stakes, mission failure.
LOSS OF IDENTITY OR POWERS	Characters may lose identity, abilities.
EXPOSURE OF SECRETS	Secrets exposed, dire outcomes.
SOCIETAL COLLAPSE OR TYRANNY	Antagonist's win leads to chaos or tyranny.
ISOLATION AND LONELINESS	Risk of isolation due to choices.
FAILURE TO SAVE OTHERS	Failing innocents leads to guilt.
LOSS OF DREAMS OR ASPIRATIONS	Goals jeopardised by challenges.
PERMANENT CHANGE	Actions bring lasting change.

HEROIC GOALS IN YOUNG ADULT FICTION

SELF-DISCOVERY	Main character seeks identity, place.
OVERCOMING CHALLENGE	Conquer fear, trauma, limitation.
ACADEMIC SUCCESS	Excel in school, scholarship, college.
SAVING LOVED ONE	Rescue family, friend, love interest.
FINDING TRUE LOVE	Form meaningful romance.
FULFILLING PROPHECY	Achieve destiny, significant journey.
SEEKING JUSTICE/REVENGE	Justice, vengeance for self/others.
CHANGING SOCIETY/WORLD	Positive community, global change.
BECOMING CHAMPION	Excel in sport, arts, competition.
RESOLVING MYSTERY	Unravel puzzles, adventure, discovery.
ESCAPING OPPRESSION	Seek freedom from control.
REUNITING LOST LOVED ONE	Find separated family, friend.
SURVIVING HOSTILE ENVIRONMENT	Endure danger, challenges.
GAINING SPECIAL SKILL/POWER	Learn unique ability.
DEFEATING ANTAGONIST/THREAT	Overcome adversary, danger.

NOTORIOUS VILLAINS IN YOUNG ADULT FICTION

POWER-HUNGRY DICTATOR	Controls through oppression.
MANIPULATIVE MASTERMIND	Schemes for dark goals.
JEALOUS RIVAL	Competes, fuelled by envy.
CORRUPT AUTHORITY	Abuses power, harms others.
DARK SORCERER/WITCH	Wields evil magic.
BETRAYED FRIEND/ALLY	Turns against due to betrayal.
VENGEFUL ENEMY	Seeks revenge for past.
RELENTLESS HUNTER	Pursues with vendetta.
MANIPULATED PAWN	Controlled by greater evil.
TWISTED SCIENTIST/INVENTOR	Creates destructive tech.
ANCIENT EVIL	Old malevolent threat reawakens.
OPPRESSIVE SOCIETY	Represents dystopian rule.
ENVIOUS SIBLING	Seeks harm out of resentment.
IMMORTAL ANTAGONIST	Formidable, immortal adversary.
DARK REFLECTION	Represents protagonist's dark side.

THEMES IN YOUNG ADULT FICTION

COMING OF AGE	Growth through adolescence.
FRIENDSHIP AND LOYALTY	Trust, bonds in adversity.
IDENTITY AND SELF-ACCEPTANCE	Embracing who they are.
LOVE AND ROMANCE	Joys, complexities of love.
COURAGE AND RESILIENCE	Bravery amid challenges.
LOSS AND GRIEF	Coping with loss, death.
SOCIAL ISSUES AND ACTIVISM	Addressing discrimination, rights.
FAMILY DYNAMICS	Complex family relationships
FINDING STRENGTH IN VULNERABILITY	Strength in seeking help.
EMPOWERMENT AND REBELLION	Defying oppression, empowerment.
ACCEPTANCE AND INCLUSION	Embracing diversity, inclusivity.
OVERCOMING PREJUDICE	Challenging biases, empathy.
POWER OF IMAGINATION AND CREATIVITY	Creativity overcoming obstacles
QUEST FOR KNOWLEDGE AND TRUTH	Seeking truth, self-discovery.
FACING FEARS AND INSECURITIES	Confronting fears, finding courage.

TITLES

COMMON LENGTHS FOR YOUNG ADULT FICTION TITLES

On average, YA book titles tend to be relatively short, typically ranging from three to five words. Concise titles are easier to remember and more visually impactful on book covers and marketing materials.

COMMON WORDS FEATURED IN YOUNG ADULT FICTION TITLES

LEGACY	SECRETS	JOURNEY	ECHOES
SHADOWS	LOST/LOST IN	DREAMS/DREAMING	CHRONICLES
TIME/TIMELESS	PROMISE/PROMISES	FORGOTTEN	WINDS
BLOOD	SWORD/SWORDS	EMPIRE	KINGDOM

SOME INTRIGUING TITLES FOR YOUNG ADULT FICTION

WHISPERS OF STARDUST	MIDNIGHT CHRONICLES	CRIMSON VEIL	ECHOES OF ETERNITY
EMBERS OF EDEN	SERPENT'S SYMPHONY	THE FORGOTTEN KEY	THE GLASS GARDEN
SHADOWS OF THE CRESCENT MOON	THE ENCHANTED CIPHER	STARLIGHT SERENADE	GLIMMERS OF INFINITY
STARFALL ACADEMY	THE SILVER LABYRINTH	REQUIEM FOR A DREAMER	THE ORACLE'S ODYSSEY

TITLES

CREATING A COMPELLING YOUNG ADULT FICTION TITLE

CORE THEME OR ESSENCE	Identify your YA story's core theme, conflict, or unique element.
KEYWORDS AND PHRASES	Brainstorm related words, emotions, and symbols.
METAPHORS AND SYMBOLS	Incorporate metaphors for depth.
SHORT IMPACTFUL COMBINATIONS	Create concise, striking 3-5 word titles.
TEST RESONANCE	Share titles for feedback.
GENRE AND SUBGENRE	Reflect YA and subgenre.
AVOID CLICHÉS	Be original, avoid overused phrases.
MEMORABLE IMPACT	Ensure memorability and curiosity.
CONNECT TO AUDIENCE	Consider appeal to YA readers.
POLISH AND FINALSE	Refine until it fits and intrigues.

MOST POPULAR WORDS IN YOUNG ADULT FICTION

ADVENTURE	POWER	LOVE	MAGIC
DESTINY	SECRET	FRIENDSHIP	DANGER
MYSTERY	BETRAYAL	COURAGE	REBELLION
FATE	ROMANCE	DARK	SECRETS
WAR	SURVIVAL	TRUTH	QUEST
IDENTITY	SACRIFICE	CHOSEN	UNCOVER
EPIC	SUPERNATURAL	LEGACY	CONFLICT
POWERFUL	UNRAVEL	FIGHT	ESCAPE
FORBIDDEN	CHAOS	FUTURE	DISCOVER
LEGEND	WITCH/WIZARD	ENCHANT	ETERNAL
END	REVENGE	SURVIVE	BATTLE
TORN	CURSED	RESIST	PROPHECY

SYMBOLS FOUND IN YOUNG ADULT FICTION

KEYS	Representing access to knowledge, hidden truths, or unlocking mysteries.
MIRRORS	Symbolising self-reflection, identity, or the duality of characters.
STARS	Evoking dreams, aspirations, and the vastness of possibilities.
DOORS/GATEWAYS	Signifying opportunities, transitions, or crossing into the unknown.
LABYRINTHS/MAZES	Representing challenges, self-discovery, or finding a way forward.
FEATHERS	Symbolising freedom, flight, or spiritual connection.
CANDLES	Representing hope, illumination, or moments of clarity.
LOCKETS/LOCKETS	Carrying sentimental value or secret memories.
TREES/FORESTS	Symbolising growth, life, and connection with nature.
WINGS	Representing freedom, transformation, or a journey to new heights.
CLOCKS/WATCHES	Signifying the passage of time, urgency, or impending events.
BOOKS/SCROLLS	Representing knowledge, learning, and the power of stories.
DOORS/GATEWAYS	Signifying opportunities, transitions, or crossing into the unknown.
COMPASS	Representing guidance, direction, and finding one's way.

POWER WORDS IN YOUNG ADULT FICTION

ADVENTURE	Exciting and daring experiences, often involving a journey or quest.
COMING-OF-AGE	A central theme where characters experience growth, maturity, and self-discovery.
FRIENDSHIP	Strong bonds and connections between characters, offering support and understanding.
ROMANCE	Love and emotional connections between characters, often with a focus on teenage relationships.
LOVE	Affection and deep feelings between characters, both romantic and platonic.
IDENTITY	Characters' quest to understand and embrace who they are, including their values, beliefs, and personalities.
SELF-DISCOVERY	The process of characters uncovering hidden truths about themselves and their place in the world.
REBELLION	Characters challenging authority, norms, or oppressive systems.
EMPOWERMENT	Characters gaining strength, confidence, and control over their lives and destinies.
GROWTH	The development and evolution of characters, often through challenges and experiences.
COURAGE	Brave actions taken by characters, even in the face of fear or danger.
CHALLENGES	Obstacles and difficulties characters face on their journeys.
DREAMS	Aspirations and desires characters strive to achieve.

POWER WORDS IN YOUNG ADULT FICTION

FANTASY — Imaginative and magical elements, often in alternative worlds or supernatural settings.

MYSTERY — Unexplained or hidden elements that characters must unravel.

SECRETS — Concealed information or truths that have significant impact on the plot or characters.

QUEST — A mission or adventure characters embark on to achieve a specific goal.

DYSTOPIA — An oppressive or undesirable society or world.

RELATIONSHIPS — The connections and interactions between characters.

TEENAGERS — The age group of young people between childhood and adulthood.

EMOTIONS — Characters' feelings and emotional experiences.

TEEN ANGST — The turmoil and struggles often experienced by teenagers.

SCHOOL — Educational institutions where characters learn and grow.

MAGIC — Supernatural powers or elements influencing the story.

SUPERNATURAL — Beyond natural or normal occurrences, often involving mystical or paranormal elements.

JOURNEY — The characters' physical or emotional travels through the plot.

BELONGING — Characters' sense of fitting in or finding their place in the world.

Now mix and match these words to create plot twists/ and or endings:

The main character finds a COMPASS that leads to a GATEWAY where CLOCKS go backwards.

SHOW NOT TELL TECHNIQUES IN YOUNG ADULT WRITING

INSTEAD OF TELLING EMOTION

Telling: Sarah was excited about the upcoming dance.

Showing: Sarah could hardly contain her excitement as she chatted with her friends, her eyes sparkling and her laughter filling the air.

INSTEAD OF TELLING A SETTING

Telling: The forest was mysterious.

Showing: The forest, with its thick canopy and twisting paths, held an air of mystery that intrigued anyone who dared to venture into its depths.

INSTEAD OF TELLING CHARACTER PERSONALITY

Telling: Emma was creative.

Showing: Emma's room was a riot of colours and crafts. Canvases leaned against walls, and a desk covered in sketchbooks and paints revealed her boundless creativity.

SHOW NOT TELL TECHNIQUES IN YOUNG ADULT WRITING

HOW TO DO IT

USE SENSORY DETAILS	Engage the reader's senses by describing what characters see, hear, feel, smell, and taste. This adds depth to emotions and experiences.
DIALOGUE AND BODY LANGUAGE	Allow characters' interactions and nonverbal cues to reveal their emotions and intentions, creating more realistic and immersive scenes.
INTERNAL MONOLOGUE	Show characters' thoughts and inner conflicts through internal monologues or introspective narration, allowing readers to understand their emotional turmoil.

BENEFITS OF SHOW NOT TELL IN YOUNG ADULT FICTION

EMOTIONAL IMPACT	Showing emotions and experiences immerses readers in the characters' feelings, creating a deeper emotional connection with the story.
CHARACTER DEVELOPMENT	Demonstrating characters' thoughts and actions rather than telling them helps develop well-rounded, three-dimensional characters.
IMMERSIVE READING EXPERIENCE	Show, not tell, creates a more engaging and immersive reading experience, allowing readers to experience the story alongside the characters.
READER EMPATHY	By showing characters' struggles and vulnerabilities, readers can empathise with them and become emotionally invested in their journey.
AVOIDING INFORMATION DUMP	Showing instead of telling allows the story's information to unfold naturally, avoiding information dumps that can disrupt the flow of the narrative.
PROMOTING INTERPRETATION	Showing allows readers to interpret characters' emotions and motives, encouraging critical thinking and engagement with the story.

CONTEMPORARY/ WOMEN'S/ DOMESTIC

440

FICTION SQUARE

CHARACTER	SETTING	GOAL	CONFLICT	CONSEQUENCE
SINGLE MOTHER	CITY	STABILITY	EX-PARTNER	LOSS
WIFE	SMALL TOWN	ESCAPE	SELF-BELIEF	ABUSE
NURSE	MANSION	DISCOVERY	MONEY	DEPRESSION
CAREER WOMAN	COASTAL	FULFILMENT	PARENTS	STRAINED RELATIONSHIPS
DIVORCEE	OFFICE	BUILD SELF-ESTEEM	EXPECTATIONS	TRAPPED
LANDLADY	VILLAGE	BUILD BUSINESS	COMPETITION	UNFULFILLED
WIDOW	FLAT/APARTMENT	EXPLORE	MENTAL HEALTH	DEATH

	WIFE	SMALL TOWN	ESCAPE	EX-PARTNER	TRAPPED
IDEA 1	A recently divorced wife in a small town seeks escape from the clutches of her powerful ex, a man admired by all but harbouring a dark side. Struggling to be believed and receiving no support, she faces the haunting question: Will she remain trapped forever under his control?					
WHY?	In the aftermath of a painful divorce, the wife yearns for liberation from her powerful ex, whose charming facade hides a sinister truth.				
WHAT IF…?	As she grapples with the isolation of being disbelieved and abandoned by those around her, the threat intensifies, leaving her in a precarious position, financially and physically.				
AND THEN…?	Faced with the chilling possibility of enduring perpetual control, she must summon the strength to expose the dark reality, seeking allies and a way to break free before it's too late.				

FICTION SQUARE

You should have: A character, setting, goal, conflict and consequence

IDEA 2

WHY?

WHAT IF...?

AND THEN...?

You should have: A character, setting, goal, conflict and consequence

IDEA 3

WHY?

WHAT IF...?

AND THEN...?

WHAT TO DO

REALISTIC CHARACTERS	Create relatable, flawed characters.
EMOTIONAL DEPTH	Explore complex feelings, relationships.
AUTHENTIC RELATIONSHIPS	Portray genuine connections.
ENGAGING DIALOGUE	Write natural, story-moving talks.
STRONG THEMES	Address resonant themes: love, loss, growth.
CAPTIVATING PLOT	Craft compelling, paced story.
WOMEN'S EXPERIENCES	Centre on women's challenges, triumphs.
REAL-WORLD ISSUES	Tackle social themes sensitively.
EMPOWERMENT	Celebrate women's strength.
AUTHENTIC SETTINGS	Create immersive, vivid locations.
MULTIDIMENSIONAL VILLAINS	Craft complex antagonists.
FAMILY DYNAMICS	Explore relationships: mother-daughter, generational.
EMPATHY AND UNDERSTANDING	Foster understanding.
UNEXPECTED TWISTS	Surprise with well-timed surprises.
SATISFYING ENDINGS	Provide fulfilling closure.

WHAT TO AVOID DOING

STEREOTYPICAL CHARACTERS	Avoid one-dimensional, stereotypical characters.
PREACHINESS	Refrain from heavy-handed messages.
TOKEN DIVERSITY	Include diverse characters with depth.
EXCESSIVE MELODRAMA	Avoid overdone dramatic scenes.
UNREALISTIC ENDINGS	Aim for plausible, satisfying conclusions.
LACK OF CONFLICT	Keep engaging conflict.
NEGLECTING PACING	Balance pace for reader engagement.
GLAMOURISING ABUSE	Be sensitive to abuse portrayal.
UNDERDEVELOPED SUPPORTING CHARACTERS	Enhance supporting roles.
OVERLY PREDICTABLE PLOTS	Add engaging twists.
LACK OF EMPOWERMENT	Empower female characters.
IGNORING EMOTIONAL DEPTH	Explore emotions and relationships.
MISREPRESENTATION OF CULTURES	Research well for cultural accuracy.
TROPES AND CLICHÉS	Avoid overused tropes.
IGNORING REAL-WORLD ISSUES	Address real issues thoughtfully.

COMMON CONTEMPORARY/WOMEN'S/DOMESTIC SETTINGS

SMALL TOWNS	Quaint and close-knit communities that offer a sense of familiarity and community.
URBAN CITIES	Bustling metropolitan areas with diverse cultures, opportunities, and challenges.
SUBURBS	Residential areas outside of urban centres, often characterised by family-oriented neighbourhoods.
COUNTRYSIDE/RURAL AREAS	Serene and picturesque landscapes, often associated with a slower pace of life.
COASTAL TOWNS	Scenic seaside settings, offering a tranquil and beachy ambiance.
FAMILY HOMES	Intimate and familiar spaces where family dynamics and personal journeys unfold.
SCHOOLS/UNIVERSITIES	Educational institutions that shape characters' lives, relationships, and self-discovery.
WORKPLACES	Various work environments that influence characters' careers and ambitions.
COFFEE SHOPS/CAFÉS	Popular meeting spots that serve as social hubs and settings for character interactions.
BOOKSTORES/LIBRARIES	Environments that celebrate literature, reading, and knowledge.
PARKS/GARDENS	Natural and calming settings for contemplation and important conversations.
WEDDING VENUES	Symbolic locations that represent love, commitment, and family celebrations.

COMMON CONTEMPORARY/WOMEN'S/DOMESTIC SETTINGS

HOSPITALS/CLINICS	Places where characters face medical challenges and emotional moments.
COMMUNITY CENTRES	Gathering places for events, group activities, and social connections.
FITNESS CENTRES/GYMS	Locations where characters may pursue personal growth and self-improvement.
RESTAURANTS	Spaces for meals, conversations, and shared experiences.
ART GALLERIES/MUSEUMS	Places where characters can explore art and cultural exhibitions.
THEATRES/CINEMAS	Venues for entertainment, performances, and shared experiences.
CHURCHES/PLACES OF WORSHIP	Spiritual settings for contemplation, faith, and reflection.
PUBLIC TRANSPORTATION	Settings where characters encounter diverse people and experiences during their commutes.
SHOPPING MALLS/BOUTIQUES	Locations for retail therapy and shopping excursions.
CHARITY ORGANISATIONS	Spaces where characters may engage in philanthropy and community service.
BEACH HOUSES	Tranquil and relaxing vacation spots for character getaways.
RETIREMENT HOMES	Settings that explore themes of aging, family dynamics, and legacy.

CONTEMPORARY/WOMEN'S/DOMESTIC TIME PERIODS/ERAS

PRESENT DAY	Stories in modern times, reflecting current society.
LATE 20TH CENTURY	Settings in the latter half of the 20th century, capturing historical events.
POST-9/11 ERA	Exploring effects of 9/11 on characters and society.
WORLD WAR II (WWII)	Historical fiction during global conflict, women's experiences.
VICTORIAN ERA	19th-century societal norms for women.
ROARING TWENTIES	1920s, Jazz Age, changing women's roles.
GREAT DEPRESSION ERA	Fiction in 1930s economic downturn, family struggles.
1960S AND 1970S	Counterculture era, civil rights, feminism.
SUBURBAN 1950S	Post-WWII suburban life, gender roles.
EARLY 21ST CENTURY	2000s, tech impact, cultural change.
CONTEMPORARY HISTORICAL	Blend of present and history.
PRE-REVOLUTIONARY AMERICA	Colonial life, women's roles.
REGENCY ERA	Early 19th-century England, societal norms.
POST-WWII ERA	Aftermath of World War II.

KEY CHARACTER ROLES IN CONTEMPORARY/WOMEN'S/DOMESTIC FICTION

PROTAGONIST	Drives story, faces challenges.
FEMALE LEAD	Central, prominent female role.
MOTHER	Navigates motherhood, growth.
WIFE	Explores marriage, identity.
SISTER	Explores sibling bonds, loyalty.
DAUGHTER	Navigates parent-child dynamics.
BEST FRIEND	Supportive, key to protagonist.
SINGLE WOMAN	Explores single life, relationships.
DIVORCÉE	Navigates post-divorce life.
CAREER WOMAN	Focus on career.
EMPTY NESTER	Life changes after kids leave.
ELDERLY WOMAN	Wise, life-experienced.
ENTREPRENEUR	Navigates business challenges.

KEY CHARACTER ROLES IN CONTEMPORARY/WOMEN'S/DOMESTIC FICTION

WIDOW	Coping with loss, finding purpose.
GRANDMOTHER	Embraces role, family joy.
ARTIST	Artistic pursuits are central.
CAREGIVER	Themes of compassion, sacrifice.
SURVIVOR	Overcomes adversity, heals.
ACTIVIST	Advocates social change.
COMMUNITY LEADER	Local leadership, connections.
NEWLYWED	Early marriage stages.
WORKING MOTHER	Balances career, motherhood.
MENTOR	Guides, imparts life lessons.
RELIGIOUS/SPIRITUAL WOMAN	Faith/spirituality central.
INFLUENCER/SOCIAL MEDIA PERSONALITY	Navigates online influence.

CHARACTER NAMES

MALE CHARACTERS		FEMALE CHARACTERS	
JAMES	MICHAEL	EMMA	OLIVIA
DAVID	JOHN	SOPHIA	AVA
ROBERT	WILLIAM	ISABELLA	MIA
DANIEL	CHRISTOPHER	EMILY	AMELIA
ANDREW	MATTHEW	CHARLOTTE	HARPER
JOSEPH	RICHARD	ABIGAIL	ELLA
THOMAS	CHARLES	GRACE	LILY
STEVEN	BRIAN	CHLOE	SOFIA
KEVIN	MARK	AVERY	EVELYN
JASON	SCOTT	HANNAH	NATALIE

Remember that while these names are commonly used in Contemporary/Women's/Domestic fiction, there is no hard and fast rule when it comes to naming characters.

As a writer, you have the creative freedom to choose names that suit your characters and their personalities.

MOST COMMON OCCUPATIONS

TEACHER/EDUCATOR	Shapes students' lives.
WRITER/AUTHOR	Explores creativity, writing challenges.
NURSE	Compassionate healthcare workers.
LAWYER/ATTORNEY	Legal professionals, ethical dilemmas.
JOURNALIST	Reports on events, uncovers stories.
CHEF/COOK	Culinary skills, restaurants or passion.
ARTIST	Expresses creatively through art.
SOCIAL WORKER	Helps through tough situations.
INTERIOR DESIGNER	Creates functional spaces.
EVENT PLANNER	Organises events, handles emotions.
PSYCHOLOGIST/THERAPIST	Offers mental health support
FASHION DESIGNER/STYLIST	Creates unique styles.
PHOTOGRAPHER	Captures moments, emotions.

MOST COMMON OCCUPATIONS

MARKETING/ADVERTISING PROFESSIONAL	Promotes products, brands.
BUSINESS OWNER/ENTREPRENEUR	Faces entrepreneurial challenges.
WAITER/WAITRESS	Provides hospitality, builds connections.
ARCHITECT	Designs buildings, blends creativity.
COUNSELLOR	Offers guidance, support.
POLICE OFFICER/DETECTIVE	Investigates, maintains order.
RETAIL SALESPERSON	Interacts with customers, handles sales.
EXECUTIVE/MANAGER	Makes decisions, manages teams.
FINANCIAL ANALYST/ACCOUNTANT	Handles finances, analyses data.
PERSONAL TRAINER/FITNESS INSTRUCTOR	Promotes physical health.
HR PROFESSIONAL	Handles employee matters.
PUBLIC RELATIONS SPECIALIST	Manages public image, communication.

CHALLENGES AND CONFLICTS

RELATIONSHIP ISSUES	Misunderstandings, trust problems.
FAMILY DRAMA	Sibling rivalries, generational conflicts.
CAREER CHALLENGES	Job loss, workplace conflicts.
LOVE AND ROMANCE	Love triangles, long-distance issues.
PERSONAL TRAUMA	Confronting past wounds.
FINANCIAL STRUGGLES	Debt, unexpected expenses.
HEALTH ISSUES	Illnesses, mental health obstacles.
SELF-DISCOVERY	Finding true identities.
SOCIAL EXPECTATIONS	Challenging norms, desires.
PARENTING CHALLENGES	Parenting styles, decisions.
GRIEF AND LOSS	Emotional aftermath of loss.
BETRAYAL	Deception by friends, family.
LIFE TRANSITIONS	Moving, divorce, empty nesters.
CULTURAL DIFFERENCES	Navigating traditions, clashes.
COMMUNITY/NEIGHBOUR ISSUES	Conflicts with neighbours.

HIGH STAKES IN CONTEMPORARY/WOMEN'S/DOMESTIC FICTION

RELATIONSHIP BREAKDOWN	Losing a bond due to conflicts.
CAREER SETBACKS	Job loss, missed opportunities.
FAMILY ESTRANGEMENT	Disconnect from family.
LOST OPPORTUNITIES	Missing growth or success chances.
FINANCIAL RUIN	Instability, bankruptcy risk.
LONELINESS/ISOLATION	Losing connections, isolation.
HEALTH DETERIORATION	Physical, mental decline.
HEARTBREAK	Unrequited love, breakups.
MISSED PERSONAL FULFILMENT	Sacrificing dreams for others.
LEGAL CONSEQUENCES	Lawsuits, charges.
LOSS OF REPUTATION	Reputation damage, scandals.
PARENTAL ALIENATION	Losing child due to conflicts.
DISCONNECTION FROM IDENTITY	Losing self and purpose.
SOCIAL REJECTION	Rejected by peers, society.
REGRET AND GUILT	Burden of past mistakes.

HEROIC GOALS IN CONTEMPORARY/WOMEN'S/DOMESTIC FICTION

FINDING LOVE	Characters search for meaningful romantic connections.
CAREER SUCCESS	Characters pursue professional growth and dream jobs.
SELF-DISCOVERY	Characters embark on journeys of self-exploration.
FAMILY RECONCILIATION	Characters work to heal family conflicts.
PERSONAL GROWTH	Characters overcome trauma and develop emotionally.
STARTING A FAMILY	Characters aspire to become parents.
FINDING HAPPINESS	Characters seek fulfillment and joy.
BUILDING FRIENDSHIPS	Characters form deep and meaningful bonds
ACHIEVING FINANCIAL STABILITY	Characters overcome financial struggles.
FOLLOWING DREAMS	Characters pursue passions and lifelong aspirations.
REBUILDING AFTER LOSS	Characters reconstruct lives after setbacks.
OVERCOMING OBSTACLES	Characters conquer challenges and adversity.
FINDING INNER PEACE	Characters search for tranquility and contentment.
CREATING A HOME	Characters establish a loving and nurturing environment.
MAKING A DIFFERENCE	Characters aim to impact their community or world positively.

NOTORIOUS VILLAINS IN CONTEMPORARY/WOMEN'S/DOMESTIC FICTION

SABOTAGE	Villain aims to ruin protagonist's plans, relationships, or career.
REVENGE	Villain seeks retaliation for past grievances against protagonist.
MANIPULATION	Villain uses deceit to control or harm characters.
OBSTRUCTION	Villain blocks protagonist's progress and goals.
POWER AND CONTROL	Villain desires dominance over people and situations.
ISOLATION AND ALIENATION	Villain creates loneliness or separates protagonist from support.
HUMILIATION	Villain aims to embarrass and humiliate the protagonist.
FINANCIAL GAIN	Villain seeks personal profit at protagonist's expense.
DESTRUCTION	Villain wants to ruin protagonist's reputation and relationships.
ENVY AND JEALOUSY	Villain's jealousy drives them to harm protagonist.
TWISTED LOVE	Villain obsesses over protagonist, resorting to extreme actions.
SUPPRESS INDEPENDENCE	Villain aims to control protagonist's independence.
MANIPULATE RELATIONSHIPS	Villain sows discord and breaks protagonist's relationships.
THWART PERSONAL GROWTH	Villain prevents protagonist from evolving.
INFLICT FEAR	Villain creates fear and chaos in protagonist's life.

THEMES IN CONTEMPORARY/WOMEN'S/DOMESTIC FICTION

LOVE AND RELATIONSHIPS	Exploring various types of love and connections.
IDENTITY AND SELF-DISCOVERY	Characters on a journey to find their true selves.
FAMILY DYNAMICS	Examining complexities within family relationships.
FRIENDSHIP AND LOYALTY	Celebrating genuine friendship and loyalty.
RESILIENCE AND OVERCOMING ADVERSITY	Characters conquering challenges.
LOSS AND GRIEF	Exploring the emotional process of grief.
EMPOWERMENT AND INDEPENDENCE	Characters seeking empowerment.
PERSONAL GROWTH AND TRANSFORMATION	Characters evolving through experiences.
SACRIFICE AND COMPROMISE	Themes of giving up and finding middle ground.
AMBITION AND PURSUIT OF DREAMS	Characters striving for aspirations.
COMMUNICATION AND MISCOMMUNICATION	Impact of effective communication.
FORGIVENESS AND REDEMPTION	Themes of forgiveness and second chances.
TRADITIONS AND CULTURAL IDENTITY	Exploring significance of traditions.

THEMES IN CONTEMPORARY/WOMEN'S/DOMESTIC FICTION

BETRAYAL AND TRUST	Themes of betrayal, trust, and reconciliation.
GENDER ROLES AND FEMINISM	Themes of gender equality and challenges.
BELONGING AND ACCEPTANCE	Characters seeking acceptance and belonging.
RESPONSIBILITY AND DUTY	Characters dealing with obligations.
SOCIAL ISSUES	Addressing discrimination, inequality, and mental health.
EMPATHY AND UNDERSTANDING	Characters learning empathy.
PARENTING CHALLENGES	Exploring joys and struggles of parenthood.
COMMUNITY AND SUPPORT	Importance of support networks.
HOME AND BELONGING	Themes of finding a place to belong.
EXPECTATIONS AND INDIVIDUALITY	Navigating societal expectations.
COURAGE AND BRAVERY	Themes of facing difficult situations.
REDEMPTION AND SECOND CHANCES	Characters seeking new beginnings.

TITLES

COMMON LENGTHS FOR CONTEMPORARY/WOMEN'S/DOMESTIC FICTION TITLES

The average title length typically ranges from three to five words. However, there is no strict rule, and some titles may be longer or shorter based on the impact and uniqueness they provide.

COMMON WORDS FEATURED IN CONTEMPORARY/WOMEN'S/DOMESTIC FICTION TITLES

LOVE	HOME	FAMILY	HEART
JOURNEY	SECRETS	DREAMS	FOREVER
PROMISE	REDEMPTION	EDGE	LOST
SISTERS	TANGLED	HEALING	DAUGHTER

SOME INTRIGUING TITLES FOR CONTEMPORARY/WOMEN'S/DOMESTIC FICTION

HEARTS IN HARMONY	WHISPERS OF HOME	LOVE'S RESILIENCE	PROMISES AND PETALS
JOURNEY TO BELONGING	CHASING SUNSETS	FRAGMENTS OF FOREVER	INFINITE GRACE
SECRETS BETWEEN SISTERS	BEYOND THE HORIZON	SHADOWS OF YESTERDAY	EMBERS OF HOPE
DANCING IN THE RAIN	LOST IN TRANSLATION	HOMECOMING SECRETS	THE ART OF HEALING

TITLES

CREATING A COMPELLING CONTEMPORARY/WOMEN'S/DOMESTIC FICTION TITLE

CAPTURE THE ESSENCE	Reflect the core theme or emotion of the story in a few words.
CONSIDER THE GENRE	Align with the genre, evoke relatability, and connect with the target audience.
USE EVOCATIVE LANGUAGE	Choose words that evoke strong emotions or imagery.
KEEP IT CONCISE	Shorter titles are memorable and eye-catching.
AVOID SPOILERS	Pique curiosity without revealing major plot twists.
TEST IT OUT	Get feedback from peers to find a resonating title.

A FRAMEWORK FOR A CONTEMPORARY/WOMEN'S/DOMESTIC FICTION TITLE

WORKING TITLE	Start with a title reflecting the central theme or conflict.
EMOTIONS/THEMES	List key emotions or themes, like love, family, redemption.
PLAY WITH WORDS	Mix and match words and phrases for a compelling title.
ALLITERATION AND RHYTHM	Use repetition and rhythm for memorability.
STRONG VERBS/ADJECTIVES	Add impact with vivid words evoking emotions or imagery.
CHECK FOR EXISTING TITLES	Search for similar titles to ensure uniqueness.

MOST POPULAR WORDS IN CONTEMPORARY/WOMEN'S/DOMESTIC FICTION

LOVE	FAMILY	SECRETS	HEART
JOURNEY	RELATIONSHIPS	HOME	FRIENDSHIP
ROMANCE	LOSS	REDEMPTION	IDENTITY
DREAMS	HEALING	STRUGGLES	EMOTIONS
CHALLENGES	BETRAYAL	DISCOVERY	COURAGE
CONNECTION	SACRIFICE	BELONGING	HOPE
FORGIVENESS	END	REGAIN	DASH

SYMBOLS FOUND IN CONTEMPORARY/WOMEN'S/DOMESTIC FICTION

HOME/HOUSE	Represents a sense of belonging, safety, and family.
FLOWERS	Symbolise beauty, growth, and renewal.
JEWELLERY	Often represents love, relationships, and emotional connections.
DIARY/JOURNAL	Signifies self-reflection, personal growth, and hidden emotions.
PHOTOGRAPHS	Symbolise memories, nostalgia, and the passage of time.
CANDLES	Represent hope, warmth, and solace during difficult times.
LETTERS	Symbolise communication, hidden feelings, and connections.
FOOD/COOKING	Represents nurturing, family gatherings, and love.
DOORS/GATEWAYS	Symbolise new opportunities, transitions, and journeys.
MIRRORS	Signify self-reflection, identity, and introspection.
KEYS	Represent access to hidden knowledge, secrets, or new paths.
RAIN/STORMS	Symbolise emotional turmoil, cleansing, and renewal.
BLANKETS	Represent comfort, safety, and emotional support.
BIRDS	Symbolise freedom, transformation, and new beginnings.

POWER WORDS IN CONTEMPORARY/WOMEN'S/DOMESTIC FICTION

PASSION	Intense emotion and enthusiasm for something or someone.
HEARTFELT	Sincere and deeply felt, often used to describe emotions or sentiments.
INTIMATE	Close and personal, often relating to personal relationships or experiences.
EMPOWER	To give someone the confidence and authority to take control of their life or situation.
UNVEIL	To reveal or make known something that was previously hidden or secret.
EMBRACE	To hold or hug warmly, or to accept and adopt something willingly.
TENDER	Showing gentleness, affection, or care.
YEARNING	Strong and persistent longing or desire for something or someone.
INTRIGUE	To arouse curiosity or interest in something mysterious or fascinating.
CHERISH	To hold dear and deeply value someone or something.
RESILIENT	Able to recover and bounce back from difficulties or setbacks.
REVEAL	To disclose or make known something that was previously hidden or unknown.
CAPTIVATE	To enchant or attract someone's attention and hold it in a compelling manner.
WHISPER	To speak softly or in a hushed voice, often conveying intimacy or secrecy.

POWER WORDS IN CONTEMPORARY/WOMEN'S/DOMESTIC FICTION

SERENITY	Calmness and tranquillity, a state of being peaceful and undisturbed.
ENCHANT	To delight or charm someone in a captivating and magical way.
VULNERABLE	Open to being hurt or emotionally affected, often associated with emotional exposure.
RADIANT	Shining brightly, often used to describe someone's happiness or beauty.
YEARN	To have a strong and persistent desire or longing for something.
UNBREAKABLE	Unable to be broken or destroyed, often used to describe unyielding strength or resilience.
ENRAPTURE	To captivate or enthral someone completely.
SUSTAIN	To maintain or keep something going, often used in the context of support or endurance.
INSPIRE	To motivate or encourage someone to do or achieve something meaningful.
EVOKE	To bring forth emotions, memories, or reactions in someone.
INTERTWINE	To twist or weave together, often used to describe closely connected relationships or elements.

Now mix and match these words to create plot twists/ and or endings:

The main character visits a LIBRARY with her class and discovers a book where a LETTER falls out. It's from a woman desperate to escape and she writes about the location of some KEYS.

464

SHOW NOT TELL TECHNIQUES IN CONTEMPORARY/WOMEN'S/DOMESTIC WRITING

EMOTION	TELL	SHOW
SADNESS	She was heartbroken.	Tears streamed down her cheeks as she clutched the old love letter to her chest, her breath hitching with every painful memory.
MESSY	The kitchen was a mess.	Piles of dirty dishes teetered precariously on the countertops, and an overturned flour bag created a powdery mess on the floor.
NERVES	Sarah was nervous about the interview.	Sarah's palms were sweaty, and her stomach churned with butterflies as she rehearsed her answers for the job interview in front of the mirror.
HAPPPY	The baby was happy.	The baby's face lit up with a toothless grin, giggles filling the room as she reached out to grab her favourite toy.
ANGER	He was angry at his brother.	He clenched his fists, his face turning red, as he confronted his brother about the broken promise.
BEAUTY	The room was beautiful.	Sunlight streamed through the sheer curtains, casting a warm glow over the meticulously arranged vases of fresh flowers and the ornate tapestries adorning the walls.
TIRED	She was tired after a long day.	She dragged her feet up the stairs, each step heavier than the last, her eyes drooping with exhaustion.
LOVE	He loved her deeply.	He brushed a strand of hair away from her face and gazed into her eyes with a soft, tender expression, his heart swelling with love.
GUILT	She felt guilty.	She avoided making eye contact with her friend, her hands fidgeting with her shirt hem, unable to meet her gaze after the argument.

SHOW NOT TELL TECHNIQUES IN CONTEMPORARY/WOMEN'S/DOMESTIC WRITING

HOW TO DO IT

USE SENSORY DETAILS	Engage the reader's senses by describing what characters see, hear, feel, smell, and taste. This adds depth to emotions and experiences.
DIALOGUE AND BODY LANGUAGE	Allow characters' interactions and nonverbal cues to reveal their emotions and intentions, creating more realistic and immersive scenes.
INTERNAL MONOLOGUE	Show characters' thoughts and inner conflicts through internal monologues or introspective narration, allowing readers to understand their emotional turmoil.

BENEFITS OF SHOW NOT TELL IN CONTEMPORARY/WOMEN'S/DOMESTIC FICTION

EMOTIONAL IMPACT	Showing emotions and experiences immerses readers in the characters' feelings, creating a deeper emotional connection with the story.
CHARACTER DEVELOPMENT	Demonstrating characters' thoughts and actions rather than telling them helps develop well-rounded, three-dimensional characters.
IMMERSIVE READING EXPERIENCE	Show, not tell, creates a more engaging and immersive reading experience, allowing readers to experience the story alongside the characters.
READER EMPATHY	By showing characters' struggles and vulnerabilities, readers can empathise with them and become emotionally invested in their journey.
AVOIDING INFORMATION DUMP	Showing instead of telling allows the story's information to unfold naturally, avoiding information dumps that can disrupt the flow of the narrative.
PROMOTING INTERPRETATION	Showing allows readers to interpret characters' emotions and motives, encouraging critical thinking and engagement with the story.

PARANORMAL

467

FICTION SQUARE

CHARACTER	SETTING	GOAL	CONFLICT	CONSEQUENCE
GHOST HUNTER	CITY	HELP SPIRITS FIND PEACE	DARK FORCES TOO STRONG	CURSE
WITCH	SMALL TOWN	LIFT CURSE	LACK OF BELIEF FROM OTHERS	INJURY
INVESTIGATOR	CAVE	UNCOVER SECRETS	RUNNING OUT OF TIME	DEATH
MEDIUM	HOUSE	SOLVE CRIME	POWERS FADING	TORMENT
TIME TRAVELLER	HIDDEN COMMUNITY	LEARN MAGIC	SPIRIT TOO SMART	UNREST
DETECTIVE	WOODS	PREVENT DARK FORCES REIGNING	BETRAYAL	INSANITY
CURSED PERSON	VILLAGE	DEFEAT THE ENEMY	RUNNING OUT OF IDEAS	DARK MAGIC WINS

	MEDIUM	SMALL TOWN	HELP SPIRITS FIND PEACE	DARK FORCES TOO STRONG	TORMENT
IDEA 1	A determined medium, desperate to bring peace to lingering spirits in her small town, finds her abilities strained as dark forces intensify. Facing the looming threat of eternal torment for both herself and the trapped spirits, she must navigate the growing malevolence and uncover the source behind the strengthening dark forces before it consumes them all				
WHY?	Driven by an innate compassion for the restless spirits and haunted by a personal connection to the supernatural realm, the medium seeks to bring solace to those trapped between worlds				
WHAT IF...?	However, her efforts awaken malevolent forces that threaten to overpower her abilities and trap both the spirits and herself in eternal torment.				
AND THEN...?	As the darkness intensifies, the medium must confront her own fears, unravel the origin of the encroaching malevolence, and strengthen her connection to the spiritual realm to ensure the salvation of the trapped souls and her own soul's survival.				

FICTION SQUARE

You should have: A character, setting, goal, conflict and consequence

IDEA 2

WHY?

WHAT IF...?

AND THEN...?

You should have: A character, setting, goal, conflict and consequence

IDEA 3

WHY?

WHAT IF...?

AND THEN...?

WHAT TO DO

UNIQUE SUPERNATURAL WORLD	Develop an original and well-defined paranormal realm with its own rules and creatures.
INTRIGUING SUPERNATURAL ELEMENTS	Introduce captivating paranormal beings and phenomena.
RELATABLE PROTAGONIST	Create a relatable protagonist with clear goals and vulnerabilities.
TENSION AND MYSTERY	Maintain an air of tension and mystery to keep readers engaged.
EMOTIONAL DEPTH	Add emotional depth by exploring the characters' fears, desires, and struggles.
BALANCED WORLD-BUILDING	Balance world-building with reader imagination for a sense of wonder.
STRONG SUPPORTING CHARACTERS	Develop well-rounded supporting characters that contribute to the story.
CONFLICT AND CHALLENGES	Present significant conflicts, both supernatural and personal.
FORESHADOWING	Use foreshadowing to hint at upcoming paranormal events.
CREATIVE SUPERNATURAL ABILITIES	Showcase inventive use of supernatural powers to drive the plot.
RICH ATMOSPHERE AND SETTING	Set the tone with a vivid, mood-enhancing setting.
TWISTS AND SURPRISES	Include unexpected twists to keep readers engaged.
RESEARCH SUPERNATURAL LORE	Ground paranormal elements in well-researched lore or inventive twists.

WHAT TO AVOID DOING

OVERUSED TROPES	Avoid clichéd paranormal tropes like chosen one, love triangles, or all-powerful protagonists.
INFO DUMPS	Gradually reveal paranormal world details, avoiding info dumps.
INCONSISTENT RULES	Keep rules consistent, avoid sudden power introductions.
IDEALISED CHARACTERS	Create relatable characters with flaws, not perfection.
POORLY DEVELOPED ROMANCE	Build believable chemistry, avoid rushed relationships.
LACK OF TENSION	Maintain conflict, avoid prolonged inactivity.
WEAK ANTAGONISTS	Develop compelling antagonists with clear motives.
UNRESOLVED PLOT THREADS	Tie up loose ends for satisfying conclusions.
UNDERDEVELOPED SIDE CHARACTERS	Give purpose and growth to supporting characters.
INCONSISTENT CHARACTER BEHAVIOUR	Ensure consistent character actions.
IGNORING EMOTIONAL DEPTH	Address characters' emotional impact from paranormal events.
EXCESSIVE GORE OR VIOLENCE	Balance dark themes, avoid excessive violence.
TROPES AND CLICHÉS	Avoid overused tropes.
LACK OF ORIGINALITY	Strive for unique paranormal elements and plot twists.

COMMON PARANORMAL SETTINGS

HAUNTED HOUSES/ MANSIONS	Eerie locales with ghostly history.
SMALL TOWNS	Ordinary towns concealing supernatural secrets.
URBAN SETTINGS	Modern cities with supernatural elements.
FORESTS/WOODS	Enchanted or eerie woods.
GRAVEYARDS	Sites of paranormal activity.
OLD LIBRARIES/ BOOKSTORES	Hubs of hidden knowledge.
ABANDONED ASYLUMS/ HOSPITALS	Creepy, dark past locations.
MYSTERIOUS ISLANDS	Isolated islands of legend.
MAGICAL SCHOOLS/ INSTITUTES	Supernatural learning centres.
UNDERGROUND TUNNELS/ CATACOMBS	Ancient passageways.

COMMON PARANORMAL SETTINGS

CARNIVALS/FAIRS	Reality and fantasy merge.
TIMELESS CASTLES	Centuries-old secrets.
OTHER DIMENSIONS	Parallel worlds.
ANCIENT TEMPLES/RUINS	Sites of ancient power.
GOTHIC CATHEDRALS/CHURCHES	Paranormal and religious convergence.
COASTAL VILLAGES	Seaside towns with maritime legends.
PSYCHIC READING SHOPS	Seek guidance from psychics.
WITCH COVEN HIDING PLACES	Secret spots for witches.
UNDERWATER WORLDS	Oceans with mystical creatures.
PARALLEL DIMENSIONS/ALTERNATE REALITIES	Supernatural and reality merge.

PARANORMAL TIME PERIODS/ERAS

VICTORIAN ERA	Mysterious and gothic (1837-1901).
ROARING TWENTIES	Jazz, flappers (1920s).
MEDIEVAL TIMES	Knights, dragons (Middle Ages).
REGENCY ERA	Unique charm (1811-1820).
WORLD WAR II ERA	Wartime intrigue (WWII).
ANCIENT EGYPT	Mysticism, mythology.
PIRATE AGE	Cursed treasure, pirates (1650-1730).
WILD WEST	Frontier, folklore (19th century).
PREHISTORIC TIMES	Ancient spirits, creatures.
FUTURE/FUTURISTIC WORLDS	Advanced technology, paranormal.
RENAISSANCE PERIOD	Art, alchemy (14th-17th centuries).
SALEM WITCH TRIALS	Haunting, witch hunts (17th century).
WORLD WAR I ERA	Ghosts, wartime (WWI).
POST-APOCALYPTIC WORLDS	Disasters, paranormal (dystopia).
PRE-COLUMBIAN CIVILISATIONS	Mythology, folklore (Americas).

KEY CHARACTER ROLES IN PARANORMAL FICTION

THE CHOSEN ONE	Destiny-bound saviour of the world.
THE INVESTIGATOR/DETECTIVE	Unravels supernatural mysteries.
THE WITCH/WARLOCK	Master of magic and spells.
THE VAMPIRE	Immortal with blood thirst.
THE WEREWOLF	Human-beast dual nature.
THE GHOST	Seeking closure or revenge.
THE PSYCHIC/MEDIUM	Communicates with spirits.
THE SHAPESHIFTER	Identity-shifting challenges.
THE DEMON/HALF-DEMON	Good vs. evil struggle.
THE GUARDIAN/PROTECTOR	Defender against threats.
THE HYBRID	Unique mixed abilities.
THE WITCH HUNTER	Eliminating dangerous beings.
THE RELUCTANT HERO/HEROINE	Unwilling destiny embrace.
THE CURSED ONE	Seeking curse resolution.
THE TIME TRAVELLER	Historic paranormal encounters.

CHARACTER NAMES

MALE CHARACTERS		FEMALE CHARACTERS	
ETHAN	CALEB	ISABELLA	LUNA
SEBASTIAN	GABRIEL	AURORA	SERAPHINA
LUCAS	ALEXANDER	CELESTE	WILLOW
ADRIAN	DAMIEN	AMARA	GENEVIEVE
NATHANIEL	EZEKIEL	EVANGELINE	ARABELLA
PHOENIX	ORION	FREYA	SELENE
ASHER	TRISTAN	OPHELIA	CALLIOPE
XAVIER	DANTE	PERSEPHONE	GWENDOLYN
CASPIAN	JASPER	ESME	ROWAN
ALISTAIR	ZEPHYR	VIVIENNE	ELARA

Remember that while these names are commonly used in Paranormal fiction, there is no hard and fast rule when it comes to naming characters.

As a writer, you have the creative freedom to choose names that suit your characters and their personalities.

MOST COMMON OCCUPATIONS

PARANORMAL INVESTIGATOR/DETECTIVE	Unveils supernatural mysteries.
WITCH/WARLOCK	Magic practitioners, spellcasters.
VAMPIRE HUNTER	Eliminates dangerous vampires.
MEDIUM/PSYCHIC	Communicates with spirits, foresees events.
OCCULT BOOKSTORE OWNER	Reports on events, uncovers stories.
WEREWOLF TRACKER	Expert in werewolf incidents.
DEMONOLOGIST	Studies and deals with demons.
GHOST TOUR GUIDE	Leads haunted tours, shares tales.
EXORCIST	Expels malevolent spirits.
WITCH COVEN LEADER	Guides witchcraft practices.

MOST COMMON OCCUPATIONS

CRYPTID RESEARCHER	Studies mysterious creatures.
ARTEFACT CURATOR	Safeguards supernatural artefacts.
POTION SHOP OWNER	Sells magical remedies.
OCCULT LIBRARIAN	Preserves ancient supernatural knowledge
PARAPSYCHOLOGIST	Studies paranormal phenomena.
HAUNTED HOUSE GUIDE	Shares ghost stories.
SPIRIT MEDIUM THERAPIST	Aids troubled spirits.
WARD SPECIALIST	Counters magic with wards.
FORTUNE TELLER	Offers divination-based guidance.
SACRED SITE GUARDIAN	Protects mystical locations.

CHALLENGES AND CONFLICTS

SUPERNATURAL THREATS	Combat dangerous entities.
UNCONTROLLED POWERS	Master unpredictable abilities.
CURSED OBJECTS	Break malevolent curses.
PARANORMAL INVESTIGATIONS	Face scepticism.
SPIRITUAL WARFARE	Battle dark forces.
MYSTICAL ARTEFACTS	Protect powerful items.
SECRET IDENTITIES	Conceal true nature.
LOVE AND RELATIONSHIPS	Navigate supernatural romances.
BETRAYALS AND ALLIANCES	Manage shifting loyalties.
PROPHECIES AND DESTINY	Confront prophetic paths.
COVENS AND RIVALRIES	Handle faction conflicts.
SPIRIT POSSESSION	Fight malevolent spirits.
ETERNAL LIFE	Endure centuries.
PARALLEL WORLDS	Navigate alternate dimensions.
ANCIENT CURSES	Break haunting curses.

HIGH STAKES IN PARANORMAL FICTION

LIFE & LOVED ONES	Characters risk lives battling supernatural threats, endangering loved ones.
ETERNAL DAMNATION	Characters risk eternal damnation or spirit world entrapment.
HUMANITY LOSS	Disconnect from family.
WORLD'S END	Characters prevent global destruction, dark force release.
ANCIENT EVILS UNLEASHED	Characters risk ancient malevolent entity release.
FAMILY LEGACY	Characters face ancestor actions' fallout, supernatural heritage.
ISOLATION	Protagonists isolate due to supernatural nature.
LOVED ONES ENDANGERED	Characters protect family, friends from supernatural dangers.
SUPERNATURAL BALANCE	Characters disrupt supernatural-human world balance.
BETRAYAL	Characters betrayed by trusted supernatural community members.

HIGH STAKES IN PARANORMAL FICTION

DARK TEMPTATIONS	Characters tempted to misuse powers for gain, revenge.
REALITY UNRAVELLED	Misused artefacts risk reality fabric unravelilng.
COSMIC RULE BREAKING	Characters face consequences for ancient rule breaking.
FATE & PROPHECY	Protagonists fulfil/defy prophetic destinies.
CURSED LONGING	Characters suffer cursed existence, seek redemption.
SACRIFICE	Characters choose self-sacrifice for greater good.
TIME DISRUPTION	Characters risk altering history via time manipulation.
EXISTENTIAL CRISIS	Characters question supernatural existence's meaning.
ULTIMATE POWER CORRUPTS	Pursuit of power corrupts, humanity loss.
SEALING EVIL	Characters seal away dangerous entities permanently.

HEROIC GOALS IN PARANORMAL FICTION

DEFEAT SUPERNATURAL FOE	Characters combat harm-causing entities.
MASTER POWERS	Protagonists control newfound abilities.
BREAK A CURSE	Characters free selves, kin from curses.
UNRAVEL MYSTERIES	Protagonists decipher paranormal puzzles.
PROTECT KIN	Characters shield family, friends from supernatural peril.
FIND ARTEFACT	Protagonists seek potent, risky artefact.
SEEK REDEMPTION	Characters atone for supernatural wrongs.
RESTORE BALANCE	Protagonists mend supernatural-human equilibrium.
PREVENT APOCALYPSE	Characters halt supernatural-fuelled catastrophe.
RESCUE CAPTIVE	Protagonists free those held by supernatural entities.
UNCOVER LORE	Characters reveal ancient knowledge, family legacy.
DECODE PROPHECY	Characters interpret predictive supernatural signs.
CLOSE PORTAL	Characters shut inter-world gateway to bar malevolence.
LEAD SUPERNATURAL WORLD	Protagonists aspire to guide community.
RECOVER MEMORIES	Characters retrieve lost supernatural past.

NOTORIOUS VILLAINS IN PARANORMAL FICTION

DARK SORCERER/SORCERESS	Sinister magic wielder, aims to rule with dark rituals.
MALEVOLENT SPIRIT	Vengeful ghost seeks retribution, harms the living.
DEMON/DEMON LORD	Otherworldly entity causes chaos, tempts mortals.
VAMPIRE LORD/LADY	Ancient vampire desires human world dominance.
WEREWOLF ALPHA	Dominant werewolf leads aggressive pack, threatens all.
DARK WITCH/WARLOCK	Nefarious magic practitioner with sinister aims.
CURSED ENTITY	Cursed being seeks revenge through malevolence.
ROGUE WITCH COVEN	Forbidden magic coven harms for power.
MAD SCIENTIST	Scientist experiments with dangerous supernatural forces.
CORRUPTED HERO/HEROINE	Protagonist manipulated by dark entities.
SHADOWY ORGANISATION	Secretive group controls supernatural realm, manipulates humans.
TRICKSTER SPIRIT	Mischievous spirit sows chaos among mortals.
NECROMANCER	Dark necromancer controls undead for sinister purposes.
MALICIOUS DEITY	Deity demands sacrifices, manipulates mortals.
POSSESSING ENTITY	Malevolent spirit seeks human vessel.

THEMES IN PARANORMAL FICTION

GOOD VS. EVIL	Eternal battle between light and darkness, often through supernatural beings.
IDENTITY & SELF-DISCOVERY	Protagonists finding themselves amid supernatural traits.
LOVE & SACRIFICE	Love's trials, especially among immortal beings.
MORTALITY & IMMORTALITY	Challenges of eternal life or facing death among immortals.
POWER & CORRUPTION	Temptation and fallout of supernatural power.
FATE & DESTINY	Coping with prophecies tied to the supernatural.
REDEMPTION & FORGIVENESS	Seeking pardon from malevolent forces.
SECRETS & KNOWLEDGE	Unveiling supernatural truths.
BALANCE & HARMONY	Maintaining natural-supernatural equilibrium.
ISOLATION & BELONGING	Finding community amidst humans or the supernatural.

THEMES IN PARANORMAL FICTION

PARALLEL WORLDS	Exploring alternate realities.
DECEPTION & ILLUSIONS	Magic's use for manipulation.
CURSES & REDEMPTION	Breaking curses, seeking salvation.
SURVIVAL & PERSEVERANCE	Overcoming supernatural threats.
LEGACY & INHERITANCE	Inheriting supernatural roles.
MYSTICISM & SPIRITUALITY	Unveiling mystical aspects.
ACCEPTANCE & PREJUDICE	Humans' bias against supernatural beings.
ETERNAL LOVE & LOSS	Immortal love, enduring grief.
ETHICAL DILEMMAS	Moral challenges tied to powers.
ANCIENT PROPHECIES	Deciphering old predictions, seeking artefacts.

TITLES

COMMON LENGTHS FOR PARANORMAL TITLES

Paranormal fiction titles typically range from 2 to 5 words. While shorter titles can be concise and impactful, longer titles offer more opportunity to convey atmosphere and depth.

COMMON WORDS FEATURED IN PARANORMAL FICTION TITLES

SHADOWS	SECRETS	BLOOD	MOON
CURSE	WITCH	DARK	MAGIC
GHOST	FATE	SOUL	CHRONICLES
PROPHECY	LEGACY	ENCHANTMENT	HAUNTED
FORBIDDEN	IMMORTAL	SACRIFICE	ETERNITY
VENGEANCE	WHISPERS	COVEN	AWAKENING

SOME INTRIGUING TITLES FOR PARANORMAL FICTION

WHISPERS OF THE MOON	DARK ENCHANTMENT	THE IMMORTAL CURSE	HAUNTED SHADOWS
WITCH'S LEGACY	SACRIFICE OF SOULS	THE FORBIDDEN SPELL	ETERNAL VENGEANCE
BLOOD MOON CHRONICLES	BEYOND THE HORIZON	SHADOWS OF YESTERDAY	AWAKENING THE SPIRITS

TITLES

CREATING A COMPELLING PARANORMAL FICTION TITLE

NOUN + DESCRIPTIVE WORD	Combine a powerful noun representing a supernatural element with a descriptive word to evoke intrigue. **Examples:** "Moonlit Whispers" and "Cursed Legacy."
ADJECTIVE + NOUN	Start with a strong adjective to set the mood, followed by a noun relating to the paranormal theme. **Examples:** "Dark Secrets" and "Enchanted Soul."
NOUN + ACTION VERB	Use a significant noun combined with an action verb to convey the central conflict. **Examples:** "Blood Moon Rising" and "Sacrificing Shadows."
THE + NOUN + ADJECTIVE	Employ "The" to add weight and importance to the supernatural element. **Examples:** "The Haunted Chronicles" and "The Forbidden Spell."
ALLITERATION/ ASSONANCE	Combine words with the same initial consonant sound or similar vowel sounds for a memorable title. **Examples:** "Mystical Moon" and "Whispers of the Witch."

MOST POPULAR WORDS IN PARANORMAL FICTION

MYSTERIOUS	SUPERNATURAL	HAUNTED	DARK
ENCHANTING	MAGICAL	EERIE	OTHERWORLDLY
SECRET	CURSED	GHOSTS	COVEN
WITCH	SORCERY	ANCIENT	LEGACY
SACRIFICE	PROPHECY	IMMORTAL	FORBIDDEN
POWERS	CURSE	PARANORMAL	HAUNTED
CHILLING	SUPERNOVA	MYTHICAL	APOCALYPSE
PHENOMENON	POSSESSED	ELDRITCH	WRAITH
OCCULT	WHISPERS	PHANTASMAGORICAL	PANDEMONIUM
ARCANUM	BEWITCHED	CATACLYSMIC	UNEARTHLY
SPECTRAL	TWILIGHT	EPHEMERAL	TWISTED
SACRIFICIAL	RESONANT	WITCHING	VAMPIRE

SYMBOLS FOUND IN PARANORMAL FICTION

AMULET/TALISMAN	An object imbued with magical properties for protection or power.
CAULDRON	Used in magical rituals and associated with witches and potions.
CRYSTAL BALL	Used for scrying and divination, revealing visions of the past, present, or future.
PENTAGRAM/ PENTACLE	A five-pointed star symbol often used in protective and magical rituals.
OUIJA BOARD	A tool used to communicate with spirits or the supernatural world.
BOOK OF SHADOWS/ SPELLBOOK	A book containing magical spells, rituals, and knowledge.
WAND	A magical tool used to channel and direct supernatural powers.
MIRROR	Often used for scrying, revealing hidden truths or reflections of the supernatural.
BLACK CAT	A symbol of mystery and witchcraft, often associated with magical beings.
BROOMSTICK	A mode of transportation for witches and a symbol of their craft.
MOON	Symbolises magic, transformation, and the supernatural cycle of life.
CROSSROADS	A place where spirits and supernatural entities are believed to gather.
HOURGLASS	Symbolises the passage of time and can be associated with magical rituals.

SYMBOLS FOUND IN PARANORMAL FICTION

RUNE STONES	Used in divination, each rune symbol has a specific meaning and power.
TAROT CARDS	Used for fortune-telling and gaining insight into the supernatural.
CRESCENT MOON	A symbol of transformation and connection to the supernatural realm.
SKULL	Often associated with death and the supernatural, symbolising mortality and power.
FEATHER	Symbolises messages from the spirit world or supernatural beings.
TRISKELION	A three-legged symbol representing the past, present, and future in Celtic mythology.
TAROT CARDS	Used for fortune-telling and gaining insight into the supernatural.
VIAL OF LIQUID	Potions and elixirs often play a significant role in paranormal fiction.
RITUAL CIRCLE	A sacred space where magical ceremonies are performed.
MYSTICAL DOOR/GATE	A portal between worlds or realms of existence.
SIGIL	A unique magical symbol used to represent supernatural beings or entities.
CANDLE	Used in various magical ceremonies and as a symbol of enlightenment.

POWER WORDS IN PARANORMAL FICTION

ENCHANTING	Filled with charm and magic, captivating and delighting the senses.
ETHEREAL	Delicate and otherworldly, having a ghostly or celestial quality.
MYSTICAL	Relating to the supernatural, mysterious and imbued with spiritual significance.
SUPERNATURAL	Beyond the laws of nature, involving forces or beings beyond the ordinary realm.
ENIGMATIC	Mysterious and puzzling, difficult to understand or interpret.
EERIE	Creating a feeling of unease or spookiness, suggesting the presence of ghosts or the supernatural.
OTHERWORLDLY	Pertaining to a realm or existence beyond the physical world, magical or extraterrestrial.
HAUNTING	Evoking a sense of lingering, often ghostly presence or memories.
CHILLING	Sending a shiver down the spine, causing fear or unease.
CURSED	Subject to a spell or malevolent enchantment, bringing bad luck or misfortune.
SPECTRAL	Relating to or resembling a ghost or apparition.
ARCANE	Known or understood by only a few, mysterious or secret.
SPELLBINDING	Captivating and holding the attention as if under a magical spell.

POWER WORDS IN PARANORMAL FICTION

SORCERY	The practice of magic, especially involving the invocation of supernatural powers.
PHANTASMAGORICAL	Characterised by a fantastic sequence of dream-like images, surreal and mysterious.
MYSTERIOUS	Full of intrigue and secrets, not easily understood or explained.
OCCULT	Relating to supernatural phenomena, involving hidden knowledge or esoteric practices.
UNEARTHLY	Supernatural or out of this world, beyond normal human experience.
WITCHING	Involving witches or witchcraft, possessing a magical quality.
EPHEMERAL	Fleeting or short-lived, existing for only a brief moment.
IMMORTAL	Possessing eternal life or being beyond death.
APOCALYPTIC	Relating to the end of the world or a catastrophic event.
CATACLYSMIC	Involving a violent upheaval or catastrophe, suggesting immense destruction.
ELDRITCH	Weird and eerie, suggesting a supernatural or otherworldly origin.
UNCANNY	Strange or mysterious in an unsettling way, seemingly beyond natural explanation.

Now mix and match these words to create plot twists/ and or endings:

The main character plays around with some TAROT CARDS and discovers their name on them and hears WHISPERS. There's an EERIE feeling around her.

SHOW NOT TELL TECHNIQUES IN PARANORMAL WRITING

EMOTION	TELL	SHOW
FEAR	She was terrified of the ghost in the haunted house.	As she entered the old house, her heart pounded against her chest, and her breath quickened. Every creak and whisper made her skin crawl, and her eyes darted nervously around, searching for any sign of the ghostly presence rumoured to haunt the place.
MAGIC	He had powerful telekinetic abilities.	He extended his hand toward the book on the shelf, and without touching it, the book levitated, gently floating into his grasp. The pages turned as if moved by invisible hands, demonstrating the extent of his telekinetic powers.
LOVE	The vampire was incredibly attractive and alluring.	His eyes locked with hers, and she felt a magnetic pull toward him. His voice, smooth like velvet, sent shivers down her spine as he leaned in, revealing sharp fangs glistening in the moonlight.
SAD	She was devastated by the loss of her magical amulet.	She clutched her chest, tears streaming down her cheeks as she stared at the empty space where her amulet had once hung. Without it, she felt vulnerable and powerless, a part of her essence now missing.
ANGER	The werewolf was angry.	His muscles tensed, and his growls filled the air as his eyes glowed with fury. With a fierce snarl, he lunged forward, ready to confront the one who dared challenge him.
EERIE	The haunted forest was eerie.	The trees seemed to lean in, casting long shadows that danced in the moonlight. The wind whispered through the leaves, producing an eerie melody that sent shivers down their spines. Every rustle and crackle heightened their sense of foreboding.

SHOW NOT TELL TECHNIQUES IN PARANORMAL WRITING

HOW TO DO IT

USE SENSORY DETAILS	Engage the reader's senses by describing what characters see, hear, feel, smell, and taste. This adds depth to emotions and experiences.
DIALOGUE AND BODY LANGUAGE	Allow characters' interactions and nonverbal cues to reveal their emotions and intentions, creating more realistic and immersive scenes.
INTERNAL MONOLOGUE	Show characters' thoughts and inner conflicts through internal monologues or introspective narration, allowing readers to understand their emotional turmoil.

BENEFITS OF SHOW NOT TELL IN PARANORMAL FICTION

EMOTIONAL IMPACT	Showing emotions and experiences immerses readers in the characters' feelings, creating a deeper emotional connection with the story.
CHARACTER DEVELOPMENT	Demonstrating characters' thoughts and actions rather than telling them helps develop well-rounded, three-dimensional characters.
IMMERSIVE READING EXPERIENCE	Show, not tell, creates a more engaging and immersive reading experience, allowing readers to experience the story alongside the characters.
READER EMPATHY	By showing characters' struggles and vulnerabilities, readers can empathise with them and become emotionally invested in their journey.
AVOIDING INFORMATION DUMP	Showing instead of telling allows the story's information to unfold naturally, avoiding information dumps that can disrupt the flow of the narrative.
PROMOTING INTERPRETATION	Showing allows readers to interpret characters' emotions and motives, encouraging critical thinking and engagement with the story.

GLOSSARY OF KEY TERMS

AN A-Z OF SHORT STORY WRITING

GLOSSARY OF KEY TERMS

A	ANTAGONIST	The character or force that opposes the protagonist, creating conflict and obstacles in the story.
B	BACKSTORY	The background information about characters or events that occurred before the story's main events.
C	CONFLICT	The central problem or struggle that drives the plot and characters' actions.
D	DIALOGUE	The spoken or written conversation between characters that helps develop their personalities and move the story forward.
E	EXPOSITION	The initial part of the story that introduces the setting, characters, and basic information.
F	FORESHADOWING	Hints or clues about future events in the story to create suspense and intrigue.
G	GENRE	The category or type of fiction the story belongs to, such as romance, mystery, sci-fi, etc.
H	HOOK	The opening line or sentence that grabs the reader's attention and entices them to keep reading.
I	IMAGERY	Vivid and descriptive language that appeals to the senses and paints a clear picture in the reader's mind.

GLOSSARY OF KEY TERMS

J	JUXTAPOSITION	Placing two contrasting elements side by side to highlight their differences and create meaning.
K	KALEIDOSCOPIC CHARACTERS	Characters with diverse and multi-faceted traits that make them well-rounded and realistic.
L	LOGLINE	A brief summary of a story's key elements used for pitching or describing a movie, TV show or book.
M	MOTIVATION	The reasons and driving forces behind a character's actions and decisions.
N	NARRATOR	The voice or perspective from which the story is told, such as first-person or third-person.
O	ONOMATOPOEIA	Words that imitate the sound they represent, adding sensory depth to the writing (e.g., buzz, bang, hiss).
P	PROTAGONIST	The main character of the story who faces the central conflict.
Q	QUEST	A journey or mission that the protagonist embarks on, often leading to personal growth.
R	RESOLUTION	The final outcome or conclusion of the story where the conflict is resolved.

GLOSSARY OF KEY TERMS

S	SYMBOLISM	The use of objects, actions, or characters to represent abstract ideas or themes.
T	TONE	The writer's attitude or mood conveyed in the story, influencing how readers feel while reading.
U	UNRELIABLE NARRATOR	A narrator whose credibility is compromised, leading readers to question the accuracy of their account.
V	VOICE	The unique style, personality, and perspective of the narrator or characters in the story.
W	WORLDBUILDING	Creating a vivid and immersive setting that brings the story's world to life.
X	X-FACTOR	The unique and intriguing element that sets the story apart from others and makes it memorable.
Y	YEARNING	The intense desire or longing that drives the protagonist's actions and emotions.
Z	ZEITGEIST	The prevailing mood or spirit of a particular time or era, influencing the story's themes and context.

Remember that short story writing allows for creativity and experimentation, so don't be afraid to explore different elements and techniques to craft compelling and captivating narratives.